SUN RAYS AT MIDNIGHT

SUN RAYS AT MIDNIGHT

One Man's Quest for The Meaning of Life,
Before, During and After The Holocaust

Norbert Friedman

To order additional copies of this book, contact:
Xlibris Corporation
1-888-795-4274
www.Xlibris.com
Orders@Xlibris.com
29184

DEDICATION

I dedicate this book to the memory of my Mother, Gusta Friedman and my brother Oskar, and to all the other members of my family, who have perished in the Holocaust.

To the unfulfilled potential of my peers, whose lives were terminated in the most brutal manner.

And to all the survivors who had the courage to break out of the prison of their memories and despite the pain that it creates for them, dedicated themselves to give witness to the events of that faithful era and to draw positive lessons from Man's most tragic experience.

INTRODUCTION

As soon as my children understood that a part of my life differed significantly from the lives of most people, they began trying to persuade me to record my experiences in writing.

"Why don't you write a book about the war, Daddy?" they would ask. They were gentle, but persistent, and I wanted to do as they wished.

But I never tried. I had many convenient excuses: my deficiencies in writing skill, my shortcomings in the command of the English language. A more substantial reason was that it seemed impossible or perhaps not completely honest for one person to presume to describe something as tremendous as "the Holocaust experience." How could any single voice speak for all those thousands and millions who suffered and perished each with a particular kind of anguish and pain? How could I speak for Hungarian Jew who suddenly found himself under the German occupation in 1944 and was immediately shipped to a concentration camp? For the partisans and fugitives who lived in forests and fields, dodging detection by the Nazis and sometimes betrayal by people of their own nationality? I could only speak for a single Polish Jew who was pinned under the heel of the German boot from 1939 until liberation in 1945. And even for that person, myself, I doubted my ability to give a complete account.

As the years went by and the events of the Holocaust grew distant in time, more and more people became familiar with the major outlines of the experience. I heard them saying: "I read about the Holocaust . . . I am familiar with the Holocaust because I studied it . . . I know all about the Holocaust." These declarations frequently came from people who had read several books or attended lectures and believed they had been "initiated" into the evils of that complex and horrendous period.

Considering the profusion of literature, scholarship, museums, and research on the subject, it is not hard for one to believe himself or herself an "expert." Of course these people are sympathetic, and many of them had relatives who perished during the war. And as they absorbed a great deal of information, including the testimonies provided by survivors, each of them came away with a certain image or story that formed their own private understanding. They clearly saw a few threads of a particular color and texture, but they could not possibly see the whole fearsome tapestry that was the Holocaust.

How was I any different? I could not shoulder the awesome responsibility of weaving a complete tapestry out of my few threads and colors, of trying to tell the "whole truth" for every survivor. How could I presume in good conscience to provide the binding warp for all that pain and anguish, for the agonizing terrors and the last thoughts of all those who perished? What could I do but add my own few threads and leave them hanging loosely and wanting, bereft of the binding truth that might achieve the comprehension and closure so many of us longed for?

The silt of memory at the bottom of one's psyche, when stirred surely hides and distorts much of what actually happened. Surely I would never be able to see through to the landscape of fear, apprehension and confusion that clouded our lives; to express adequately the pain of despair and hopelessness, the degradation and dehumanization; to portray the terror caused by pathological sadism and bestiality; to depict the eventual numbness, self-doubt, unworthiness, cynicism and resignation, the not-always-successful attempt to crawl into a protective shell of uninvolved indifference.

And so for many years I abstained from writing. My psyche found therapeutic outlet in oral presentations, mostly at *Yom Hashoa*, Holocaust Memorial Day observances or witness giving and teaching sessions at educational institutions before classes of students ranging from elementary schools to colleges. I became a gallery educator at the *Museum of Jewish Heritage, A Living Memorial to the Holocaust* in New York City, where I was able to talk to many groups of interested people over the years. In fact, once my early silence was finally broken, I tried to share my experiences with anyone who would listen, preferably young students.

I told myself: The last word about this tragedy is for the future to utter. The why and the how will eventually be accepted, but it will depend on the still-to-be-told contributions of eyewitnesses, the ongoing research of historians, the images created by generations of artists.

In the meanwhile, I was convinced that every attempt to encapsulate or portray the catastrophe that was Shoah invariably failed. Whenever a tangible product was conceived and put in concrete form, be it in literature, visual art, stage or screen, it always fell short, at least in my perception. Likewise I was convinced that any effort of mine could never begin to approach the enormity and total tragedy of even one moment of one victim's pain and despair. Most

NORBERT FRIEDMAN

of the saga, I told myself, may always be un-revealed, unfinished, open to questioning, to the endless process of pondering with which we regard the great mysteries.

I can remember when my thinking began to change, when I began to take my children's request more seriously. First it was when I gave testimony to the Steven Spielberg Shoah Foundation, and later when I had a chance to review the video of my testimony. As I was watching I realized that, writing or not, I had already recorded some of my experiences, and as I had feared, the words I used to describe them were sadly inadequate and sometimes even misleading. Yet these words would be preserved and they would contribute to what I had always been most fearful of: an inaccurate portrayal of the history of Shoah. I longed to do better.

But the most important influence was my conversations with the adult groups and the children—especially the children—which I guided around the Museum of Jewish Heritage and talked to in the schools. Of all the thousands of questions submitted to me in the course of my speaking, the one most frequently asked was: "How did you survive?" The children wanted to know that, and they asked it over and over.

For me it was the most difficult question to answer. I knew that it was not my youth and my physical good health that were the reasons for my survival; hundreds of thousands of others who were as young and healthy as I had perished. And in the course of events my youth vanished and my good health had dwindled.

I knew also that it was not my guile or street smarts that kept me alive, for thousands of others more cunning than I, and with more life experience, did not live to see the day of liberation.

Finally, I knew it was not my vocational skills that were the key to my survival, my ability to operate certain machines and tools. Many others with more valuable skills did not survive, while some without any qualifications of use to our captors managed to live.

Divine providence or chance notwithstanding, which for me was not an adequate answer, I finally came to another factor that was at least partially responsible for my survival. And that was the ability to seek out and cleave to the rare people of true compassion and nobility of spirit. Some of these people literally saved or spared my life; others uplifted my sagging spirits by their example. And once I recognized that truth, that it is the greatness in other human beings, which allowed me to survive, then I recognized why I would have to write this book. I had to write this book because I had found for myself a truth about the human condition, something more basic and important than anything else I have discovered in my life.

So I have written these memoirs because I wanted to express this truth and this discovery. I realized in answering the schoolchildren's questions that I wanted this truth to be known—that the goodness of one person can be life saving in its power. That it can save life even in that quagmire-like, suffocating existence of the camps; that even in the dark abyss we could find islands of bright sanity and precariously cling to them. We saw flashes of mercy and we managed, in our desperation, to share that mercy among us. Thanks to these sparks of spirit, our past and our future could hold the possibility of meaning and hope.

It is true that the world of the Holocaust victim was one continuous, dehumanizing experience, so poignantly expressed by the writings of Eli Wiesel, Primo Levi and others. But I cannot agree with those who saw only darkness. I cannot agree with the belief expressed by Lawrence L. Langer, in *Preempting the Holocaust,* that "there are no redeeming lessons to be learned from this atrocity." I cannot agree that the human spirit failed utterly. I do agree that the overwhelming majority of experiences were grim, that humans behaved badly and betrayed each other. I know that the experiences of compassion I refer to are the exceptions, the all-too-rare instances when dignity and honor and faith rose above the odorous vapors of evil, the animalism of primitive behavior, and shone through the darkness.

As I reviewed my private memories and the recordings of my public testimonies, I saw again and again evidence of saintliness, this faint but distinctive force against the barbarous norm. And so I chose to write this book by the light of those examples, and to dedicate it to their souls.

NORBERT FRIEDMAN

MEMORIES OF CHILDHOOD

The chaos in the village square was punctuated by the wailing of the women and intensified by the prodding and shouts of the soldiers.

The two trucks, carrying about one hundred men, destined for the labor camp and followed by a staff car with two SS officers, were about to depart.

I watched my mother as she stood with her hands on my little brother's shoulders. At the age of only forty-two, her lovely face was wrinkled from all the hardships and worries of recent years. With tender and resigned sadness, with tears in her eyes, she seemed to be saying "Farewell my son, I will always love you."

And then we left. As we traveled, bouncing on the rough Polish country road, I thought about the vulnerability of my existence, my un-lived adolescence and my already-distant childhood.

CHAPTER I

I was born December 20, 1922 in the city of Krakow, Poland. My parents, Josef and Gusta, product of an arranged marriage, had been wedded for two years by then. My father was twenty-four years of age and my mother twenty-two at my arrival.

My first recollection of life is the sensation of warmth and peace derived from lying close to my mother's body and holding my hand under her soft breast.

I also remember sleeping with my father; I remember the smell of his body, an unmistakable scent, a mixture of the cigarettes he smoked (his favorite gold-tipped brand) and the butcher-shop odor of meat, bones and animal fat which permeated all his clothing. I can still feel the warm sense of protection and security I enjoyed when nestled in the crook of his short but powerful arms. And I re-live the long moments of darkness, anger and despair while waiting for my father to come home, late into the night. But all was forgiven; though not forgotten, when he would arrive at last and put his arms protectively around me after he climbed into bed.

I remember the ever-present cup of sweetened tea with milk at my bedside, there to quench my thirst should I happen to wake up in the middle of night. I can still feel the touch of my mother's hand when she put my hand over my eyes and helped me to recite the *Kriath Shmah*, the prayer before retiring. I do not remember whether my years of infancy were spent in the home of my mother's parents, but the memories of that apartment are so overwhelming that it might as well have been so.

I do remember living in other places, such as the house on the outskirts of Krakow. I remember the name of the street *Krolowa Jadwiga* several blocks from the streetcar stop. A large back yard and shady trees, a place where I learned to kick a rubber ball and where we held outdoor picnics, usually followed by picture-taking. My uncle would hide his head under a black cloth, stick out his hand, and yell, "Smile now!" and a light would flash, scaring me enough to prompt a crying spell. I remember that a large tannery was located on the other side of the street. The Jewish workers employed there were guests at our table on the Sabbath and holidays.

I remember the first day of school and my new yellow plywood back-satchel, the long trip by streetcar, with my mother accompanying the petrified yet excited child, the tears of departure in front of the classroom, the joy and relief at seeing my mother again after that first day. All my courage having returned, I was again the bubbling hero on the hour-long trip home. I remember the sight of my German shepherd Rex, waiting for us at the streetcar stop and his licking my face while wildly wagging his tail, expressing his joy at seeing me again, which triggered another outburst of crying on my part.

So has ended my first day in school. In the evening when my father returned from his butcher shop a decision must have been made that I would have to travel by myself as soon as possible. The memories of my travels on that streetcar, enduring the taunts of other children either because I was Jewish or because of my brand new, eye-catching yellow back-satchel, are always a painful companion to the otherwise cheerful recollections of that period of my life.

Not until much later in life did I understand why we always found ourselves living somewhere on the outskirts of town. My mother always longed for bucolic surroundings—an expression of her striving to shed the ghetto environment with all its indigenous smells, its mode of dress, its provincialism and lack of fresh air. She yearned for the country sites described in the novels and poetry of that time. Her romantic soul longed for an escape from the drudgery of the everyday struggle for existence in some pastoral setting amid stately trees and fields of wildflowers. In contrast, the house of my maternal grandparents stood in the center of the Jewish quarters of Krakow, on 16 Josefa Street, a large three-story stone structure with a cobblestone courtyard, each floor with its own L-shaped balcony facing the yard. Behind the yard was another building of the same height. The latrines were at one end of the balcony, while the front of the inverted L contained the entrance to my grandparents' apartment. In the corner of the L was the water faucet.

A double glass door led to the large kitchen. At its entrance, next to the door, was a large double glass window. In wintertime grandmother would keep milk and butter between those windowpanes. We children would exhale warm breath on them, creating clear circles in the oddly configured ice crystals.

A large coal-burning stove stood in the left corner past that window, a well-stacked wooden coal bin next to it. Three large burners with several removable steel rings that served as lids regulated the amount of flame or heat needed for cooking. The heat was drawn to the chimney through an insulated compartment called the *Szabasnik*, used for baking and keeping food warm for the Sabbath. Most of the cookware was kept on the stove or stored on top of it. Water for cooking and washing was kept in a covered pail next to the stove. The salting and washing of meat, known as Koshering, was done over another pail on a wooden grate. In winter the faucet outside had to be left slightly open to allow a flow of water; otherwise it would freeze, causing serious problems.

Laundry was done in a large round wooden tub, which doubled as a bathtub for the whole family and served sometimes as a fish tank. I remember taking baths in that tub. I even remember scrubbing my grandfather's back on occasion, although I remember that he would also go regularly to the *Mikvah,* the ritual bath, as well as to the public Roman baths. I do not remember the women of the house taking their baths; we children must have been kept out of the kitchen or the house on those occasions. The women also went to the *Mikvah* on a regular basis.

A large wooden table where meals were taken most of the time, a bench and some chairs, a brass bed and a large wardrobe completed the furnishing of the kitchen. At the other end of the kitchen, a door led to the second room, which served as bedroom, sitting room and formal dining room. As one came into the room, in the left front corner stood a tall, coal-heated tile oven that reached the ceiling. In winter grandmother and grandfather would stand with their backs to it, hands behind them touching the stove, trying to stay warm. When one came in from the cold outside, his first reaction would be to run to the oven and put his hands to it to warm up. Everyone would make sure that the stove was always well stoked. Evenings, grandfather would bake potatoes in its hot ashes and serve them with a dash of salt.

The room was furnished with two beds next to each other with night tables on either side and at their feet an ottoman. On the right stood a secretary in mahogany wood and a large crib. A large, formal dining table, its top always covered with a white lace tablecloth, surrounded by chairs, dominated the room. The windows of that room looked out on the street and on the life of the Jewish quarter of the city. From there I remember watching children playing hop-scotch on the sidewalks, rolling their wooden hoops and chasing each other in what seemed like an endless game of "You are it."

I remember watching from those windows the gradual ebbing of the day's activities on Friday afternoons as Sabbath approached and the transformation of life on those streets. The very same men who during the working week were feverishly pursuing the evasive *"Parnassa"* (sustenance or income), at the same time trying not to neglect their prayers and the study of the Talmud, now appeared in their Sabbath finery their black satin coats sashed with heavy braids, wearing white socks and lace-less boots. Their feet moved now with a different rhythm, their heads bedecked with fur-brimmed hats. At their sides, their offspring dutifully accompanied them to evening services. I would wait, dressed in my Sabbath outfit, to hear my grandfather call out to me in Yiddish, *"Nachum, lo meer gayn,"* "Norbert, let's go," and then I would proudly follow him to his house of prayer.

I watched from that window the arrival of horse-driven wagons in which farmers would bring produce into town and the thieves who cleverly stripped them of some of their stock.

I watched the funeral processions on their way to the cemetery and would always wonder; "Did I know that person?" Perhaps I was trying to readjust the size of the small world of a growing child.

I remember watching the funeral of my grandfather, his plain wooden coffin borne on the shoulders of the pallbearers. I can still hear the heart-rending wails of the women, and the pleas for alms from the poor. I was considered too young to attend the funeral and was told to stay home with my cousins and watch my grandfather's cat that had been acting very strangely since my grandfather had become bedridden. She would stay under the bed and refuse to come out. As soon as his body was taken out of the house, the animal ran following it into the street, trailed the funeral procession to the cemetery and never came back. Some said that for a long time it could be seen at the cemetery, sitting by my grandfather's grave.

I also remember watching from those windows in the winter of 1939, the German troops marching through the Jewish quarter chanting the *Horst Wessel Lied,* their heavily studded boots pounding the street while they ominously sang, *"Wen Judenblut vom Messer Spitze spritzt . . ."* "When Jewish blood from the edge of the knife spurts . . ." Sowing paralyzing fear into the hearts of the Jews of the town.

The halls of my grandfather's building were dimly lit by kerosene lamps which were the responsibility of the superintendent. Twenty-four steps to each of the floors, seventy-two in all. The wooden balustrades were smooth and shiny, polished by the endless sliding of the children who lived in that house. We would run up the stairs quickly, wondering at the slow pace of the adults' progress. On the way down we would either slide down the balustrades, pretending to be Icarus in flight, screaming with fright and excitement, or we would jump two or three steps at a time, daring each other to jump more then that. The games we played were simple children's games: hop-scotch, soccer, kicking a rubber ball or one fashioned from old socks; and hide and seek, which sometimes ended up in dark corners as the sexually exploratory games that curious little boys and girls play. Our sex education stemmed from distorted stories and descriptions we told each other. The stork theories caused some snickers, but were never totally discarded. We loved to listen to tales of demons, dragons, mighty warriors, and magical witches. The "Baba Jaga" tales were guaranteed to strike fear and terror in our little hearts.

The stories of creation taught in our religious schools were also received with a good dose of skepticism. One such discussion led to my questioning the way in which Adam and Eve's children produced offspring. "Whom did they have children with?" I asked the rebbe, "their own mother and sisters?" That earned me a week's suspension and an invitation to my father to come and discuss the conduct of his heretic son. It also earned me a good licking from my father, as well as reprimands and reminders of the respect and deference due to teachers and rabbis. The teachers themselves would also frequently dispense corporal punishment using a thin bamboo stick, a ruler, or just a simple sharp pull of the ears.

The teaching in the *Heder*, the religious school I entered at the age of four, was done by rote. It consisted of a monotonous recitation of lines from the Pentateuch and translation of them into Yiddish. The mischief brought on by the boredom and restlessness of children studying in this fashion would result in corporal punishment by the rebbes. The only rewards for this study, it seemed to me, were the sweets that my grandfather would offer me after examining my weekly progress every Sabbath afternoon.

I loved those Saturday afternoons in my grandparents' home. My grandmother would hold court in the large room with her daughters, her sons and their spouses when they visited. All the problems of the family would be addressed, the financial and marital disputes would be discussed, and grandmother's decisions dutifully followed. The needs of other relatives would be debated: raising a dowry for a poor girl; finding lodgings for a relative from out of town who was seeking employment or attending a yeshiva in the big city; making matches for eligible youngsters.

All this would take place in the big room while we, the children, were left to ourselves to play, but only after grandfather would drill the boys about their progress in the study of Torah. "So what have you learned this week?" he would ask. "You cannot let the time pass idly by, there is so much to know." He would reward us with candied fruits and other sweets specially obtained for these occasions and then release us to go and play. It must have been at one such Saturday afternoon session, after the passing of my grandfather that the decision was made to take me out of the Heder and, at the age of six, place me in the second grade of the Hebrew day school—a decision that must ultimately have affected the direction of my religious life.

What was the tone of my religious life as I remember it? My maternal grandfather, Reb Hersh Mandelbaum, was an orthodox Jew whose graying beard enhanced the effect of his handsome face and who always wore the garb of the *Hassidim* of his time: dark clothes, white, tie-less shirts buttoned under his chin. The shape of his cap revealed his place of origin and his allegiance to a specific rabbi. He was born in the second half of the 19th century in a small village outside the town of Nowy Sacz in the southern part of Poland, a part of what was then the Austrio-Hungarian Empire. I do not know the extent of my grandfather's religious education, but I know that he was well-versed in the Talmud, for on many occasions when I went with him to the house of study and prayer, the *Beth Midrash*, others would besiege him with Talmudic questions and problems which he would answer only after much deliberation and stroking of his beard. His life revolved around his business and the house of worship and study. He fathered nine children, six of whom survived infancy: four daughters and two sons. The religious laws and holidays were strictly observed both in his home and in the marketplace. He was known as a *"Frume Yid,"* a pious Jew, one who lived according to the *Halacha,* Jewish law. But there must have been tensions and adjustments in his religious philosophy because of his life with my grandmother.

I loved my grandmother dearly, and in turn I was the apple of her eye despite her equal affection for her other grandchildren. Grandmother Esther Bochner-Mandelbaum was a diminutive woman but a giant in moral stature. She was a fourth-generation, direct descendent of a famous Hassidic Rabbi, the *Chrzanover Tzadik* (Righteous One), himself a descendent of the founder of Hassidism, the revered *Ba-al Shem Tov.* In her thought and behavior she was far ahead of her time. Strictly observant, she was apparently also sympathetic to the thinking of the *Maskilim,* the adherents of the *Haskalah,* the progressive movement of religious enlightenment. Despite her traditional upbringing and marriage to a strictly orthodox man, she nevertheless ensured a secular education for all her children. It was almost unheard of in those times for this to be done in a traditional Jewish home. Her daughters attended "*Beth Jakov*" religious schools but also enrolled later in secular middle schools.

My mother, for instance, attended a Jewish *Handelschulle,* a Jewish commercial school. Besides speaking the usual Yiddish, Polish and German, which most Jews in that part of Poland were fluent in, and the language of the Torah, the *Lashon Kodesh* (holy tongue), Hebrew, my mother also studied English, French and Esperanto. Esperanto was the language of the post-World War I era and was thought to represent hope for a peaceful world through communication in one universal tongue. (I remember how proud she was to wear the little pin in her lapel that indicated her membership in the world community and mastery of Esperanto.)

Grandma was so very well-versed in the Talmud that she sometimes offered counter-arguments to Grandpa, who would shake his head in disbelief and leave the room, not wanting to engage in a Talmudic dispute with a woman, even if she was his wife. He must have suffered terribly on those Friday nights when, after the traditional supper and our singing and rejoicing a black-clad figure would appear at the door of the kitchen. It would be the parson of the large church complex across the street whom my grandmother sometimes invited to their home, especially during the period of Christian Lent, for a fish dinner and some theological discussion.

My grandfather would greet the priest with a polite nod of his head; a Jew could ill afford a sign of disrespect for Catholic clergy in Poland. Then he would retire to the other room, locking the door and leaving my grandmother to her own designs. After the meal, washed down by some of my grandfather's schnapps, my grandmother would engage the priest in animated discussions of differences between the faiths and interpretations of the Bible. The priest was well versed in Hebrew, a skill of many religious Catholic scholars of that time, and the text would be studied in the original instead of the sometimes inaccurate translations. My grandmother thoroughly enjoyed those evenings, while my grandfather must have suspected her of heresy, although he never said so. She would amaze the Polish girl who used to come on Saturday to light the stove and perform some chores by telling her what the Sunday sermon in the church would be. Some nights during the week my grandmother would leave the house to collect charity funds from her friends and her husband's business cronies. Many were the needs that the women of *"Gemilat Hessed"* (the welfare committee) tried to fill: dowries for poor maidens, funds for widows, help for the sick and aged, and even tie-over moneys for people in business trouble. The precepts of Torah concerning charity were for these women a way of life. They sought no recognition; the reward would be given to them in the world to come. Many a night grandmother would get back after ten o'clock and have to ring the concierge to open the gate of the house for her. (According to an ancient ordinance, all houses in Krakow had to have their gates closed at ten p.m.) Grandfather would grumble under his beard, bemoaning the tip that had to be handed to the super for his efforts, who in turn cursed the Jews under his alcoholic breath for the meager pittance he would receive.

Thursdays and Fridays for my grandmother were the days of baking the Chalah and cakes for the Sabbath, of planning the dishes that had to be cooked, and of helping her husband on his busiest days of the week. There was a rhythm to the life of a Jew then; holidays, births, circumcisions, *Bar Mitzvoth*, weddings and funerals, all controlled by religious customs and observances. The holidays were the centerpieces of one's existence. Families planned and looked forward to them, saving as much as they could to be able to celebrate them in style.

Grandfather was a wholesale fish dealer. He would travel into the countryside to visit landowners who raised fish in specially constructed ponds; mostly carp, some pike and other popular varieties. The fish would be loaded into water-tank railroad cars and then unloaded into wooden casket-like containers at the banks of the Vistula River. There they would remain in the water for several weeks so as to have the mud of the ponds washed out from them. In the summertime it was great fun for me to accompany my grandfather and sometimes my father (who would help him) to the Vistula River and watch them take the fish out of the floating boxes and load them into wicker baskets. The poor fish would jump high into the air and fall on the ground, and it would be my job to put them back into the baskets so they could be weighed for the waiting retail dealers. I was swift and skillful, putting my hand under their gills and throwing them into the writhing swarm of other fish.

NORBERT FRIEDMAN

Winter was quite another story. I had to beg grandpa to be allowed to accompany him to the river. Splashed water would freeze instantly in the severe cold of the Polish winter, when temperatures of -30° C were not uncommon. Grandfather's first task upon arriving at the river would be to select a fat carp, slice it open and rub its fat on his hands and nose to protect them from frostbite. (No one had heard of Lanolin yet.) We would vigorously stamp our feet and wave our arms across our bodies to try to keep warm. On the way home we would stop at a familiar inn for a piece of grilled goose and a shot of hot mead, the popular honey wine. My reward would be a sip of the beverage, which heated my insides and released a warm glow throughout my entire body. I was very proud that at that young age I was accepted and the adults seemed to take note of me.

Naturally the kitchen in my grandmother's house reeked of fish and the frequency of fish dishes at grandma's table turned me away from eating fish until my advanced adulthood. Sometimes there would be an especially rare specimen of fish, sent to my grandmother by a landowner, swimming in the kitchen in the wooden tub. I would grow fond of the fish, only to see it a few days later on the Sabbath table. I would search for wild excuses not to have to eat it.

My playmates were mostly my two cousins Wilek and Dolek, along with some second cousins; most of them named Samek. Sometimes for the holidays of Rosh Hashanah and Passover my uncle David would visit from Czechoslovakia and his son, cousin Gerd would join us. Cousin Wilek was only ten weeks older than I. Of ruddy complexion and a strong physical presence; he was extremely gentle and considerate. He had a brother, Tobias, some eight years older than he was. They were the children of my mother's oldest sister, Aunt Pepka, and her husband Srulek, who married at the advent of World War I. The marriage became a family legend. My uncle was promptly marched away and declared missing in action. Shortly after his departure my cousin Tobias was born. According to the legend, some returning soldiers reported seeing my uncle fall in combat, but my aunt refused to believe the reports and faithfully anticipated his return. Every Friday she baked his favorite poppy-seed cake, expecting his arrival. The story ended happily when after a five-year absence he finally walked in on a Friday evening, having spent most of the war in a Russian prisoner-of-war camp in Siberia.

My Uncle Srulek was a corpulent man with a deep bass voice. He sang in the choir of the Progressive (Reformed) Temple in Krakow. His claim to fame was that the choir once performed for the Krakow radio station. On that occasion the entire family gathered in a neighbor's house to share the earphones of the crystal radio to hear uncle Srulek's voice. He was a maker of bootlegs (tops for shoes), a profession which he taught his older son Tobias, who subsequently became a designer for high-class ladies' shoe manufacturers. The family lived on the outskirts of Krakow in a neighborhood where only one other Jewish family lived. It was an hour's walk to the Jewish section of town, and sometimes on holidays they would walk the distance and stay over with my grandmother until the end of the holidays.

My aunt Pepka and my uncle Srulek were most hospitable despite the economic hardships of a working family and a modest apartment. On High Holidays my cousins and I would walk over to the Progressive Temple and sneak in to hear the choir dominated by my uncle's voice. We made sure that our grandfather would not know about it. To him, entering a Reformed house of worship was no different from entering a church, an act unheard of for a traditional Jew of those days.

Cousin Dolek, a year older than I, was the ringleader of our little gang, introducing games and setting the tone of our activities. His hair even in childhood was ash-blond; he was called the "White Sheep." There must have been a little mean streak to him. I remember his forcing our grandfather's beloved cat onto the ledge of the balcony, then giving it a push with his foot, which sent the screaming animal three stories down to what we believed would be its end. To our surprise the cat landed on its feet, wailed for a while in pain and then in the evening showed up before the door, waiting to be let in. Dolek made us swear us not to mention the incident to anybody or he would not let us play in his house.

Dolek's younger sister Hela would sometimes join the boys in their games, but always with little interest. She preferred the company of her oldest sister Tosia, a dark-haired, blue-eyed beauty loved and admired by every member of the family and by her peers as well. Three years older then Dolek, she was of a most pleasant and agreeable nature, always smiling, always ready to listen. As the oldest child of Uncle Michal, she was the apple of his eye. Uncle Michal was very strict with his children and even with us, his nephews, but cousin Hela as the youngest child enjoyed certain privileges and would get away with mischief or failure to do her homework.

Dolek's mother, Aunt Rozia, was the second oldest of my mother's siblings. Corpulent and stately, she exuded authority. Whenever she addressed us or one of her children she would put the pince-nez on her nose, peer intently and then make her point. Her husband Michal Ehrlich was a self-educated man who rose to the position of director in a company which held partnerships in lumber mills and coal dealerships and owned a fleet of barges that transported commodities up and down the Vistula River. In his youth he belonged to the P.P.S., the Polish Socialist Party, in the time around 1918 when the Polish Republic was coming into being. He was an associate of the future leader of Poland, Marshal Jozef Pilsudski, whom he never forgave for leaving the party and forming the BBWR, the Independent Block. Years after Pilsudski's death we were still not allowed to visit the Memorial Mound erected in his honor.

In the earliest days of my childhood, Uncle Michal Ehrlich lived on Piekarska Street. Cobble-stoned and dusty, it housed several brick homes and some small industrial buildings. On the other side of the yard from where my aunt lived was a soap and candle factory whose smells permeated the neighborhood. Across the hall from the Ehrlichs lived an elderly widow, Mrs. Jary, who would always invite my mother into her house whenever we visited my aunt Rozia. Her apartment was beautifully furnished with dark English furniture. She served tea, delicious cookies and biscuits with jams. The quiet elegance of those Saturday afternoons in that dimly lit setting would later come back to me in dreams in the most unsuitable places, under the least serene circumstances. Not far away on Bochenska Street lived our second cousins, the Bochners, with whom we would wage competitions, playing games of various kinds.

By existing standards Uncle Michal was affluent. He and his family later moved into a new section of town, between the old Jewish quarters and the Planty a beautiful tree-lined grassy mall built on what was once the moat encircling the Old Town of Krakow. The new apartment of aunt Rozia and Uncle Michal was large and modern. The Ehrlichs enjoyed a state-of-the-art bathroom, a telephone and a modern stove. The balcony had flowerpots and in the basement Uncle Michal made wine and liqueurs out of different fruits. A family visit to the Ehrlichs was an excursion into the never-to-be-reached but always coveted world of prosperity.

Wide and filled with benches under the old chestnut trees, the Planty was the favored place for children to play, for lovers to meet and for the social life of the community to be conducted. One could see on Sabbath afternoons men dressed in their holiday finery, ranging from black Hassidic garb to modern suits of the latest cuts, walking side by side, gesticulating, arguing about abstract political or Talmudic topics. The women would sit on benches discussing fashions, their children and general gossip. It was a tranquil and pastoral setting, occasionally disrupted by gangs of young Poles running through it, shouting insults and obscenities at their targets, the Sabbath-peace-seeking Jews.

My mother's youngest sister, Hela, the most progressive of the siblings except for her rebellious brother Jacob, got married as soon as the year of mourning for my grandfather was over. He would surely have objected to that union, for Hela's husband Israel Icheiser was not only clean-shaven but also bareheaded and quite secular. He was a member of the *Bund*, the irreligious Jewish workers party. After the wedding, Aunt Hela and Uncle Israel Icheiser moved in with my grandmother.

The ceremony took place on the grounds of the *Kehila*, the Jewish autonomous community council, under starry skies. The *Huppa*, the wedding canopy, was held above the wedding party, with light supplied by scores of candles. I remember holding a candle high above my head and despite all my efforts, being unable to keep the candle wax from dripping on my festive clothing. I remember riding from the wedding, for the first time in my life, in a large black automobile. For the wedding reception my Grandma persuaded her next-door neighbor, Mrs. Zelnick, to open the door dividing the two apartments, stack the furniture from both dwellings in the corridor, we then used the two large rooms for music and dancing and the two kitchens for cooking and serving.

None of this would have been possible while my grandfather was alive. His feud with Mr. Zelnick was legendary in the house where they lived. They did not speak to each other at all. They would not even nod as they passed on their way to the balcony latrines, though they were intimate with each other's *krechtzin* (groaning), being neighbors in latrines as well as apartments.

Only on *Rosh Chodesh Elul*, the first of Elul, the month preceding the Jewish New Year that signaled the *Yomim Noraim*, the Days of Awe, would my grandfather knock on the door in the large room dividing his apartment from Mr. Zelnick's, and yell, *"Reb Zelnick, zeit meer moichu!"* ("Mr. Zelnick, forgive me!") It is customary for all Jews to seek forgiveness and do *Tshuva* (penance) during the Days of Awe so as to be favorably inscribed in the Book of Life. However, on the last day of the holiday season, on *Shanah Rabba*, my grandfather would again knock on Mr. Zelnick's door and yell, *"Reb Zelnick ich bin weiter broigez mit ach!"* ("I am again cross with you!"), negating the chance for reconciliation. No one ever knew the source of this discord, though its details were the stuff of myth.

My mother's older brother, Uncle David, lived in Teplitz Schoenau, Czechoslovakia. He was a furrier. He married a cousin with whom he had two children: Gerd, two years younger than I, and a daughter, Ruth, born on the same day as my younger brother Oskar. They would come down to Krakow to visit, usually on holidays. From the way they dressed I assumed that they were well to do. Uncle David was of slight build, very nattily attired and a disciplinarian. We would often see Gerd standing in the corner for some minor infraction of family rules.

My mother also had an older brother between her and Uncle David in age. Uncle Jacob, the black sheep of the family, was a member of the PPK, the Polish Communist Party. He refused to serve in the Polish army and might even have done time in Bereza Kartuzka, the infamous Polish concentration camp of the 1920's. He later went to Czechoslovakia, worked as a tailor and had uncle David help him out when in need. He married an artist of some kind, Aunt Lola, an agnostic like him. I remember that when he came to see his father, my grandfather, on his deathbed, he came bareheaded, a sign of disrespect and belligerence painful to my grandfather. When he refused to put on a head covering despite my grandmother's urging, my father became so outraged that he chased him around the apartment to mete out physical punishment.

I missed my grandfather. After his death I would attend my father's shul more often. The house of prayer was in the home of Rabbi Lipschutz, the rabbi from my father's town of birth, Wielopole. He was therefore called the *Wielopole Rov*, even though his flock was in Krakow, and his followers were called the *Wielopole Hassidim*. I well remember the services in that small congregation, especially on the holidays—loud and full of fervor. Oh, how joyous were the *Simchat Torah* observances. The dancing by that entranced and slightly inebriated gathering was an unending round of total abandonment of earthly cares and a flight towards sensuous unity with the Almighty. And if in the process they trampled a fallen youngster, such as myself, G'd would forgive them. After one such celebration, my father would not take the chance again and I was not allowed to attend the next *Simchat Torah*.

My father's butchering business, which he conducted in a small rotunda in the market square, could not have been too successful, for after my grandfather's death he closed it and helped my grandmother in her wholesale fish business. We had moved from the suburbs closer to town. Mother found an apartment across from the Wawel, the fortress-castle and seat of Polish kings since early times, a block from the banks of the Vistula River.

Once a year on June 24th, Saint John's day, there would be a great festival on the banks of the river. Garlands of flowers would be thrown on the Vistula in memory of a beautiful Polish maiden, Wanda, who drowned herself rather than wed a Germanic conqueror. Fireworks would follow the festival and the vendors with their stands offered a multitude of colorful pastry and cotton candy. My mother had promised to take me to the next fair. When my grandfather died, my mother was in mourning and with deep regret informed me that she would be unable to keep her promise. In my grievous disappointment I decided to appeal to my grandmother. Her judgment was swift and in the opinion of my young self, most just:

"You made the promise to the child before your father died," she ruled. "The boy does not understand. Take off your mourning garb and dress normally so people will not talk. You do not have to have a good time there, but you must take the child."

The view from the balcony of our apartment on Groble #5 offered a glimpse of the barracks of a garrison of the Polish army and one of the bridges on the Vistula River. Two Polish University students occupied one of the apartments on the same floor, with a window facing our balcony. They wore their university caps at a rakish angle on the side of their heads and proudly displayed fencing scars on their cheeks, badges of courage in their anti-Semitic academic circles. On the same floor lived a young couple, the Piureckis. He was a pilot for Lot, the Polish airline, she a rather attractive woman, most of the time dressed in a morning housecoat over her nightgown.

I remember seeing her sometimes through the window in the students' apartment, but as a child of seven drawing no conclusions. I liked when my mother would visit with Mrs. Piurecki, for she always served delicious cookies with tea and would affectionately gather me to her bosom. She had no children of her own; her kisses would always be a little warmer and a bit longer after she had downed a few shots of liquor. Once during such a visit she suggested that I go up in an airplane with her husband and promised to speak to him about it.

To fly in an airplane in 1929 was an adventure beyond a little boy's dreams and almost deeper than his reservoir of courage. However, the response of my

NORBERT FRIEDMAN

cousins and friends when I mentioned the possibility to them, their shrieks of excitement and awed disbelief, the looks of admiration from the girls in my crowd, gave me the impetus to press Mrs. Piurecki for such an opportunity. Finally one day I was to go up with Mr. Piurecki for a spin in an aircraft of some sort. My mother was to bring me to the airfield on the outskirts of town early one Sunday morning. We boarded the bus in the bus depot. After having ridden in it for about an hour, my mother timidly addressed the Polish bus driver: "How much longer is it to the Rakowice Airport?"

"We are not going to the Rakowice Airport," was the curt reply. "This bus is going to the military airfield."

We had boarded the wrong bus. My opportunity to fly went down in flames, and I had to wait forty years before I again had a chance to fly.

In those days traveling long distances was an undertaking that demanded long preparation, much time and great expense. In 1928 my parents received a postcard (telegrams were reserved for extreme emergencies) from my paternal grandfather. We were summoned to come as soon as possible. My great-grandfather's health was fading and he wanted to see us. My grandparents lived in the small village of Zablocie, next to the small town of Zywiec. They were allowed to do business in Zywiec but not to live there. The town belonged to the Archduke of Zywiec and he barred Jews from residency. Zywiec was about eighty miles south of Krakow and it took some four hours by train to get there.

It was my first visit to my paternal grandparents' house and my first opportunity to meet my father's family, his brothers and his one sister. I had only known one brother, a butcher who also lived in Krakow. His name was Nathan, the oldest of my father's siblings from my grandfather's second marriage. His younger brother was my Uncle Henry. My father's mother had died after giving birth to my Uncle Henry. After my paternal grandmother's death, my grandfather married his wife's younger sister, as was the custom amongst traditional Jews following a biblical tenet. Out of that union came seven more children: Nathan, Lipek, Tulek, Aciek, my Aunt Netka, Slomek and Uniu. The last six were still living at home at the time of our visit.

After the customary greetings, hugs and kisses, my father and I were led to a small chamber where my great-grandfather was lying. A pale old man, toothless with a gray beard resting on the featherbed, his almost transparent hands fidgeted with the bedcover. After I was introduced to him, the purpose of our visit was explained to me, I was the first-born son of a first-born son of a first-born son of his, he himself having been a first-born, so I was the carrier of the primogenitureship of my family. My great-grandfather had requested my presence so that he could bless me before his death.

I was asked to bow and lay my head on the bed. My great-grandfather put his hands upon my head in biblical fashion and in mumbled tones pronounced his blessings upon me in Hebrew. (My father later told me that he implored a Guardian Angel to watch over me.) He then reached under his pillow and handed me an apple. He must have put it there when he first sent for me, for by now the fruit was completely brown and decayed. Petrified and overwhelmed by the whole setting, I took the apple and kissed my great-grandfather's hand. I bowed down and backed out of the room, earning a pat on the head from my grandfather and a favorable comment from him: *"Oy, ah sahn klieg yingelle!"* ("Such a smart little boy"). He believed that I had tactfully accepted the rotten apple, not realizing how terrified and tongue-tied I was.

I do not remember our return voyage, but I remember my father telling me shortly thereafter that my great-grandfather had passed on. My acquaintance with my father's family was to be renewed later when I reached the age of eight and we moved to Bielsko-Biala, closer to Zywiec.

The winter of 1929-1930 stands out in my memory for several reasons. The weather was severe, temperatures dropping to -35°C the air so cold it would freeze one's nostrils. The water in the teapot froze solid inside the baking compartment of the stove. The snow squeaked underfoot in the frozen rhythm of quickened steps. I remember the silhouettes of scurrying figures against the whiteout of the landscape. The economy was in a *Krizis*, a crisis, reflecting the worldwide economic Depression. The relationship between my parents became strained by the economic pressures and my grandmother's failing health. In 1930 my grandmother passed away after a brief illness. Her last act was to knit me a woolen set of gloves, earmuffs and scarf in a pinkish-coral color, upon completion of which she reportedly put away her knitting needles and her wool, folded her hands and expired. Whenever I encounter apparel in that pinkish-coral color I envision my grandmother's tiny body lying in her bed and knitting for her favored grandson.

Although I was not aware of it at the time; her death marked for me the end of a very special source of moral and ethical teaching; anchored in the tradition of the Talmud. She always saw and interpreted people's behavior in the light of Jewish ethical dictates; actions were either right or wrong and you simply did not do what was wrong.

That year my father started to look for employment. His butcher shop in Krakow was failing. He found a job managing a large butcher shop in the town of Bielsko, sixty miles southwest of Krakow. I remember going to a post office with my mother to receive a telephone call from my father. The communication was arranged a week in advance and we were notified about it via postcard. I remember the animated conversation and my mother's subsequent grim announcement: "We are moving to Bielsko-Biala."

My whole being rebelled against the prospect of being uprooted from my beloved city; from my cousins; my playmates and all the places to which I had by then developed a deep attachment. From the parks where in fall we would gather chestnuts and golden leaves from the various trees, inhaled the scent of linden flowers, and gathered them to make herbal tea, the best remedy for winter coughs. I would miss the meadows called Blonie on the outskirts of town where we would picnic, play soccer, or just lie, lazily sucking on a piece of straw; the army parades on the state holidays and the religious processions on Christian festivities; the feast of *Lykonik* commemorating the invasion of the Tartars, with a colorfully dressed man portraying the invader by running around inside a wooden horse. I would miss the magic winter wonderland; the mystical glow of gas lamps; the sleds swiftly racing through the snow-covered streets, preceded by the sound of sleigh-bells; the never-never land of shop windows with their Christmas displays.

And most of all, I would miss the haunting sound of the trumpeter who played every hour on the hour from the Marian Tower in the center of town. Its dramatically interrupted clarion call reminded everyone of the brave herald whose warning of the enemy army's approach was halted by a Tartar's arrow through his throat.

CHAPTER II

I do not remember when we moved to Bielsko-Biala, but I remember entering a spacious, newly furnished apartment, its wide windows looking out at a garden full of fruit trees. The house was situated on the outskirts of the town of Biala, a fact that apparently pleased my mother. For my father it was a long walk to work. He would get up very early in the morning and come home late in the evening. He worked in a large kosher butcher shop, the owner of which seemed like a shrewd business man. Mr. Glotzer had a contract with the Polish army garrison for the hindquarters of the slaughtered animals, the parts that were impractical to devein, so as to meet the *kashruth* requirements. The front parts he either sold to Jewish butchers or retailed in his own butcher shop. My father managed the operation and was promised a percentage of it if he invested part of his wages in it. He furnished our new apartment by buying furniture on time, expecting great things from his new job. It was a happy beginning for my mother. The challenges of a new start were exciting and promising.

I was enrolled in a Jewish Public School in the adjoining town of Bielsko, which was a bilingual town having been awarded to Poland as part of the World War I plebiscite and which still had a large German-speaking population. German was taught in school using the old German Gothic alphabet. I had to learn German quickly in order to do well. I excelled in the subjects taught in Polish and Hebrew, for those were the main languages in the school that I had left in Krakow.

The walk to school took 40 minutes. Those of us who lived in Biala would pick each other up on way to school. The walk back always took longer, for we would gawk at the store windows, get into mischief, play games and sometimes even discuss homework. The class consisted of more than forty boys; girls attended separate classes until the seventh grade. One of the very few pre-war pictures that I have is of my fourth-grade class, showing forty-two pupils, less the few that were absent on the day of the picture taking.

My parent's good fortune did not last long. My mother became pregnant and then lost her baby in the later months of her pregnancy. I remember being placed with our neighbors when she went to the hospital and my father's despair when he returned from the hospital and told our neighbors that my mother had lost the baby. I had never seen my father cry before and certainly not in that fashion. He howled like a wounded animal, banging his head against the doorpost, pounding his chest and crying, "It's my fault, it's my fault!"

We went to see my mother in the hospital the next day. She drew me close to her breast and sobbed briefly, and then dried my tears of sympathy, which I had shed without really comprehending the situation. She lifted my chin, and consoled me: "You still are my only son, my *Jedynak*." We took her home the next day.

Some months after, men in uniform came and sealed our apartment and a few days later put everything up for auction. Once again I watched my mother in tears and my father in despair. This time there was fury and frustration in the tone of his cries. He had been betrayed by his employer, who went into bankruptcy and failed to pay my father his back wages, causing forfeiture of payments on our furniture.

We lived in a barren apartment for a time, while my father again looked for employment. My mother's eyes were often red from crying. Sometimes all she could muster for my school lunch was a piece of bread with some jam. She tried to compensate for this meager meal with a special hug added to her customary kiss. I could almost hear the onset of the weeping which would start after my departure.

A year and half later on October 1, 1932, my mother gave birth to my brother Oskar. My father had opened a butcher shop but the income was hardly enough to pay for rent and not enough to pay for my tuition. It must have been very humiliating for my mother to have to go to the principal of my school to plead poverty. But was told not to worry, her son was an excellent student and there would be no problem in waiving the tuition for him.

As if to prove the point, the school awarded me that year and every subsequent year a modest scholarship prize, of which my mother was very proud. But the articles of clothing that sometimes came with the prize she considered a humbling reminder that the award might be due to our financial situation as much as a reward for my scholastic excellence.

My own sense of embarrassment came less from the clothes I wore, whether they were a gift or not, than from the quality of lunches I brought to school and ate mostly out of sight of others.

My economic plight did not escape the attention of some of my school friends. I would get invited to their homes and asked to stay for supper more frequently than others. Sometimes because of the lack of observance of *Kashruth* in the homes of some of my friends, I would not dine with them or would accept only a glass of tea and some fruit. The mother of one of my schoolmates, Herbert Reisfeld, discreetly rectified this problem. On the evenings that I would be invited to play and study with Herb, she would send the maid for salami from a kosher butcher and serve it with bread and tea for all present. She was a beautiful divorced woman who had the exclusive representation for Poland of the 4711 cosmetic products. They lived half a block from the school in a modern villa. German was spoken at their home and I was welcomed to help Herb with his school assignments in Polish. There were always little favors of cosmetic products for me to take home, mostly for my mother.

My father, meanwhile, started to come home late, hanging out with people we didn't know, playing cards in coffee houses and in the game rooms of the two hotels in town. My parents quarreled more frequently. My poor beleaguered mother sought counsel from her sisters through the mail. She must have felt the loss of my grandmother and her moral support more intensely then ever.

I offered to help my father as much as I could; I even suggested quitting school to help him in the butcher shop. (He had had to let his assistant go.) My father did not allow me to quit school but accepted my offer of help. I would get up very early in the morning to go to the icehouse with him, load the meat for the day's sales onto a hand-drawn wagon, harness the rope on my shoulder, grab the thill and help to pull the wagon to the butcher shop, run home and then run to school. Afternoons I would deliver the meat to the customers and on Thursdays I would also try to collect from those who bought on credit, a chore I greatly disliked. In winter, when the temperature at 3 A.M. was rather severe, my father would encourage me to have a shot of vodka before we left the house as a protection against the bitter cold. He would temper the sharp drink with a bit of raspberry syrup and a bite from an egg cookie that my mother had baked.

In the summer of 1933 my father opened a butcher shop in the nearby resort village of Bystra for the vacation season. We rented a farmer's house and since business was good my father decided to move us there permanently. Bystra lay in the foothills of the Beskidy Mountains. It had a sanitarium for people afflicted with tuberculosis and was a summer resort frequented by Jews from Bielsko-Biala and from the towns of Sosnowiec and Bendzin. Of all the year-round inhabitants of Bystra there was only one other Jewish family living in our neighborhood. They owned a grocery store and had no children my age, so my playmates were the children of the Polish farmers and blue-collar workers who lived in the area. Some used to take the same train I did to attend school in town. Through those relationships I was introduced to the habits of rural life. The games that we children played were simple and mostly took place outside. I learned how to fish bare-handed for trout; walking upstream, wiggling my fingers and looking under rocks and river banks, sometimes coming up with a crab hanging onto my finger instead of a fish. I rediscovered the joy of eating potatoes baked in an open fire plain or sometimes with their taste enhanced by a dash of salt if I was able to sneak some from home. Still today I enjoy baked potatoes with salt as the only flavoring.

I continued to attend the Jewish public school in Bielsko, commuting by train. It was a fifteen-minute walk to the railroad station, and a twenty-five-minute ride to town. When I heard the whistle of the train coming around the mountain bend I knew that I was late and wouldn't get to the station in time. It would be an hour and a half of brisk walking to school and I was sure to miss at least the first class. If I missed the train on a snowy winter day, I would put on my skis and either hook onto a passing horse-driven wagon or sled or just ski to town. I had learned how to ski from my playmates. I fashioned my second set of skis with one of my friends from some ash tree lumber and shaped them in his basement. We competed in cross-country races with some success. After the war I read about this friend, Janek Kula, winning one of the events at the European FIS (International Ski Federation) championship in Zakopane, Poland.

In summer the rhythm of my life changed completely. I would be busy either helping my father in his butcher shop or working in the fields with the peasants, especially during the harvest, digging for potatoes or cutting and gathering hay and grain. The soles of my feet became as tough as leather from working barefoot between the harvesters, gathering the stalks and tying them in bundles. I remember my initial panic at working between the fast-moving scythes, their swift semi-circular motion threatening but never injuring my bare legs, their blinding gleam in the sunlight compounding my fear, which I had to conquer and which I was ashamed to share with the boys and girls working with me. At noon we would rest, exhausted, and enjoy the farmer's reward of cool buttermilk.

The work with my father was of an entirely different nature. I helped him in the slaughterhouse, tying up the animals for the slaughter and cleaning up afterwards. Sometimes I went to a village with my father to see a farmer with an animal for sale.

I was proud to witness the peasant's trust during their bargaining sessions with my father. A slap of one hand against the other would seal the deal and a drink of vodka from a bottle, which my father usually produced from his pocket, would make it an amicable transaction. Sometimes I would be entrusted with leading a purchased calf to the shed next to our butcher shop.

I did not like this particular chore. The young animal was never willing to be dragged the few kilometers to its destination and would buck, trying to drag me by the rope. The only sure way to make it follow was to put a few fingers in its mouth and let it suck on them. By the time the trip was over, the fingers of both my hands would be bleeding badly. The farmers would usually bring the older cattle to us themselves.

The animals were slaughtered by ritual slaughterers who would have to travel from the city, and who were under the supervision of the *Kehilla* (Jewish community) in town. The *Kehilla* paid the slaughterer in monthly wages and the butcher would in turn pay the *Kehilla* for each animal serviced. The lung, the liver and the spleen of the animal were also traditionally part of the payment to the *Shohet*, the ritual slaughterer. Since sometimes the *Shohet* had to come after the end of Sabbath and then either stay overnight or go home very late (the Sabbath ends late in summer), they would try to relegate the assignment to the youngest among them. One man was in his thirties, a redhead, very arbitrary and generally incompetent. He would supplement his income as a slaughterer by being a watchmaker. The standard joke about him (in Yiddish of course) was "when he fixed a watch it would stop dead, and when he slaughtered an animal it would keep going."

On one Saturday night the moody young man very reluctantly agreed to come down to the village to slaughter a young heifer. After the act, during the ritual of examining the slaughtering instrument, the *Halef*, he declared the animal *Treif*, not kosher.

The section of *Halacha*, Jewish law, which was formulated to insure as painless a death for the animal as possible, states that if after the act of cutting the animal's throat there is a nick on the very sharp *Halef*, the animal is not Kosher, for it might have suffered by having its windpipe torn rather then cut. My father, being a butcher, of course knew the laws of slaughter in minute detail, set out in the tractate *Chulim* of the *Gemarah*. His father, his brothers and their grandfather had all been kosher butchers and were required to familiarize themselves with those ordinances.

"How do they test the nick?" the law asks. "Some on their fingers, some on their tongues, some by putting it in the water." "And what is considered a nick big enough to render it as causing a rip?" The law as interpreted by the Ashkenazi Rabbis states: That if you can remove the nick by non-mechanical means the animal is *Kosher*. So my father asked the watchmaker/*Shohet*, who obviously did not seem positively inclined to his assignment, to try to take the nick out by repeatedly dragging the knife on the palm of his hand. After a while the *Shohet* defiantly declared that the knife still had a nick. My father, who would face a financial crisis of sorts without any merchandise for the start of the week, and sensing that the young man might be intentionally trying to declare the animal *treif,* opened the icebox and shoved him in, instructing him to try again.

At first, after a short time came the retort: *"Yossel,"* Josef, "the animal is still *treif.*" But my father refused to let him out and insisted that he try again. After about ten minutes came the resigned announcement: "I got it out, it's kosher now." The frozen, shaking young man came out of the freezer, hastily put on his coat on and left.

After that the *Kehilla* somehow found it possible to send the older and more experienced slaughterers to my father.

There were also occasions when we had no cattle to be slaughtered on Saturday night, but there were some chickens that my father had promised to his customers for Sunday and they had to be taken care of. I would have to put the live chickens in a basket and carry them on my shoulders the seven and a half kilometers to town. I could not take a bus for there was none available at that time. I would get back home with the slaughtered chickens around midnight, my shoulders sore and raw from the weight of the birds. I was not even twelve at the time.

There was another significant aspect to my life in Bystra. There were two Jewish hotels, better termed boarding houses, in the village. They were called *Pensjonat* and offered room and board. One of them was run by the family Neufeld. To this *Pensjonat Neufeld,* Rabbi Twersky from the town of Kielce, a member of one of the prominent rabbinical dynasties of Poland, would come to stay for the summer. Rabbi Twersky suffered from tuberculosis and during the week he spent much of his time in the local sanitarium for tuberculosis patients. Located on a hill overlooking the village, it was known throughout Poland as a center for treatment of tuberculosis. The rabbi was an outpatient of the institution, living with his family in the *Pensjonat*. There was always a large contingent of his Hassidim, followers who would come to Bystra to stay with the rabbi.

One of the larger rooms in the boarding house was turned into a *Beth Midrash* where the rabbi and his followers would pray and study. My father and I would regularly attend the Sabbath services there and sometimes the weekly morning or evening prayers.

On Saturday between the afternoon and evening services the rabbi would deliver a talk on a Talmudic subject and a lively discussion would follow. Afterwards the rabbi would fall silent. He would close his eyes, sway back and forth, strike his beard and then initiate a melody. Sometimes it was familiar and sometimes a new one, which he would compose in those moments of repose, sometimes to the words of familiar *Zemiroth*, Sabbath hymns, and sometimes just a melody to hum to. Often, if he were in a pensive mood, this would be a slow-starting, melancholy, haunting tune. Sometimes the tune would be fugue-like and repetitious and then evolve gradually into a joyous, rhythmic beat accompanied by hand clapping and table banging. The Hassidim would join in, swaying their heads, their curly *payhot* dangling from side to side, their spirits lifted to a sacred merger with their God.

Before the *Zemiroth*, the traditional Sabbath third meal, the *Suda Shlishit*, would be served, usually in the form of a *Nuddel Kugel*. The Hassidim would lunge aggressively with their bare hands to partake of the dish after the rabbi had pronounced the blessing over the food. I did not participate in that act, for I did not care for that kind of *Kugel*, prepared in the manner of the Jews from Central Poland and Lithuania with salt and pepper. I was accustomed to the Galician kind of *Kiegel*, sweet with raisins, like my grandma used to make.

Of the rabbi's children I remember two. David was several years older than I, a studious, serious young man who participated in the table discourse. The rabbi would sometimes question him publicly during debates about the talmudic approach to a problem and occasionally let him lead the services. The other son, Mottel, was closer to my age, more restless and more inclined to fraternize with someone like myself who was not a part of the Hassidic circle. We would sometimes sneak out for a walk when the rabbi was sleeping or preoccupied with his Hassidim. Mottel would ask me about my life, the things I did, games and associations that were off-limits to him. I, in turn, would question him about his family life and his relationship with his father.

NORBERT FRIEDMAN

We would watch peasants working in the fields, his curiosity centered on the young girls, their sunburned legs showing from under their skirts when they bent over.

When the summer started I would look forward to the Twersky clan's arrival. I enjoyed the atmosphere of joyous and scholarly piety, of respectful conduct and reverence that the family and the visiting followers displayed toward the rabbi. While I was a window onto the more modern life of a Jewish youngster for Mottel, he and his surroundings revealed all the joy, serenity and beauty of the Hassidic world to me.

In 1996 while paying a Shiva-call (a visit to a person in mourning) to a friend of mine who had lost a sister, I noticed that the family's name was Twersky. I asked my friend if they were any relations to the Kielce Rov, the Rabbi of Kielce, Twersky. When he said yes and I found that his sister's husband's name was David, I realized that I was in the house of Mottel's brother. I had no idea that any of the members of the family had survived. I approached David and introduced myself. We had not seen one another for 60 years.

At first he did not remember me, but after I mentioned my father's name it came back to him: "You are the butcher Yossel's son! You were a friend of Mottel's." He called his grandsons, all of them obviously yeshiva students, and introduced me to them, pointing out that I once knew their great-grandfather and used to pray with him, ages ago in another world, in another time. The young men listened respectfully, eyeing the modern dressed old man who was not a part of their world. Their mode of dress and their uncut earlocks nonetheless reminded me of what their grandfather and his brother looked like when I knew them. Mottel's name was not mentioned in the introduction. Only when I inquired about his fate did I find out that he had also survived and was living in Los Angeles. Later I found out from my friend that Mottel had left the Hassidic community after the war and led the life of a non-Orthodox Jew.

As I was leaving the house of mourning my thoughts went back to the prewar universe of the Hassidic world in Poland, a world never to be duplicated or even fully appreciated, and I realized that my romantic attachment to that life was to a great degree the result of my exposure to the house of the Kielce Rov, Rabbi Twersky Z'L. of blessed memory

CHAPTER III

In the winter of 1934-35 my parents decided that we had to move back from Bystra to Bielsko-Biala. I was to become *Bar Mitzvah* in the winter of 1935 and a tutor had to be engaged. At that time I was attending the seventh and last grade in the Jewish School.

In May 1935, Marshal Josef Pilsudski, the military leader and de facto ruler of Poland, died suddenly. His death marked the beginning of the end of the enforcement of the laws and ordinances that had been installed to protect the Jewish minority. Marshal Pilsudski was the checking force to the attempts of the declared anti-Jewish elements to deprive the Jews of their rights.

We moved back to Bielsko-Biala after the summer season. My father found a one-room apartment on the outskirts of the town of Biala in a house owned by a Seventh-Day Adventist, a religious sect of Christians who also observed the Sabbath and who also were in disfavor with the Polish Roman Catholic faithful.

The house stood at the end of a short, tree-lined street, elevated and looking out on a large rolling meadow—A perfect location to suit my mother's idea of a place to live.

The landlord lived on the ground floor. The top floor had three tenants, each occupying one-room apartment. To the left of us lived a widow with two sons, Wladek and Wojtek, both of whom worked as locksmiths. All were devout Catholics, good though simple souls.

To the right of our door was an entrance to the attic and a small room with a slanted ceiling where a single pretty young woman lived who used to entertain gentlemen on regular basis. She supposedly worked as a dancer in a nightclub.

Our room had a coal stove, a table, four chairs and two beds, one on each side of the window at the end of the room. When we moved in there was no electricity in the house; two kerosene lamps supplied the light. Later on, the owner installed electricity with the help of the two men Wladek and Wojtek.

A single bulb with a dish-like reflector hanging over the table illuminated the apartment and there was a bulb in the foyer over the stairs as well.

Water was drawn from a hand-pumped well downstairs and stored in a pail. Dirty water and waste was simply dumped into the gutter. The outhouses stood next to each other and offered little privacy because of the cracks between the wooden boards. In wintertime the cold wind would blow ferociously through those cracks, inducing the tenants to use the pail or the chamber pot in the comfort of the house.

Each tenant owned a bin downstairs for supplies such as wood, coal and potatoes. A coal-carrier would supply coal; an elderly forward-bent man, always black from the coal dust, he would carry it in a basket on his back. A full basket contained about one hundred pounds of coal. At the onset of winter we would order several hundred pounds and the dealer would bring it in a horse-driven wagon. Wood for fuel was bought by the yard and long sections would be cross-stacked outside, to be cut and chopped when needed.

My father and I, and sometimes one of the neighbors, would saw the wood in quarter-yard-long pieces and chop them with a large ax on a wooden block. I liked that particular chore; although it was tiring, it was also invigorating and strength-building. I liked the smell of the wood and the sense of power that the handling of it gave me. I would look out for sap-containing logs and save them for kindling to start the fire, which would be my responsibility most of the time.

A barrel or two of sauerkraut would also be prepared for the winter and kept in the cellar. The sauerkraut and potatoes were the staple of our food in the cold winter months, which lasted from November trough April.

Because of the uncertainty of our economic situation and having had to endure other inconveniences already, my mother had apparently learned to accept conditions that her background did not prepare her for. Under those circumstances she was happy to accept her new abode, except that we were the first Jews to move into the vicinity and I was not welcome among the kids of the neighborhood.

The first beating put me to bed for a couple of weeks. I did not expect such a fierce reaction. The non-Jewish children that I had played with in Bystra were less averse to Jewish playmates, because all the summer vacationers in Bystra were Jewish and there were many economic benefits derived by the parents of my playmates from the presence of those vacationers. Slowly, however, I started to form friendships in my new neighborhood with individual boys, sometimes even resorting to bribes in the form of candies or cookies surreptitiously sneaked out from the house. Later my willingness to blend in with the gang and to participate in their activities, as well as my ability to play goalie on their soccer team (I was mortified to let in a goal and contribute to a loss) gained me acceptance by the gang. All but one: Tadek Malecki, a combative, moody, always—ready-for-a-scrap young fellow, who was never pacified by my attempts to befriend him. Although less then twelve years old, he would often carry a bottle of vodka and always a knife in his pocket.

His brother, Janek Malecki, the leader of the gang and several years older then most of us, was already working in a machine shop, trying to support his widowed mother who did laundry for the people in the neighborhood. Janek, who had to leave school at an early age to work, possessed inborn intelligence and a drive for knowledge. He and I spent a lot of time together.

Saturday afternoon after services and the Sabbath meal, I would bring down to Janek a piece of cake or a portion of *Cholent* (a traditional dish of meat, beans or potatoes, stewed in a pot in a baker's oven over Friday night and eaten on Saturday). On Sunday after he returned from church I would keep him company even when he would drop into the neighborhood inn for a shot of vodka followed by a glass of beer or two. (Apparently there were no age restrictions on alcohol consumption; if there were, they were not enforced.) We would discuss various subjects: sports, movies, religion. I would encourage him to read, but he always claimed that he had no time for it, and insisted instead that I tell him about the books I read.

When I complained to him about his brother's behavior, he would usually grow silent, but finally he confided in me. Their father had been an alcoholic who physically abused their mother and the boys until one day while in a post-binge depression he hung himself. Tadek was never able to handle the way that he lost his father. Janek himself had difficulty controlling his temper, which became apparent when he got into an altercation. His fighting skills and his fearless battles with members of other gangs were legendary in our area; they earned him the respect of young and old, and sometimes a round of drinks at the pub.

In his relationship with me he was gentle and considerate. He respected my father greatly after my father once defeated him in arm wrestling and bought him a beer. His friendship eventually won me the total acceptance and protection of the group. Still, they would have preferred that I was one of them and that I was a Christian.

One time they decided among themselves to baptize me. In their juvenile minds they concocted a procedure which they thought would elevate me to their Christian status. They ganged up on me, threw me to the ground and pinned down my arms. They unbuttoned my fly and spat at my private parts, thus nullifying in their minds the act of circumcision. Then they held my nose until the lack of air made me open my mouth and they forced a piece of pork into it, pushing it down and making me swallow it. This they felt validated my "conversion." After they released me I got sick and vomited. Ever since, when I am forced against my will to violate my religious convictions I can imagine the metallic taste of salted pork in my mouth.

Still, the bond of friendship between my neighborhood peers and me grew stronger. In the winter we would often go skiing together. Sunday mornings we would hire a horse-driven sled with a driver, hang on to a knotted rope and ski, ten or twelve of us, all the way to the base of the *Klimczok* Mountain. On the way to the slopes the boys would stop sometimes in the church to attend mass. I would go in with them, but I would stand in the back without kneeling.

Once on such a Sunday while standing in the back of the church and witnessing the services, I received a violent blow to the back of my head. The accompanying curse, "Down on your knees, you Jewish son-of-a-whore," shouted at me by a rather large, young Polish man, impressed upon me that I was not a welcome visitor in the church. From then on I preferred waiting in the freezing cold for my friends to the risk of brutal rejection.

The following spring our gang was shocked by a terrible accident. While working on a lathe, Janek Malecki had his shirtsleeve caught in the lathe's head. His forearm was mangled and had to be amputated below the elbow. I visited him in the hospital every day and tried my best to cheer him up. I brought him books to read, but he still insisted that I read them to him. One day the nurse who took care of him in the hospital explained that he was nearsighted but refused to wear glasses.

In the hospital Janek was very concerned about his earning ability and his ability to play soccer. He starred as the left wing on the local team. But not long after he got out of the hospital he rejoined the team. One could see him flying down the field and dribbling around his opponents, his empty shirtsleeve flapping around as if looking for the body part that it once adorned. He had received a small compensation from the company he worked for, but his job was gone. This affected him for a while, driving him into the shelter of the pubs and the solace of alcohol. Then one of the patrons of his sport club helped him to get a job in a haberdashery store, where he was well liked by the customers; he sincerely and politely tried to be of assistance. He was happy to be working and be able to help his mother.

Meanwhile I was preparing for my *Bar Mitzvah*. Reb Mayer, who came to tutor me, was a small bearded man dressed in the traditional garb of the

Hassidim. At first he was greeted with a barrage of stones on the way to my house, but after I had informed the boys that he was my tutor he was left alone. They would even silence the verbal abuse of the elderly passing Poles.

My Bar Mitzvah took place in my father's house of prayer. It was a rather Spartan little shul, with wooden benches and tables; a calico sheet partitioned off the women's section. I read the week's whole Torah portion as well as the portion of the Prophets, the *Haftorah*. After the services, schnaps and honey cake were served. There might even have been some herring, I do not remember. Maybe three or four of my schoolmates were invited to the house. Some nuts and candy were hurled at me; egg-cookies and milk were served. On Sunday, the following day (for you are not allowed to handle a writing instrument on the Sabbath) a fountain pen, courtesy of my relatives in Krakow, was presented to me. It was nothing special; my friends did not have anything much different at their Bar Mitzvahs.

At that time I was attending the eighth grade of a public non-Jewish school in Bielsko. It was a difficult environment; one I never really became comfortable with. The first problem for me and the five other students from the Jewish school, stemmed from our refusal to join others in the Lord's Prayer in the morning and to clasp the palms of our hands in the common gesture of Catholic worship. The teacher of our class, Professor Dombrowski, hurled insults at us and threatened us with expulsion. Unmoved, we went to the principal of the school, Mr. Suhon, who was a liberal and reasonable man. We explained to him that we Jews prayed at home before we left for school and that the text of the Lord's prayer was contrary to our belief and that we could not comply. He solved the problem by having us enter the class after the morning prayers were said.

Later that year a contest among the students of the eighth grade was held for a speech to be given to greet the visiting governor of the state. He was coming to visit the school on the occasion of the installation of a short-wave radio station, which also connected all the classes by a communication system. It was the first such installation at any school in the state.

I had entered the contest and Mr. Suhon called me into his office. After sitting me down, he told me that my speech was chosen as the best of the lot. But for reasons that I would understand, he said the school would have someone else read it to the governor during his visit. I suspected the reason, but I wanted the principal to spell it out, so I asked him for it.

"Well," he halfheartedly stated, "you do have a little bit of a Jewish accent,"

When I protested, insisting that I spoke Polish more correctly than the majority of other children, he embarrassingly stated, "Your name is Jewish, and because of that, one might perceive a slight accent in your delivery."

"But you have not heard me reading this speech, so how can you say that? And besides," I added angrily, almost in tears, "if you want someone else to read the address, let him write one."

The principal knew that I was right, but apparently he was under pressure from other teachers.

"I will let you know," he concluded as he escorted me out of the room.

Three weeks later I delivered my address to the governor. He was impressed apparently, for he called me to the principal's office and in Mr. Suhon's presence presented me with an autographed volume of Polish history and pledged a full scholarship to the state gymnasium upon my graduation. My parents, who were present at the ceremony, were immensely proud and moved. My mother envisioned her son graduating from the gymnasium and continuing on to a university. My father declared that he would never from now on let me handle a knife in the slaughterhouse or in the butcher shop. He must have been nursing ideas of breaking me into his profession, just as his father did for him.

But I had other plans for my future. At the early age of ten I had joined a Zionist-Socialist youth group, not because of ideological leanings or opinions (I doubt that a ten-year-old has any), but because most of my schoolmates belonged to one. Membership in Polish Boy Scout troops was denied to Jewish youth and the Zionist youth groups offered Jewish children parallel programs and involvement. There were many such organizations with different ideological loyalties. I joined the *Shomer Hatzair* movement, not because of its ideology, but because they had a large playing area in front of their meeting place—a former potato field which now served as a soccer and athletic field. I also joined because of the rumors that *Shomer Hatzair* practiced free love among their members in their *Kibbutzim*, the farm co-operatives in Israel.

The unit that I belonged to, the *Kvutzah* was recruited mostly from among my schoolmates. We participated in discussion groups, which were mostly indoctrination sessions about the philosophy of the organization and its view of world affairs, with an eye to its ultimate goal, of settling in *Eretz Yisrael*. We were to liberate the Arab farm and city workers from exploitation by their employers and have them join the struggle for a just socialist state.

Excursions into the mountains and overnight hikes with all the usual instructions that the Polish scouts received were intended to develop a hardiness suitable for the severe conditions in Palestine. To those exercises were added martial art instructions as preparation for possible para-military service in the *Palmah*, the Jewish Defense Force. Every summer we would be encouraged to attend a sleep-away camp lasting from two to eight weeks someplace in the country. At the age of twelve I spent four weeks in such a camp, and then again in the summer of 1939, the last summer before the war.

Despite its agnostic view of religion, the organization strongly believed in historical ties and the right of the Jewish people to the land of what was then called Palestine. The major requirement of members was *Aliyah*, the emigration to Palestine. The young members of my group, despite the constant indoctrination into atheism and doubts placed in our minds about our beliefs, could not divorce ourselves from the restrictions imposed by tradition. For instance, on Saturday evenings, when we would gather for a discussion group, we would not light the kerosene lamp until at least two of us could verify three stars in the sky, signaling the end of the Sabbath. On cloudy evenings we would send someone a block away to check if the lights in the nearest Jewish house had been lit. My Zionist tendencies were reinforced by frequent anti-Semitic incidents I encountered in my everyday life: being called a dirty Jew on the street; having insults and rocks hurled at me while passing through strange neighborhoods; noticing the official discrimination that a Jew had to deal with every day of his life.

After graduating from the eighth grade I decided to apply to a four-year polytechnic middle school which offered an engineering technician's degree. I opted for this instead of taking up the offer of a full scholarship to the state gymnasium because of my plans to go to Palestine and help build an industrial-agricultural Jewish society.

I knew the difficulties of passing the entrance exam and I worked hard to prepare myself for it. The school had four departments: mechanical, textile, dyeing and chemical. I applied to the mechanical department. Applicants had to undergo two days of written tests and, a week later, two days of oral exams. Based on the excellence of our written test results, three others and I, from a group of two hundred hopefuls, had our oral exams waived. The results were to be announced a week after the oral exams. For two weeks I lived in hopeful confidence of being accepted. Why not? Only four of us were good enough to have our oral exams waived.

On the day that the names of the accepted students were to be announced my mother and I dressed in our Sabbath clothing and cheerfully went to the auditorium to hear the verdicts. The dean of the Mechanical faculty called out the names, announcing: "Passed and admitted," or "Not passed." He came to my name and called out: "Passed, not admitted." I was shocked. My mother's head slumped on her chest and tears of hurt ran down her cheeks. All she could say through her sobbing was, "my son, there must be some mistake."

It was no mistake; it was the dreaded *Numerus Clausus* applied to Jewish applicants in all institutions of middle and higher learning. Only one Jewish applicant was admitted to the class that I tried to be admitted to and he was someone from Turkey who probably had influential backing. All appeals on my behalf from my teachers, from the Rabbi of the community and even the most forceful intervention from the principal of my last school, Mr. Suhon, were in vain. Afterwards, they all tried to have me reconsider my choice and attend the state gymnasium.

My mind was now more made up than ever. I was leaving the country that I was born in, where I was not wanted despite the fact that my people had been its inhabitants for ten centuries; despite the fact that my father and my uncles had served in its army, and that so many of my people had dedicated their lives to its cause throughout its existence. I was learning the meaning of the term second-class citizen. My mother got in touch with her sisters in Krakow; there was a slight chance that I might get in into the Poly-Tech there, but that also fizzled for the same reason. The Polish government had instituted a policy that despite a terrible shortage of engineers in Poland restricted the percentage of Jewish engineers to the percentage of Jews in Poland. There was one last alternative—the Jewish Vocational School in Krakow, an annex to the Hebrew Gymnasium, where I attended my second and third grade of public school. But there the tuition was high and if we had to pay for room and board, my parents would not be able to afford it. It seems that the teachings of my grandmother had left their intended imprint on her daughters, for after a family consultation, my aunts in Krakow decided to share among themselves the responsibility for my room and board. I was to sleep and have breakfast at my aunt Hela's home, in what used to be my grandmother's house, the nearest location to the school. Lunch and supper I was to have at my aunt Rozia's house. Friday eve and Saturday I was to go to the suburb of Lobzow where my aunt Pepka and cousin Wilek lived.

Before my departure, my parents spent a lot of time instructing me how to act when away from home; be polite and well-mannered, they said and never, ever talk back to my aunts. My father suggested that if I should ever be in a financial squeeze I should visit his only full brother, my Uncle Henry. Uncle Henry lived in a town called Jaslo, several hundred kilometers from Krakow, but he had an office for his trucking company in Krakow and could be found at a certain restaurant where he hung out. My father claimed that his brother was a generous man and could be counted upon. My mother disagreed; she had a different opinion of her brother-in-law, one that her correspondence with Uncle Henry's wife helped to reinforce. My mother considered him a phony and an untrustworthy person.

I left for Krakow and my first stay away from home. I was not even fourteen.

CHAPTER IV

How changed was my grandmother's house, and how much smaller did every thing look to me now! The wooden bench, which we would turn upside down and take on trips to all those strange places. The three of us, Wilek, Dolek and I once fit into the upturned bench, making it a vehicle to travel to the exotic countries of our dreams: To a land called America, to fight against, or sometimes with, the colorful Indians, like chief Winetou or his trusted companion Old Schatterhand of Karl May's tales. Sometimes the bench would be a vessel for a trip down the Nile to the Egyptian Sphinx, built by our ancestors in the time of Moses. Now the bench looked so small and so insignificant. The shelf under the large wooden table, where we would huddle to stay out of the way of the adults, seemed narrower now, too, cluttered with bundles of wool or cotton waste.

Only the burned indentation in the front right-hand corner of the table top, where my grandfather would spill and light a little of the schnaps used in the *Havdalah* service, creating a bluish flame that added to the mystical moment when Sabbath would depart, reminded me of all the blissful weekends spent at my grandparents' house.

Aunt Hela's husband Israel, was a quilt-maker by profession, and the cotton or wool waste under the table was used as stuffing for the quilts he crafted. In one corner stood a forbidding hand-driven machine used for tearing cotton or wool fiber into a fine downy substance, a task which later became my regular chore. In the center of the large kitchen stood the *Krosno,* an adjustable wooden frame with hooks on which the material for the quilt would be spread, the filler evenly distributed with repeated striking of a bamboo rod and then another sheet of material hooked over it. Then the design to be embroidered into the quilt was chalk-drawn with the aid of a ruler and compass. His father, a slight, energetic man, and my Aunt Hela, who had learned to sew the embroidery and add the finishing touches, especially to the more expensive quilts, assisted my uncle. My uncle's family loved music, and there would be whistling and singing during work. They would be able to complete a set of quilts in a day.

Towards evening the quilts would be folded and delivered to the customer. On Thursdays and Fridays my Aunt Hela would sometimes help out in a large fish store, called *Hala Rybna* in Polish. The store belonged to a man who used to be my grandfather's customer and who was willing to provide my aunt with additional income.

I liked staying with Aunt Hela, a tall, pretty woman who as a youngest child had apparently acquired a reputation of being selfish; it was often mentioned that when asked to share some candy, she had replied "How can I, I only have six pieces for myself?" She generally tried to be fair towards me, but when it came to the handling of her daughter Nusia, she could not help but show favoritism. My cousin Nusia was much younger than I. She was always affectionate towards me when we were alone. She would sit in my lap, lovingly leaning her cheek against mine when I would read or tell stories. She would wait for me when I came home to show me her schoolwork, and expected praise from her cousin eight years her senior. When her parents were present, however, especially her mother, Nusia acted bossy and scornful, ordering me to do chores for her and treating me with contempt. Occasionally she would throw a tantrum or break into a crying spell, accusing me of insolent conduct toward her, all calculated to gain advantage with her parents and make me aware of my lowly station in her house. It was a painful situation for me and the awareness that I had no choice in the matter added to my dismay.

I used to look forward to the visits of my uncle's brother and his wife. My Uncle Israel's brother was a lanky, handsome man with long loose limbs and a prematurely wrinkled face without any beard-growth. His wife was also tall and very beautiful. They always dressed according to the latest fashion. There were rumors about his manliness, which I could not believe—about a man with such an attractive wife. She had a great voice and he played the mandolin, joining my Aunt Hela and her husband in renditions of popular songs. On such evenings they would sometimes send me down to buy refreshments: the sweet-tasting sauerkraut from Mr. Kleinzeler's store across the street, freshly roasted chestnuts or pumpkin seeds from the street vendor or some halvah from the corner store. I would always hurry back, so that I would not miss too much of those pleasant moments.

During my lunch break at school I would run to Aunt Rozia's house. Sometimes, when Uncle Michal could make it home or when any of her children were home for lunch she would have a hot meal ready for me; other times I had only a sandwich prepared by her servant. On those evenings when I was asked to come to supper it was quite another matter. The whole family would be present: Uncle Michal, Aunt Rozia, cousins Tosia, Dolek and Hela. The meal would be rather formal and served by the servant. All the required table manners were observed and the children spoke very little, only when addressed by their elders.

I looked forward to the times after supper when I would be able to observe and sometimes be involved in the social lives of my cousins and their friends who would come to visit. The friends of my cousin Tosia especially impressed me. They were mostly seniors in the Jewish *Gymnasium,* the Jewish High School. In my eyes they were mature individuals getting ready to enter centers of higher education in Poland or abroad, and some of them were planning to go to Palestine. They were the avant-garde of the Zionist youth in Poland; most of them were members of the *Akiba* a Zionist centrist movement. They were drawn to the beauty and sweet, friendly disposition of my cousin Tosia and to the hospitality of my Aunt Rozia's house.

Dolek and Hela, meanwhile, were being tutored. On those evenings when they were to have their lessons I tried to be present even when I was not invited, to the consternation of my Aunt Rozia. After a while it became apparent to my aunt that it was my hunger for additional education and not the food that brought me there and she did not object to my unsolicited presence.

I envied without rancor my cousins' good fortune, their bright modern home, their apparent prosperity and most of all their opportunity for education. Although sometimes I felt out of place in my worn-out clothes and would be ignored by some of the visitors and even excluded by my cousins, it only served to strengthen my resolve to excel in my own studies and succeed in my plans to leave Poland, with all of its prejudices and the shame of being poor.

The school week ended Friday at noon. After lunch at Aunt Rozia's I would run home to Aunt Hela, change into my Sabbath clothes and get ready to go to Aunt Pepka's. It was a very long walk through town, about five kilometers. Sometimes when they were in a charitable mood, Aunt Hela or Uncle Israel would stake me to ten *groszy* for the streetcar fare. And sometimes on a hot day when I was broke—which was most of the time—I would spend the money on an ice cream cone and walk the whole distance to my aunt's house.

It was the home of a blue-collar family, modestly furnished but warm and hospitable. My Aunt Pepka, the oldest of my mother's siblings, was the practical, resolute and outgoing matriarch of the clan now. It was her sense of family responsibility that secured my lodging arrangement, for she was never averse to telling others what was the right thing to do.

The Richter-Schwetzreichs, my uncle's family, were one of only two Jewish families living in that suburban area. A block down the street was a farm and garden establishment where my aunt would get her milk and other dairy products as well as her vegetables. The owners, the Koniks, were friends of my aunt, and their two boys were cousin Wilek's school and playmates. Downstairs lived the owners of the house, whose daughter Kasia was also Wilek's schoolmate. Wilek was very comfortable in the company of his non-Jewish friends and seemed to have been well accepted.

Wilek did not have too much time for play, for at that time he was starting his apprenticeship in a plumbing concern. He would come home Friday afternoon a little earlier, but between running errands and performing chores for Aunt Pepka we would have little time to play or exchange details about our doings of the week. Friday nights, after the traditional Sabbath supper, we would help with clean-up and then share our experiences. Wilek would relate his newly learned trade terminology (couplings, elbows, tap and thread sizes) and I would share with him what I had learned in the vocational school.

Saturday we would sleep late. Aunt Pepka did not insist that we go to services and the nearest house of worship was quite a distance away. She celebrated the Sabbath by abstaining from work and having her family with her. Her other son, Cousin Tobias, was serving in the Polish army at that time and could visit only infrequently.

Saturday night after Sabbath was over and the lights were turned on, Uncle Srulek would start his working week. He allowed me to try to help him; patiently teaching me some of the less skill-demanding steps in the making of the shoe tops. I loved to sit next to him, inhale the smell of the leather and glue and listen to him sing in his beautiful bass voice. I especially loved the Russian songs he had learned while in a Prisoner-of-War camp in Siberia. His rendition of "Volga, Volga" still rings in my ears.

Aunt Pepka would always give me the money for the streetcar ride back to Aunt Hela's house and I always tried to take the last streetcar. I loved staying with Aunt Pepka; there was an aura of serene stability in her house where I never heard a quarrel or even an angry exchange.

The school week started Sunday morning with four hours of shop instruction, a break for lunch and then four hours of what was known as theory. This included history, geography and languages but emphasized subjects related to trade skills, such as physics, mathematics and the science of materials. Tired from the four hours of shop (which included three-month-long alternating assignments in the blacksmith, machine and locksmith shops), where skills foreign to most Jewish youth had to be mastered, we did not pay the necessary attention to the afternoon subjects, which frustrated our teachers.

The school tuition had to be paid monthly. At first the funds came regularly from home but after the few first months there was a disturbing delay in their arrival. When I went home for the holiday break I realized that the economic situation in my house had gone from bad to worse and I also found that my parents had to borrow money to pay for my school.

I lied to them, claiming I had applied for and would receive a scholarship and that I would not need any money from them. When I returned to Krakow I tried to get tutoring jobs and when that was not enough to pay for my tuition I just stopped paying. Before the end of the school year I was informed that I would not be allowed to finish unless I met my financial obligations. So a month before the end of the school year I stopped attending. To the dismay of my schoolmates and the probable relief of my aunts, I started to make preparations to return to Bielsko-Biala and my parents' home.

I was sorry to have to leave my new friends, especially those from the Krakow branch of my Zionist youth organization. I had met many wonderful, bright young people from backgrounds comparable to my own who shared similar visions for their futures. We promised to stay in touch and continue our goal of emigration to Palestine. I knew I would also miss the company of my cousins with whom I was developing warm relationships. The only thing I was glad to leave was the degrading sense of dependence on the charity of my mother's family.

I packed my books and my few articles of clothes and took the train back home to my parents and my little brother. I was apprehensive about their reaction to my lying about the money, but they must have felt guilty themselves, for it was not mentioned.

Shortly after my return home—before the end of the school year—my cousin Tosia Ehrlich died of meningitis. She never had a chance to attend the university in Krakow where she had been admitted. We were told that the whole Jewish Gymnasium attended her funeral, a testament to her personality and popularity. The whole family was in deep mourning. It was as if a dark curtain had shut out the sunshine in their lives. I could not believe that I would never again hear her laughter and see her sweet smile and the wonderful sparkle in her eyes.

I would look up continuously the little picture of her with her brother and sister that I had brought with me from Krakow.

CHAPTER V

Things had gotten much tougher at home since I had left. In 1936 the Polish government passed a law severely limiting the number of cattle that were allowed for ritual slaughter. The government initially intended to prohibit it entirely, and only after a protracted, bitter fight in the Polish Senate a compromise was reached. The amount of beef that my father was allotted to sell did not generate enough income to support a family.

I got a job as an apprentice in a machine shop owned by a Jewish engineer. We did all kinds of work: plumbing, locksmithing, forging wrought-iron gates and fences and assembling bicycles. The work that I hated most was repairing in winter the cracked steel springs of the mechanism that lifted the storefront jalousies. Even when my hands would freeze to the steel housing my foreman would not allow me to wear gloves on the job.

The foreman's name was Schultz, a beer-drinking ethnic German who hated apprentices and made my life miserable. He was a Jack-of-all-trades and believed that a Jew could never master his skills. I suspected that dripping of the hot lead on my hands when I held the plumbing pipes for him to solder was not an accident and that his violent outbursts of temper were not a result of poor workmanship on my part, but an expression of his contempt for Jews, which he did not try to conceal.

The work was hard, the pay practically non-existent. I would get two Zloties a week, which I would turn over to my mother, who in turn would give me 10 groszy every day for my lunch. It was enough money to buy a roll and a pickle. I would go to my uncle Tulek, my father's younger brother who worked in a nearby butcher shop, and he would cut me a piece of salami. A cup of tap water completed my lunch.

Once when delivering assembled bicycles to a large sporting goods shop for which we worked, I was approached by the owner and asked if I knew how to install spokes into bicycle wheels and center and calibrate them. "Of course," was my reply, for I sensed an opportunity for additional income. So I started to take work home. When my boss found out that I was in competition with him he fired me. I did not care, since I made more money freelancing and had more time to help my father.

When the butcher shop did not generate enough income, my parents opened a fruit and vegetable stand in the market square. For my mother this meant entering a whole new experience, spending five days a week on her feet hawking produce and trying to compete with all the other similar stands. At the top of her voice she would praise her wares to attract customers. In all kinds of weather she would stand there, a far cry from the educated and poised young woman that I remembered from my earlier days. I was both embarrassed and infuriated by what I saw as her humiliation and I hated my father for being the cause of it. I tried to ease her burden by not allowing her to lift or carry anything. In the morning I would go with her to our warehouse, a dark, damp cellar room where we stored the fruit and vegetables, load them on a pushcart, take them to the market and arrange them on the stand. If it looked like rain I would spread the tarpaulin over the roof of the stall to protect the merchandise. I would relieve my mother occasionally and man the stand. I truly hated every minute of it. I also had to take my brother to and from school, run to the butcher shop and help there when necessary and come back in the evening to load and take the merchandise back into storage.

Soon my father had to close the butcher shop and devote his time to the fruit stand. On Thursdays and Fridays he kept another stand with live fish for the Sabbath and I had to expand my efforts at both stands, depending which one was busier.

While my friends were either advancing their education or learning a trade, I was stuck in an endeavor that had little to do with preparation for life in Palestine, which I saw as my future. Little did I realize that I was getting a lesson in the hardships and realities of life that later became vital to my survival.

In the fall of 1937 an event took place in Bielsko-Biala which cemented my determination to leave Poland. A Jewish innkeeper in a fight with a drunken customer shot and killed the man. Anti-Semitic riots broke out in town, evolving into a major pogrom. Thousands of men and women, some from as far away as 30 kilometers, descended on the twin communities, plundering and killing. Gentiles put crosses and holy pictures in their windows to indicate they were Christian homes, while Jewish homes and business establishments were broken into and destroyed. Jews were dragged out of their homes, beaten and wounded. Our family and our landlord cowered in the cellar for three days while my friends, led by Janek Malecki, stood guard at the entrance to our street to keep the screaming mob out, claiming there were no Jews living on that block. The blood curling screams *Bij Zyda, Bij Zyda* (kill the Jew, kill the Jew) echoed in my ears for years to come. Janek Malecki's action on behalf of his Jewish friend was certainly an act of courage, but under the circumstances and the prevailing climate of anti-Semitism it was much more than that. Janek performed an act of immense loyalty to another human being in face of taunting and criticism by the people of the neighborhood. In a sea of violent antipathy toward Jews, this uneducated urchin demonstrated a valor and nobility that so many others would fail to show in the not-too-distant future.

I threw myself into the activities of my Zionist youth organization with renewed vigor. Despite the fact that even my mother did not want to see me leave Poland, I was determined to do so. It did not occur to me that my designs for the future might be self-serving and egotistical.

In 1938 Germany invaded Czechoslovakia and Poland took advantage of the situation to grab a piece of disputed land called Zaolzie from the Czechs, some twenty miles from where we lived. Soldiers and anti-aircraft guns on constant alert were stationed behind our house, bringing the specter of imminent war close to home. I began planning in earnest to emigrate. The leaders of my Zionist organization assured me that sometime in the winter of 1939 or the beginning of 1940 I would leave for *Eretz Israel*, for Palestine, legally or not.

Meanwhile, in the summer of 1938 a tragedy struck my father's family in Zablocie-Zywiec. My Uncle Lipek suffered a fatal heart attack while swimming, and my grandparents, especially my grandmother, were inconsolable. My whole family went to pay a *Shiva* visit, a condolence call. The house was in deep mourning; there was not a happy voice to be heard in it. My six-year-old brother Oskar tried his best to cheer up his grandmother (she was the only grandmother he knew), and when we were ready to leave she asked if we could leave him with her for the summer months. My mother did not have the heart to say no. Although she had only a peripheral relationship with my father's family she treated her in-laws with respect.

The oldest of my father's brothers, and his only full brother, Uncle Henry, had married the same year as my parents, and my mother struck up a close friendship with his wife, Idka. They corresponded and shared their marital problems. Uncle Henry lived in the small town of Jaslo and seemed to have done all right for himself. He was in partnership with another man in a trucking company that owned six Chevrolet trucks and, according to the information in his wife's postcards, was also a shareholder in two oil wells. His wife operated her own photo studio and my mother was rather envious of her apparent financial independence.

Uncle Henry was sometimes absent from home for prolonged periods. He would claim to be away on business, but my mother believed that he was some place on a card-playing binge. When I went to Krakow to go to the vocational school, I went to see him as my father suggested. After several visits to the coffeehouse, where I was not even allowed to enter the room for the high stakes card players, he finally came out to see me. He impatiently acknowledged who I was, gave me a two zloty silver piece and suggested that I come to see him some other time. Despite the temptation of the money that I could expect, I never went to see him again. I had decided that my mother was right and that he was a phony.

Uncle Henry had two children. His daughter Lusia was borne the same week as I and his son Zev was five years her junior.

Next in age in my father's family was Uncle Nathan. He was a butcher by trade and lived in Krakow. He was married and had two boys. For reasons unknown to me the relationship between him and my father was rather cool. I remember visiting him in his butcher shop when we still lived in Krakow. He was the first-born of my father's stepmother, who was also my father's aunt. Perhaps there were some sibling rivalries or resentments, for shortly after the birth of Uncle Nathan my father at age nine was sent to work and live with a family who owned a provision store in a nearby village. He became a delivery and stock boy, sleeping in the warehouse on sacks of beans and flour and doing chores, all of them too hard for a child of that age. He might have blamed his lot on uncle Nathan's arrival, but uncle Nathan was not even close to his own family; he seemed bound to his wife's clan.

My paternal grandparents occupied a large house in Zablocie-Zywiec; six of their children lived there with them. Uncle Lipek, who died of the heart attack and was next in age, was my grandmother's pride and joy. He apparently had attended a trade school and studied to be an accountant, for he eventually became the comptroller of a large lumber mill. He was a modern man; an elegant dresser always in a shirt and tie and an Alpine felt hat with a little feather. He seldom came home for supper, arriving late, claiming to have had a lot of work in the office. He drove a motorcycle which made a loud noise that you could hear a distance away, and as soon as grandma heard it, she would rush to set the table with Uncle Lipek's favorite cake and coffee. He seems to have been the most generous financial supporter of the household and his word carried a lot of weight. The rumor was that he was having a tryst with the mill owner's wife. It was she whom he was rowing around on the river before he dove in to cool off and suffered the coronary. My grandmother always blamed her for his death.

Next in age was Uncle Tulek, an easy-going, husky and handsome man; he was my mother's favorite. He worked in a butcher shop in Biala, and on those weekends when he did not travel to his parents he would eat at our house, never coming empty-handed. He always had a little gift for us, a book for my mother or a ball for me or my brother Oskar. He also turned over most of his earnings to his mother who would save the money for him as she did for her other working children. Strong as a bull, he enjoyed carrying my brother and me on his shoulders or chasing and kicking a ball with us. My mother always asked him why he did not get married, since he loved children so much. He was going out with a nice young lady, but the relationship must have been based more on friendship than love.

My father's only sister, Netka, who also lived at home and worked as a secretary in Uncle Lipek's firm, was a pretty young woman in her late twenties, full of life and modern ideas. She dressed well and went out with young men in the enlightened, progressive circles. She did not hesitate to criticize her brothers or her mother's leniency towards them. She got part of her education in a Catholic high school which she was proud of, relaying the nuns' emphasis on discipline to my grandmother whenever she thought it was applicable.

In the winter of 1937, on one of our visits to my grandparents, Netka asked me if I would be her guest on a skiing vacation to the Czech border. Not until we got on the train did I realize that I was being used as an unofficial chaperone so that my aunt could get permission to go. The young man who joined us on the train must have been an intimate acquaintance of my aunt because they greeted each other like old lovers. My aunt and I had adjoining rooms in the lodge and I really did not care what she did with her time. In my opinion she was old enough to be responsible for herself, and besides I liked her very much and wanted her to have a good time. I went my own way, skiing as much as I could.

The only time we spent together on the slopes was a few hours on New Year's Eve, when we all skied down into Czechoslovakia with torches. It was an unforgettable scene; scores of skiers sliding down the slopes in darkness, the only light coming from the hand-held torches and the full moon. The silhouettes of the skiers and their dancing shadows sketched an eerie sight, while occasional yells of *uwaga*, attention, mixed with joyous cries of "Happy New Year." In Czechoslovakia we had hot cocoa and delicious pastry in a lodge. There were no border guards to bother anyone and we bought oranges and bananas to take back to Poland. Early in the morning we got on a bus to go back to our lodge. The next day I went straight back to my home in Biala while my aunt Netka went to hers. My grandparents never asked me about the time in the mountains.

Netka was probably as shaken by the death of her brother Lipek as her mother was. They had been close friends besides being siblings. They had more in common with each other than with any other members of the family. They worked in the same company; Uncle Lipek included her in the part of his life that he led outside the family. They spent a lot of their social life together. He obviously adored her, for he always referred to her as "my beautiful sister." And now the important decision-making; that modern life demanded of their family had to come from my aunt, as her mother would turn to her for counsel more and more often.

Uncle Aciek, only a couple years younger that Netka, was a constant source of tension and disappointment in the family. A card-playing bon vivant without a trade, he ran around with unsavory crowd, gambling in the pool-parlors, going out with non-Jewish girls. The only positive things that could be said about him were that he did not drink and he played soccer with Uncle Lipek and Uncle Tulek on the soccer team *Maccabi Zywiec*.

The "Three Friedmans," as they were known, were the core of the team. They all played attacking forwards and were responsible for most of the goals scored by their team. Playing against other teams in the league, however, meant always fighting gentiles on the opposing teams, in the stands and even among the referees. After a victorious match they would not bother to go to their dressing rooms to change but would run straight to their buses to avoid being attacked by the spectators who couldn't accept defeat by a Jewish team. But the glory of soccer could not support Acieck's gambling needs, so he was constantly coming to grandmother for money, always promising that this was the last time he would incur debts. On occasion money or valuable items were missing from the house, but he always denied responsibility. After every such incident my grandmother's eyes would be red from crying. She could not accept the fact that one of her offspring was a good-for-nothing *Ledig-Geier*, a bum. Aunt Netka advocated his expulsion from the house, especially when after Uncle Lipek's death he appropriated his belongings.

There were two more sons in the family, Slomek and Uniu. Uncle Sol, five years older than I, was an agile young man, hoping to exceed his brothers on the athletic field. He excelled in gymnastics, his specialty being the bar exercises. In 1935 he was scheduled to compete in the Maccabian Games in Palestine, but while training for the events he suffered a fall and broke his right arm and elbow. The family took him to a peasant woman who was a renowned bonesetter. It was said that on that visit she was unfortunately sober and miss-set Uncle Sol's elbow. It grew crooked, and subsequent surgery could not correct it. Down the drain went his dreams for fame in athletics, and Uncle Sol went to work for Uncle Henry as his personal driver. Besides owning the fleet of trucks Uncle Henry also owned a Citroen sedan for his private use. The accident and the disappointment left my Uncle Sol a subdued person for the rest of his life.

Uniu (I cannot bring myself to call him uncle for he was only two years older than I), being the youngest of the lot, expected special consideration from the family, but the only person who favored him was my grandmother. He did not like to help his father in the butcher shop, he did not want to seek advanced education and he was not allowed to accompany his brother Aciek in his escapades. So he hung around the house, a spoiled child running meaningless errands for his mother, always trying to ingratiate himself with her. My grandmother knew his game but was not willing to pressure him toward any gainful pursuit. Once he was sent to live with us and help my father. I did not like his slothful attitude and I would tell him so, sometimes very forcefully. Once a fight broke out between us, and after I pummeled him well, he went to my father to complain. My father scolded me halfheartedly, "How dare you beat up my brother?" My mother chimed in, "How can you hit your uncle?" and that was it. Uniu was shipped back to his parents.

As soon as the school year ended in 1939, my brother Oskar went back to grandmother in Zablocie-Zywiec, to stay with her for the summer. I kept working with my father, at the same time devoting all my free time to the affairs of my Zionist organization, running the local branch. Most of the older members from our town had left that year for Palestine, making their way through illegal channels. Great Britain was making it increasingly difficult for Jews to go to Palestine. I had made plans to attend the summer camp for future leaders of our movement in July of 1939. To save money I arranged for a lift to Krakow with one of Uncle Henry's trucks when it was passing our town; from Krakow I was supposed to be the beneficiary of a special offer of

NORBERT FRIEDMAN

the Polish Railroad, which allowed one free rider to every group of ten paying passengers.

That spring, my father invested in a venture in which he had been a partner a year before, with good financial rewards. He bought the fruits of an apple orchard while the trees were still in bloom. It was a risky undertaking with potential high returns—or loses. You had to be able to estimate the amount of what you would harvest from the richness of the bloom. Your profit depended on weather conditions, tree disease and defense against vandals. At harvest time one needed watchmen to guard the orchard night and day, and also a trustworthy person to watch the watchmen.

I had notified my father about the scheduled date for my vacation and had promised to be back before the apple harvest time. He must not have been listening to me; however, for when the day came for me to leave, he refused to let me go and we had a terrible exchange of words. It took place in the Market Square at the side of our fruit and vegetable stand. Finally I said I was going, I kissed my mother goodbye and turned to leave. After a few steps I heard my father cursing me and I felt a tremendous blow to my back. When I fell to the ground I saw the two-pound metal weight which was the cause of my pain.

Having been under severe economic stress and financial difficulties, my father in his frustration and disappointment that his son would not be with him to share those burdens, had hurled the object nearest to hand. I got up and, without looking back, went home, grabbed my already-packed rucksack and met the truck. I was on my way to Krakow and to what I swore to myself was to be the beginning of my freedom. I was not coming back to my house ever again.

CHAPTER VI

When I arrived in Krakow, after a four-hour, bone—jostling trip on my uncle's truck, I went to Aunt Hela's home to drop of my rucksack. I went looking for my comrades and found them in the offices of the *Shomer Hatzair.* The train was leaving next morning, and I was to meet them at the station. I was told to wear my scout uniform. Fortunately I had packed it with my other items.

I knew most of the other boys and girls that I was traveling with. The group was led by a *Rosh G'dud* the head of a larger unit. Leibek A., several years older than most of us, was the leader. I was probably the youngest of the group known as *Bogerim,* adults, in the hierarchy of the organization.

We were going to the city of Lvov where we were to be joined by more young people traveling to the *Moshavah,* the summer camp in Skole. We occupied two Pullman railroad compartments and spent the long, ten-hour trip singing the Hebrew songs of the young Zionist movement some brought from Palestine.

And when we ran out of those, we would have discussions or simply exchange stories. I spent part of the trip sleeping, my head resting in the lap of the girl who least protested.

In Lvov we slept on the premises of the local *Shomer Hatzair* and in the morning we proceeded to the railroad station there, where more young people joined us. The time that we spent on the *Moshavah,* was filled with discussions on the political and social problems that we would encounter upon arriving in Palestine. At the same time the *Sheliah,* the messenger from Palestine was warning us about the imminent conflict that was rising on the horizon and attempted to impress with the imperative to maintain contact and solidarity with each other.

When I got back to Krakow four weeks later, I found out from my Aunt Hela that Aunt Pepka has found a job for me in a machine shop across the street from her and that I would move in with her to live. My mother must have had informed them about my encounter with my father.

A Jewish engineer owned the small shop that I was to start working in next Monday, one Mr. Rosenberg. It specialized in work similar to what I had done in Bielsko and also in rewinding electrical motors, something that I was totally unfamiliar with. But Mr. Rosenberg needed a helper and I was to be it. He paid me five zloties a week, which I turned over to my aunt for room and board. This time I did not want to be a "charity case" again.

The work was demanding, which I did not mind, but I resented being made to baby-sit for engineer Rosenberg's children when he went out with his wife. I considered it labor exploitation, unrelated to my job, and my socialist soul rebelled against it.

The political situation in Europe was deteriorating despite the fact that the Polish foreign minister Mr. Beck went hunting in the Polish forest with the German foreign minister Mr. Ribentrop. We felt that something was brewing.

The German Jews of Polish origin who were pushed into Poland in fall of 1938 before the *Kristallnacht* and who never the less expressed awe and admiration for the new German might, had predicted that: *"Unser Hitler"* "Our Hitler" would annihilate the Polish army in three weeks time. They were to be proven right, that's how long it took for the victorious German campaign in Poland to be completed.

Cellars in certain buildings were designated as bomb shelters and blackout exercises were being held at night. The newspapers reporting on the political situation would come out with many blank pages, as a result of government censorship.

On Thursday night August 31, 1939, I went to my Uncle Jacob and his wife Lola for supper and stayed overnight. I was to go straight to work from there. However, in the early morning the air sirens sounded, indicating either an exercise or a true air raid.

Within minutes we had the answer as the air shook with the roar of the diving airplanes, mixed with loud explosions that shattered the windows and splattered the glass all over the apartment. We hid under the beds, and then, when the sirens of the ambulances replaced the din of the explosions we looked out the windows. We could see the dead and the wounded being carried on stretchers from the army barracks, which were situated next to my uncle's house.

World War II had broken out. My life as I had lived it until then was ending, my plans and the dreams for the future never to be realized. It was the end of my childhood.

TWILIGHT

CHAPTER VII

Friday September 1st 1939 marked the beginning of World War II. For mankind it was a turning point in history and the beginning of changes in the norms of human conduct. For me personally it marked the end of innocence and the beginning of my descent into a darkness from which I have never completely emerged.

September 1, began as a beautiful fall morning in Krakow, cool and almost cloudless. It quickly disintegrated into shock of carnage with the bombing attack by the German Air Force on the Polish army barracks situated on the street where my Uncle Jacob and Aunt Lola lived and where I had spent the previous night.

The sight of blood and death was to become my companion in the years to follow, and with the passage of time it would gradually lose its shocking impact, but not on this morning.

I became frightened and agitated, and the only thing I could think of to do was to run right away to Aunt Pepka's house seeking the comforting stability of her council.

Aunt Lola was rather high-strung and Uncle Jacob reflected her demeanor. In the confusion of screams and orders from the army barracks below and the shattered windowpanes in my uncle's apartment, breakfast was not even suggested. I ran the whole distance to my aunt Pepka's house, a good half-hour, on an empty stomach.

There I discovered that my cousin Wilek had gone to work as usual and that I was expected to do the same.

"When we know something concrete about the situation," Aunt Pepka declared, "we will decide what to do. Now go to work."

"Today is pay day," She added. "Make sure that you get paid."

Meanwhile the radio played marshal music interrupted by coded messages or announcements of air alerts. I gulped some milk, grabbed a slice of bread and ran across the street to my job at the machine shop.

We were working on a wrought-iron gate that day and it was my job to start the fire in the outdoor—open-coke stove and get the bellows ready. We had to white heat the iron bars and shape them according to a prepared pattern. The work was done outside in the yard and I could occasionally observe dogfights between German fighter planes and Polish biplanes. The out-manned Polish pilots would bravely try to out-maneuver the German aircraft and then, their planes twisting in the air, fall in flames to the ground.

In the afternoon I got paid the usual sum of five Zlotys for the week's work and went home even though the air alert had still not been called off after several hours.

In the house I noticed that the water pails were empty. I offered to go to the well two blocks away and fetch the water but my aunt was reluctant to let me go.

"Wait a little," she suggested. "I do not hear any planes, they will probably call it off very soon."

"No," I answered, "most likely they have forgotten to call it off."

I took the pails and went to the well. There was no wait at the pump at this time. I filled up the pails and turned back toward the house. At the entrance gate to the house, Kasia, the landlord's daughter asked me if it was safe to go for water. "I don't know if it's safe, but there is practically no one at the well now, so you would not have to wait," was my reply.

I had gone upstairs and started to wash up when suddenly the sound of aircraft overhead and the whining sound of falling bombs shattered the air. Then explosions shook the walls and windows. My aunt and I hit the floor under the heavy wooden kitchen table, trembling over all. "My God," exclaimed my aunt. "It was so close, it must have fallen right in our neighborhood."

We lay there on the floor, petrified, waiting for more explosions when none came, we got up to survey the damage in the apartment. The all-clear sirens sounded, but soon a more penetrating sound was heard: That of a human scream.

"Jesus, Maria, moja Kasia"; "Jesus, Maria my Kasia."

It was the landlady downstairs, wailing mournfully.

We ran down the steps, my aunt trying to find out what happened, although we already suspected the worst. I ran as fast as I could to the well where a group of people had gathered. Two bombs had fallen next to the well; three dead bodies were lying on the ground, Kasia one of them. Shocked and in a stupor I kept walking around and around the scene of the bombing, stumbling

NORBERT FRIEDMAN

at the edge of the craters. Unaware of my actions I bent down and picked up a palm-size fragment of the missile that had exploded only yards away from the well. Insensitive to the death of Wilek's friend Kasia—whom I did not discourage from going out, despite the air alert—I could think only of one thing: It could have been me, it could have been me. I had left the well only minutes before.

Dazed, I walked slowly to the house, the jagged-edged piece of metal in my hand. Guiltily I avoided going into the apartment of the landlady and walked straight up to my aunt's place.

In the evening the Polish radio assured us that the German casualties in the air were very heavy, while the brave Polish pilots emerged unscathed.

Friday night, despite the late hour, a flood of vehicular traffic came into Krakow from the west. Rumors of fighting were many and confusing. Saturday brought even more rumors and one sensed a note of desperation in the official communiqués. There were more dogfights in the sky and more Polish casualties. Saturday night my mother arrived from Bielsko-Biala with a small suitcase and a knapsack with clothing and valuables. She told us stories of neighbors and acquaintances that had declared themselves ethnic Germans, donned brown shirts the S.A. uniforms and shot Jews.

My mother and her sisters and brothers had a meeting Sunday morning. My mother, aunt Pepka and aunt Rozia decided that their sons Tobias, Wilek, Dolek and I should try to go some place in central Poland until the situation stabilized and it would be safe to return. Uncle David would not let cousin Gerd join us.

Frantically we started to pack—some clothing, socks and food. I had only one pair of shoes and so did Wilek. Dolek took along the hiking boots he used when vacationing in the mountains and some outdoor cooking utensils.

Someone suggested that maybe I should shave, so on September 3rd, 1939, I shaved for the first time. That day was to be the entrance into my adulthood in more ways than one.

My mother desperately tried to recall the addresses of my father's family who lived farther east, and with whom we might be able to stay. She wrote them down on a piece of paper and implored me not to lose them.

We hugged and kissed, and accepted some money from our parents. Tobias's young wife and their infant child joined us and we left on our journey knowing only the first destination, the village of Igolomia where Tobias's in-laws lived, and where Tobias's wife and child were to stay.

Where to afterwards? We really did not know; most likely toward the northeast, the direction that we thought would best distance us from the advancing German army.

As soon as we had left the city and entered the highway leading northeast we joined a throng of humanity, seemingly all going in the same direction. Horse-driven wagons filled with possessions and similar horse-less wagons; two-wheeled carts pushed or pulled by members of households; people on bicycles; and an occasional, infrequent motorcar, honking, trying to navigate its way through the trekking mass.

We arrived at dusk in the village of Igolomia and were welcomed in the home of Tobias's in-laws, we washed and shared a meal with the family.

My life up till then had been spent mostly in the cities of Krakow and Bielsko-Biala; both rather sophisticated urban communities for those times. I had had no exposure to the life of a Jew in a shtetl or countryside except for the summer months, which I had spent in the vacation spots of Bystra or Rabka, both typical resort villages.

The house of Tobias's in-laws was a small wooden structure with a fenced-in yard. The meal they served us was plain: bread with farmer's cheese and milk.

We were told to sleep in a barn and to show up for breakfast early. In the morning we had milk straight from the cow-barn, still warm, and again bread, this time with some plum butter. Tobias said good-bye to his child, his wife and her family. They gave us a large loaf of freshly baked country bread, blessed us and send us on our way.

The highways were already crowded with some people who had slept outside by the road and others who never stopped but continued walking. The mood had become more urgent and different rumors about the German advance and the Polish army's resistance circulated freely. Occasionally we would see soldiers on requisitioned bicycles or army officers in confiscated cars forcing their way through the throng of people, contending that they were rushing to their army units and claiming a special right.

Around noon, the column of civilians we were a part of, was attacked by three German Stuka fighter planes. With a high-pitched, siren-like noise they dived at the column, dropping bombs and strafing the people with machine-gun fire. At first we jumped into the roadside ditches. But when we saw people in the ditches being hit by bullets we decided on the advice of Tobias, who had army experience, to hide behind the trees, putting the trunk of the tree between us and the direction from which the planes were diving. It was like playing hide-and-seek, but the stakes were much higher.

The attack lasted only a few minutes, although it seemed like an eternity. In its wake it left devastation and death, all on an innocent civilian crowd of people. It took a while to overcome our panic and to regain our composure. We all felt a sudden urge to urinate and decided to get off the main highway and seek some side roads. We stopped at a farmhouse, bought some milk at an inflated price, consumed part of the loaf of bread, and asked the farmer for instructions on how to find side roads leading north.

Tobias had a map of Poland, but it showed only the main roads. Dolek had a boy-scout compass, which was helpful, but we could not consult either the map or the compass while in sight of others for fear of being accused of being German spies. We kept walking northeast, avoiding main roads but adding distance to our journey. We covered about 40km (25 miles) a day, starting out early in the morning, trying before evening to reach a larger population center where there were sure to be some Jews. We were heading toward the town of Sandomierz where we hoped to cross the Vistula River eastbound.

We had finished the jar of chicken fat, as well as the jar of plum butter. Tobias was in charge of dispensing and rationing the food as well as of making all the decisions pertaining to our travel. He was the most experienced and we accepted his authority without question.

At first we were startled by the contrast between the lifestyle and the poverty of the Jews in the villages and what we had known of Jewish life in Krakow. I remember being served tea brewed from a bit of chicory and sharing one cube of sugar among all of us. But the destitution, the dirt floors and the primitive furnishings did not inhibit the owners from exhibiting the basic tenets of Jewish tradition, that of kindness and welcoming of strangers.

We were nearing the town of Sandomierz and hoped to reach it some time the next day. This was going to be our last night on this side of the Vistula River, which would hopefully put a defensible barrier between the advancing German army and us.

The older couple at whose house we were spending the night decided to bake some bread that night, for themselves and for us to take on our journey. While we were going to sleep the old woman was kneading the dough. It was warm in the house, and tired as we were, we fell asleep rather quickly. It seemed as if we had just lain down when sounds of artillery woke us up. Tobias instructed us to get dressed quickly; he recognized the sounds as coming from nearby howitzers, most likely German.

We tried to convince our hosts to leave with us but they insisted on staying, pointing out to us that they had bread in the oven and could not leave without it. We hastily put our shoes on, grabbed our knapsacks and in the dark ran from the house.

The salvos came in series of four. We would hit the ground at the sound of the first one and get up and run after the fourth, heading in the opposite direction from the firing. We must have run several hundred yards when a round exploded near by.

We looked back, and the house, which we had just left, was ablaze. Its wooden structure and the straw roof were burning fast. We thought that we heard faint cries from the house but Tobias hurried us forward. "We must get out of here," he urged us "THEY are getting close."

We trekked through the dark in the direction of Sandomierz. At dawn we encountered a squadron of Polish Uhlans, their lances pointing forward, carbines slung over their shoulders, the hoofs of their horses wrapped in rags to silence their progress. Like some midnight apparitions or romantic Don Quixotes, they seemed to glide through the mist of the daybreak to face their tragic patriotic destinies, to confront the approaching German motorized armor. As they passed us we instinctively raised our fingers to our forehead in silent salute, somehow sensing the inevitable fate of those brave men.

Finally we reached the bridge. Just as we began to cross it, six German tanks assumed position on the embankment and began to pelt the multitude of fugitives with machine gun fire. We ran like hell, jumping over fallen bodies, ducking and weaving as if we were the only targets.

There were scores of other people trying to cross the bridge, on foot pushing possession-laden wagons; soldiers rode bicycles, and one or two had motorcycles. Everyone was trying to reach the perceived safety of the other side of the Vistula River. Before we could reach the other side, however, artillery fire from Polish position beyond the river, aimed at the tanks, presented an additional hazard.

When we finally managed to cross and arrived at a large clearing some distance beyond the river, we saw thousands of Polish soldiers bivouacked on the meadow and the grove behind it. We heard rumors that General Rydz-Smigly the head of the Polish army was amongst them. There were tables with officers behind them, set up in the meadow, and long queues of men lined up in front of them. We found out that some of the men were enlisting in the army, while others were trying to catch up to their units.

Nearby an army kitchen was set up for the refugees and the smell of the food tickled our nostrils. In the frenzy of our hasty departure and flight, we had had no opportunity to eat and now our stomachs were growling with hunger. We lined up with others and the cooks gave us a chunk of hot *kielbasy* on a piece of army bread and filled one of our mess kits with hot coffee. The hot food had a wonderful effect on us; we felt satiated and safe in the presence of so many soldiers.

The registering of recruits was still going on, when one of us meekly offered a suggestion: "Why don't we enlist? We will get uniforms, food and weapons."

"Sure, why don't we?" another one of us chimed in.

"What do you think Tobias? You have served with the army."

"Well, it was not the greatest place to be, but it must be better then what we have been doing till now."

"And besides we will get a chance to fight the Germans."

"Just don't tell them your real age, say that you are 18 years old and that you know how to fire a rifle."

We walked to the nearest table and lined up with the other hopefuls.

Tobias was first at the table; the young sergeant without looking up started the interview.

"How old are you?" was the first question.

"Twenty-five and I have already served two years in the army."

"Name!"

"Tobias Richter-Schwetzreich."

The young noncom's head jerked up. He looked at Tobias and then at the captain who was engaged in a conversation with another officer.

"Panie kapitanie!" "Captain Sir" he exclaimed and pointed at Tobias with a move of his head.

The captain looked at us briefly, noted our Jewish features, our clothing, or whatever it was that distinguished us Jews in the eyes of Christian Poles, and angrily barked:

"Get lost, we do not want any Jew-boys in our army."

Shock, hurt, shame and every other humiliating emotion made Tobias respond: "But we want to fight for our country, Captain Sir."

"Go! We do not need you, and Poland is not your country."

We turned and walked away, our faces red with shame and anger, our eyes filled with tears. Taunts and jeers by other prospective recruits in the line; *"Zyd, Zyd"* "Jew, Jew" followed us.

This land, where we Jews had lived for 1,000 years—although we were not officially welcomed until the 14th century—where we contributed to the culture and commerce to the best of our ability; this country where our fathers served and fought in its armed forces; this nation where we were now faced with a common enemy had rejected us and told us: "Go! You are not one of us, we do not want you!"

All the sad incidents of anti-Semitism that I had experienced passed before my eyes and I urged my cousins: "Come on, let us get the hell out of here."

We had hardly reached the nearest road when a squadron of Stukas with its familiar ear-splitting wail swarmed down on the area where the soldiers congregated, dropped several bombs and strafed the area with machine-gun fire. By the time the anti-aircraft flak had had a chance to fire back, the Stukas were gone, leaving chaos and destruction in the fields. Overturned field-kitchen equipment and dead horses lay strewn amongst the dead officers and enlisted men.

We reached the village of Zaklikow late that afternoon. It was Friday evening and the people in the shtetl were getting ready for Sabbath. Little did I know that the fates of war would bring me back here a couple years later under quite different circumstances.

Amongst the many Jewish families living in that *shtetl* we found one willing to put us up for the night. They lived near the synagogue and appeared to be very observant. They insisted on our washing hands and pronouncing the appropriate blessings before the Friday night meal, and after supper the head of the family engaged everyone in saying the *Birkath Ha'mazon,* the blessings after the meal and singing of the traditional *Zmiroth,* the Sabbath hymns. He was pleasantly surprised when we joined in. We knew most of the melodies and Tobias and Wilek had very good voices; Dolek and I made up with our zest and enthusiasm.

The father wore a short beard and his wife a kerchief over her wig. Their two sons, twelve and fourteen, wore the traditional garments with four fringes under their shirts and the jet-black ear-locks hanging down their faces. They struck us as simple, uneducated folks, but with a tremendous faith and trust in God. Despite our warnings and relaying of stories about the German treatment of Jews, they had no intent of leaving their home.

"Gott werd helfen," "God will help," was their response.

They offered to have us stay another day, for it was the Sabbath, but we were determined to go on. The head of the household found a Talmudic example which permitted traveling long distances on foot on the Sabbath under certain circumstances. He was silent however about the prohibition of carrying objects outside the community boundaries. However, we were not concerned about violating the Sabbath. We had seen the face of death already and were driven by different forces.

Upon awakening Saturday morning, however, we felt very tired and asked the lady of the house if we could sleep longer. Her husband and the boys had gone to their synagogue already. Shortly after we had arisen the second time and washed up, they came home. The husband was obviously pleased that we had not left and invited us to the Sabbath meal, sharing all the tid-bits with us: fish and *Chulent* and schnaps and singing and rejoicing, the last such Sabbath for a long time to come.

As we walked around the village we were sure that we heard sounds of artillery from afar. We left early Sunday morning laden with food from the good people. We had become refugees and felt no qualm in accepting handouts.

It was a week since we had left our families in Krakow and we wandered how they were coping; we had heard that Krakow had fallen to the Germans. We were nearing the town of Zamosc an old Polish fortress town known for its resistance to attacks by enemies from the east. The continuous marching had been taking its toll on our physical resources. We covered less ground per day and stopped more frequently. We also became a little short-tempered with each other and on occasion we would snap at one another. Our socks were torn and our feet swollen. Tobias had to prod us to wash regularly and I was made to take the second shave of my life.

We passed and stayed in the towns of Janow, Gorai and Szczebrzeszyn. The sound of artillery was getting closer and we tried to stay ahead of it. The air attacks were getting more frequent. One time when we were resting in a field near a schoolhouse, trying to roast a chicken we stole from a farm and whose neck Tobias had expertly wrung. The ever-present Stukas started dropping bombs. And there was no place and no time to hide. So we just lay on our bellies in the fields, covering our heads with our arms, feeling exposed and vulnerable. The length of the high-pitched whistling sound as the bombs fell to the ground indicated the distance from their targets to where we lay.

One such missile stopped whistling after a dangerously short interval and we all prayed hard, expecting it to land on or near us. I clutched the fragment of the shell that had fallen near the water-pump in Krakow and which had become a sort of talisman for me. The bomb hit the sandy ground with a loud thud some hundred feet from where we lay. We froze with fear, awaiting our end. But nothing but silence ensued; the bomb was a dud. Tobias ordered us to rise and run as fast as we could; damned be the chicken. We grabbed our possessions and ran. At the nearest stream we stripped and took a well-needed dip.

That night we sneaked into a barn next to what turned out to be a deserted farmhouse. In the morning we heard armored vehicles rumbling through the village and German voices barking commands. The rapidly advancing German forces had overrun us. We decided to stay in the barn until the Germans had passed, but they stayed around and all day we heard vehicular movement and sounds of machine-gun and howitzer fire.

At dusk Wilek decided to sneak down into the farmhouse and get some food. He came right back, telling us that the house was empty. Cautiously we went inside and started looking for something to eat. All that we found was some flour and a jar of apple butter. We made fire and on the top of the stove we baked thin cakes, not unlike the matzos we knew. We removed the white fungus from the top of the spread and made a welcome meal of it.

Dolek, who had a great curiosity for figures, found a calendar on the wall and announced that it was September 13th. Oh my G'd, exclaimed Tobias: "Tonight is *Erev Rosh Hashanah*, New Year's Eve. I was supposed to sing tomorrow with Father in the choir of the Progressive Temple!" We fell silent, each of us recalling his own memories of the holiday season spent with our families. The situation made us realize that the world we knew had changed dramatically in the last two weeks and would never be the same. A sense of uncertainty and doubts about our security and future had crept into our young, once confident minds.

Tobias decided that as long as there was gunfire to be heard we should not go outside. So we spent the two days of Rosh Hashanah 5699 in some non-Jewish stranger's house. According to tradition, this was the season when one's fate is judged and decided. Circumstances did not bode well for the future.

By the third day the sound of the gunfire had ceased. As we found out later, six Polish soldiers manning two machine-gun nests on a strategic hill had held up the advance of the German army for 72 hours before perishing at last in the superior German firepower.

We had run out of flour and jam and, because I knew German I was designated to go outside and scout for food. It was a prudent decision, for no sooner did I manage to walk a few hundred yards than a German army vehicle pulled alongside me and a *Wehrmacht,* an army, officer yelled at me: *"Was machen sie Hier?"* "What are you doing here?"

To his surprise and obvious delight, my answer came in German: "I am looking for a farmer to get some food."

"So are we," responded the officer laughing.

"How come you speak German?" was the next query.

"Oh, I come from Silesia, my friends and I. We were here on vacation when the war broke out." "Thank G`d you and the army showed up."

I lied as convincingly as I could.

"Do you speak Polish?" asked the officer "Can you help us get some supplies for the company?"

"Of course," was my happy offer.

And so on my first encounter with the invader I became an assistant to a German quartermaster. For the Germans we acquired potatoes and dairy products for cash, barter and threats. I also managed to organize enough for my cousins' and my needs.

On the third day, Otto, the officer in charge, confidentially informed me that in few days the Russian army was to come and occupy the area where we were. They were to take the eastern part of Poland all the way to the Vistula River under a pact with the German Government.

It sounded plausible; it would not be the first time that Poland would be divided between its neighbors. That night, my cousins who did not venture out, and I had a serious discussion. We had to decide whether to stay here and wait for the Russians or to turn around and go back to Krakow.

Because of my guilt feelings about the way that I had parted with my father two months before the war, I voted to go back. Everyone agreed— Tobias and Wilek because of the stories their father had told them about the hardships in the Russian prisoner-of-war camp during World War I, and Dolek because of his disapproval of Communism.

The next day I went to Officer Otto and told him that my friends and I wanted to go back to Silesia and join the German army there, like good ethnic Germans. He beamed with pride and promptly upon my suggestion made out a safe-conduct pass for the four of us, with the appropriate official stamps and recommendation for assistance.

Tobias consulted the map and decided that we should take the shortest way home, through the territory where some of my father's relatives lived. Those were the people whose addresses my mother had given me.

We started walking southwest, unaware that our encounter with Otto was not typical of what we could expect from the German army in general and the *SS Waffen,* the SS troops, in particular.

We walked through the towns and villages of Bilgoraj, Krasnobrod, Josefow and Tarnogrod. Fire and destruction, especially in the Jewish parts of the town were proof that the German conquest was not to be a benign, orderly take-over. We found ourselves on the eve of *Yom Kippur* in one of the above-mentioned shtetls; most likely it was Tarnogrod. The town was totally devastated. We could not find anybody to direct us to a Jewish home until we came across someone who used to be a *Wasser Trager,* a water carrier, in that town. He told us that on *Rosh Hashanah* the SS herded the Jews into the beautiful wooden synagogue and burned it to the ground with all the people inside. They burned the adjacent *Mikvah,* the ritual bathhouse, as well.

He gave us directions to a Jewish farm outside the town; they were good, hospitable people, he said. After a couple of kilometers we came across the road sign that the man told us to look for and found the house. A young man in his thirties in a white shirt and a black vest was leaning on the fence. When we asked him if this was the house of the family that the water-carrier had suggested, he ran inside gesticulating wildly and screaming in Yiddish: *Maloochim, Maloochim,* "Angels, angels, G`d has sent us angels."

It turned out that six men were waiting to say evening prayers. Some of them had lost next of kin in the devastation of the town and they wanted to say *Kadish,* the prayer for the departed, and needed a quorum of ten men. We were it. We were invited to participate in the washing, the afternoon prayers and then the meal preceding the fast of *Yom Kippur.* The household consisted of the owner of the house, his wife, their two sons, three daughters, two sons-in-law and another relative who seemed to be working on the farm.

It is impossible for me to describe the mood at that holiday table. Fourteen people gathered on the eve of the holiest of days in our calendar, the most solemn day of the year, when according to our tradition our fate is decided and the decree sealed. "Who shall live and who shall die . . ." We all sat silently immersed in our private thoughts, our hosts possibly contemplating their future, four strangers who had traveled some 400 kilometers on foot trying to escape the enemy, only to be overcome and forced to turn back toward where they had started. We had told them what we had heard, that the Russians were to come soon, giving them more reason to wonder.

After the meal we gathered again to pray. One of the sons led the services. We were given old, well-used holiday prayer books and joined the service. I have never in my life heard a more moving recitation of the Yom Kippur prayers. All the anxieties, uncertainties and desperate appeals for mercy and compassion from almighty G'd rang through the pleading and poignant rendition.

They wanted to put us up in one of the large bedrooms with fresh sheets, but we insisted on sleeping on the trashing floor in the barn. In the course of our journey we had picked up some itchy traveling companions; we tried to conceal our scratching but we did not want to contaminate the beds of those good people.

We spent the next day fasting and praying with the rest of the family; we broke fast without blowing of the Shofar or feeling the exhilaration that usually followed the Day of Atonement.

Next morning we left loaded up with provisions and blessings, not sure whether they still suspected us of being angels.

Apparently their blessings were still with us, however, for when about four hours down the road we were put in a dangerous situation, we were able to escape unharmed. We had stopped at the side of a road next to a well to refresh ourselves and to have some food when a convoy of Polish prisoners of war escorted by German army guards passed the spot where we had stopped.

Some of the prisoners started to point us out to the guards shouting: *Juden, Juden,* Jews, Jews. The guards paid little attention until an officer on horseback arrived. The officer turned the horse around and shouted in German: "Are you Jews?"

"Yes, but . . ." I started to answer and I pulled out the safe conduct pass. He looked at it, and returned it to me noting that it said nothing about us being Jewish and he started berating us that we were nothing but blood-sucking parasites who never worked. When I pointed out to him that we were all craftsmen, that I was a mechanic's apprentice, my cousins were plumber's helpers and a shoe maker, he simply declared that we were also liars and ordered us to run ahead in front of his horse while he hit us with his riding whip, to the delight of the Polish POWs

We ran ahead of him like that for quite a while. My chest began to hurt every time I took a breath and it became obvious that we would not last much longer. Fortunately, the young officer was called away for some reason. He instructed us to keep running, for he would be right back. As soon as he disappeared from sight we bolted away from the convoy into the adjoining woods, running even faster now with newly found energy.

"Let's run back in the direction that we came from," suggested Tobias, and we followed him.

Finally we came upon a depression in the landscape and hit the ground totally exhausted. We heard short bursts of gunfire. We did not know if it was aimed at us, but we lay there a long time before we thought it safe to proceed. The incident again brought home the realization of what we could expect from those Poles who once were our compatriots.

Still heading toward home we arrived after two days in the village of Frysztyk, near the village of Wielopole Skszynskie, where my father was born. We had by-passed the village of Wielopole without knowing that my paternal grandparents with their family and my brother Oskar had already arrived there to stay. In Frysztyk we were put up in the home of a distant relative of my father, a man by the name of Mahler, whom I later met in the United States. The family owned a flourmill and was very hospitable. They suggested that we continue to the town of Jaslo where my Uncle Henry and my Aunt Idka lived.

In Jaslo we found out that my uncle's house and my aunt's photo studio were closed. A neighbor told us that at the outbreak of the war my uncle had left in his car in the direction of the city of Lvov. When the man noticed our disappointment he directed us to my uncle's cousins' house.

The Bergers were my father's first cousins and worked in colonial wares business. I had never met them, but the mere fact that I was Josef Friedman's son and they were my cousins prompted them to become very amicable and protective of us.

We stayed with them for two days, but we wanted to get home as soon as possible. They gave us some fresh socks but our shoes were worn out, our underwear and shirts were torn from frequent washing and our stamina was wearing thin. We were really anxious to get home because of all the rumors we heard about atrocities being committed

My father's cousin David Berger was able to arrange for us a lift with a German army truck which was going south to the well known-brewery of Okocim to pick up a load of beer for the German garrison in Jaslo. This would save us at least three days of walking. It seems that Mr. Berger had dealings with the Germans supplying them with spices and other hard-to-get grocery items.

The German army sergeant in charge was a decent sort who found some boxes for us to sit on in the back of the truck. He made a stop on the way so that we could relieve ourselves, exchanging some crude jokes with me in

German. He even promised to find out for us if there would be any trucks going to Krakow.

We arrived in the brewery after some three hours, our legs stiff, and got off the vehicle to loosen up our limbs. We stayed close to the truck, waiting for the sergeant to come back. Suddenly we noticed a Polish worker pointing us out to an SS soldier in the yard and they started walking toward us. Once again we were being pointed out: *Juden, Juden*, Jews, Jews.

The young SS man lined us up against the truck pulled out his revolver and mockingly asked us: "Who wants to die first?"

When we did not reply he yelled: "You shitty, cowardly Jews, you don't even know how to die with dignity!"

He was just about to aim his gun at us when our sergeant came running, grabbed the SS man's arm from behind and yelled at us: "Run, run as fast as you can"

We did; our legs again had to rescue us from peril that our Polish co-patriots had put us in. What was happening in our country? Our own people were ganging up with the enemy against their Polish-Jewish co-citizens? Was their latent, or maybe not-so-latent hatred of the Jews greater than the natural acrimony toward the occupying foe who had laid waste to their country and killed scores of thousands of their own people?

We managed to make Krakow in two more days; we had been gone four weeks and covered 700 Kilometers. We went first to Aunt Pepka's house to find out what was the situation in town and in our families. We were greeted with joy and tears. They had had some news about us. It seems that the Mahlers with whom we stayed in Frysztyk sent news with someone to my father's brother, Uncle Nathan, in Krakow.

I found out that my father, who had come from Bielsko-Biala soon after we left, and my mother, were both staying with Aunt Hela. Dolek and I took the streetcar to our side of town. He went to his home and I went to Aunt Hela's house. My father, after greeting me warmly and hugging me with his bearish strength, could not stop crying, breaking up everyone in the house, including Uncle Israel and my cousin Nusia. My confrontation with my father before I left Bielsko-Biala had become a distant and forgotten incident.

I suggested that before I get into some fresh clothes I should take a hot bath and rub myself down with some disinfectant. So we went to aunt Rozia's home, where I was allowed to take a bath in their modern bathtub, using a very strong disinfectant soap.

I did not want to leave that hot bath, ever. But soon fatigue and drowsiness took over and I got dressed in fresh cloth, gulped some milk and went back to Aunt Hela's home. I lay down on the ottoman and fell asleep for seventy-two hours, getting up only to go to the bathroom and to have something to drink.

I had no idea of what kind of world I was going to wake up to. I could not imagine a world like the one I was about to encounter, and neither could anyone else.

CHAPTER VIII

Life in what once was my grandmother's house, open to family and guests with room for everyone, now became an aggravated existence in a very congested area.

Aunt Hela appeared to tolerate our living with them because she recognized my father's ability to provide hard-to-get necessities of life. Uncle Israel was not very resourceful or daring enough to go out and support his family. There was no need for his skills now, since people no longer purchased quilts, nor could he have found the raw material necessary for his work. He withdrew into himself afraid to go out, and spent his time reading whatever he could get his hands on. He would not pick up his mandolin and refused to play it even when his daughter begged him to.

Aunt Hela found a job for a few days a week in a pharmacy. Occasionally she would bring home some hard-to-get goodies given to her by customers who were grateful for the dispensed medicine. The bartering system was slowly becoming a way of life as currency gradually lost its value.

It was left to my father to provide the bulk of our provisions. With renewed energy, spurred by these dire conditions, he left no stone unturned as he bartered, organized and scrounged for victuals, which my mother in turn, with a great deal of ingenuity, turned into meals for the household. My father would get up early in the morning and come home with warm bread and rolls, which we would have for breakfast washed down with *Ersatz* tea made from dried strawberry or linden leaves.

If there was milk in the house we would save it for Nusia, who was the most vulnerable.

But the overall conditions were getting desperate. In October General Hans Frank, the head of the General Government (as the southwestern, occupied part of Poland was called) announced that all the Jewish males would have to work in government-sponsored jobs. Men were transported to labor camps from where they returned either every night or on weekends.

Needless to say, most men did not register, so the Germans organized occasional roundups. They sometimes used a covered van for that purpose and the mere appearance of that vehicle created panic among the inhabitants of the Jewish quarters in Krakow.

"M`hapt tzy die arbet;" *"They are catching people for labor."*

The cry could be heard on the streets as they emptied of all males. The German soldiers would jump out of the van in pursuit of the men. It was helpful to know the hidden passages in the old town in order to get away. The unfortunate ones that were caught in this fashion were subject to severe beatings, to extra hard assignments; sometimes they would not come back.

On December 1, 1939, an order was issued that all Jews—men, women and children above certain age—must wear a white armband four inches wide with a blue Star of David on their right forearm.

This demand in addition to the existing curfew, the travel restrictions and the meager food rations, gradually made life very difficult. Still, despite all of it, with every new decree there was hope that this was the last of restricting ordinances. Life somehow went on.

Because of the food shortages in the house and the resulting bickering, I started to seek the company of my comrades from the Zionist organization, most of whom were experiencing similar conditions in their homes. We would meet at the homes of Samek K. or his cousin Samek F. Their parents were poor tailors who worked very hard even before the war, but who had great empathy for the friends of their children and the common dreams that we harbored.

Now I seldom went to my Aunt Rozia's house for I knew that it would be embarrassing for them not to share their food with me. I knew that they, because of my Uncle Michal's money were able to obtain on the black market the needed provisions. Also, the Polish woman who worked for them would bring poultry and dairy products from the farm.

Distant families in general met less often, as the interests of only the most immediate relatives became principal factors in family relationships. I did, however, go frequently to my Aunt Pepka to spend time with my cousin Wilek.

One morning in the beginning of the winter, my father came home empty-handed. He was unable to obtain any bread, though he tried several sources that had been helpful before. His frustration over his failure to be the provider on whom we all depended turned to anger.

My mother went to him to soothe his disappointment. *"Jossel, Jossel,"* "Josef, Josef," do not despair, G`d will help," she pleaded.

NORBERT FRIEDMAN

"G`d helps those who help themselves," was his reply, and there was a foreboding determination in the tone of his voice. I felt moved by the scene and decided that I, too, must contribute somehow. One of our neighbors, who owned a shoe store, had removed most of his merchandise to a hiding place before the Germans installed in his shop a *Treuhander,* a trustee, a man in authority to run the business. This became the custom in all the Jewish establishments. Now this man sustained himself and his family by slowly selling off his stock to individuals at high black-market prices. He needed someone to deliver the merchandise, at the risk of incarceration or death, for it was against the law to deal in black market goods.

For a considerable fee I agreed to be the messenger boy. I would put a pair of shoes into a briefcase and, with a newly acquired bravado and pretended self-assurance I would walk confidently through the streets to make my delivery.

I discovered a hitherto unknown sense of excitement in the danger of what I considered to be a daring undertaking. I would proudly hand over the earned money to my father. Without asking questions, though he was aware of what I was doing, he would embrace me and with a silent nod of his head communicate to me all of his apprehensions and worry. I was proud and strangely happy to find concerned approval from him. A new bond was forming between us, as the perils of our existence became apparent.

But even with funds it was becoming increasingly difficult to obtain bread. One very cold winter day I heard that a bakery in the suburb would distribute bread to non-Jews. I dressed very warmly, removed the armband with the Star of David, and lined up with others in front of the bakery at about six o'clock in the evening.

The line in front of me was already considerable. As the night progressed everyone was stomping their feet and swinging their arms to keep warm. The Polish policemen who were supposed to keep order sought shelter inside the bakery while the temperature outside dropped to 30ºC below zero. The cold was penetrating to the bones despite the many layers of clothing and the constant movement.

I was tempted to leave as the early morning hours approached, but the picture of my father as he came home that one morning without any bread for the family kept me in the line. Finally at five o'clock in the morning the bakery window opened, the queue surged forward expectantly and the police had a hard time keeping order.

I was getting closer and closer to the window when, with only a few people in front of me, the window closed and someone announced that there was no more bread to be had. The angry, empty-handed people in front and back of me refused to leave and started to curse and heave rocks at the windows of the bakery.

I walked away so as not to get in trouble. The severe disappointment, which earlier would have caused me despair and maybe even a few tears, now created a new determination: that I must, regardless of any risk, take steps to insure sustenance for my family.

I acquired a pair of high boots and riding pants on the black market. A friend of mine bought for me a brown shirt like the *S.A.,* the Storm Troopers, wore and a wide belt with a swastika buckle from a young prostitute who had German customers. I had my hair cut close and I was ready to impersonate a German.

When leaving our house, I would wear my Uncle Israel's trench coat and the armband. I would board the streetcar, and once out of the Jewish area I would debark, go into a hallway, look about carefully and remove the armband with the Star of David. I then would board another streetcar to downtown and enter the German commissary wearing the trench coat wide open to expose my brown shirt and the *Hakenkreuz,* the swastika, on my belt. I would salute *"Heil Hitler"* and in German ask for bread and other items that were available to the occupiers.

On my way back I would repeat the routine in reverse and wind up at home with badly needed food. I was able to perform this ruse several times until the German civilian authorities became better organized and issued ID and ration cards to the German population in Krakow.

When I told my cousin Wilek about my escapades he asked me if I would be interested in joining a group of young patriotic people who were trying to obstruct the workings of the German occupiers. At first, when I was told that the group consisted of mostly non-Jews, I refused, but I consented when Wilek explained to me that they were mostly young Poles from socialist circles who were not anti-Semitic and who had good working relations with socialist Jewish organizations. I had visions of daring raids against the Germans, of rescuing prisoners, blowing up of trains, etc., but my work turned out to be much less dramatic. The group called itself the *Czerwony Harcerz,* The Red Scout. In our cell, besides Wilek and I, were the two brothers, Koniks, sons of the garden nursery owner with whom my aunt Pepka was so friendly. Assignments were very rare and consisted of distributing radio messages from the BBC in London, which were received on a clandestine radio and printed on onion paper. They carried mostly war news from the French front or hope-inspiring messages by General Sikorsky of the Polish Army, who spoke from London. It all seemed mundane, although we once heard that another cell executed a Polish girl for collaboration with the Germans.

There was some risk, however, because of illegality of what we did. At one point the German administration tried to limit the amount of spending money by Polish people and invalidated all the high-denomination currency—except the one stamped by the German Banking authorities. We were given a large package of 500 zloty paper notes and a counterfeit stamp and told to distribute them to other cells. Each member of a cell knew only one member of another cell so that in case of capture the disclosure would be minimal.

On one occasion I was riding a streetcar with a bundle of the underground newspapers when the street was closed by the Gestapo who were getting ready to board the streetcar. I was standing next to the motorman and to the container of sand next to the steering gear. I concealed the bundle of the onion paper in the sand and warned the motorman: "If you squeal we will kill you." I walked away into the streetcar; I slipped on my armband, praying that the Gestapo would not find the newsletters and that the motorman would keep quiet.

The Gestapo did not find the papers and the motorman did keep quiet, but nevertheless the male occupants of the streetcar were taken to the Gestapo headquarters on Pomorska 2 to be interrogated. It turned out that they were looking for certain Polish intellectuals; since that streetcar passed by the Jagielonian University they were hoping to net some. The fact that I was Jewish and had my papers in order and the fact that I spoke German got me off— after four hours of harassment, questioning and manhandling, a black eye and the loss of four teeth.

The fact that I survived that encounter with the Gestapo without endangering the unit's safety raised my status in the group. But after I had reflected on the risk involved and on my responsibility to my family I tried to avoid any further assignments.

On December 5, 1939, the area of Kazimierz where most of the Jewish population in Krakow was concentrated was surrounded by German troops who marched into the area singing the *Horst Wessel Lied: "Wen Judenblut fom Messer Spitze spritzt . . ."* "When Jewish blood from the edge of the knife spurts."

For three days and two nights a door to door search of all Jewish apartments was conducted. One was not allowed on the street or even to stand by a window for the threat of being shot. We heard intermittent rifle shots and could only wonder who was the target. The loudspeakers instructed everyone upon penalty of death to prepare to hand over to the searchers all valuables: art objects, furs, jewelry, etc.

In our apartment we feverishly tried to find secure hiding places for every prized piece; only to pull it out after awhile, unsure the place was right, and try to conceal it somewhere else.

Uncle Israel decided not to risk punishment and he put his beautiful pocket watch in full view on the night table. I took my *Tephilin,* my phylacteries, which I had not worn much lately but which still were precious to me, and hid them in the coal box beside the stove.

The soldiers entered our place on the second day, two privates and a sergeant. They asked for everything valuable to be handed over. My father told them that we were a working family and the only thing that he owned was a monkey-fur coat, well worn.

The sergeant pulled it out of the wardrobe, inspected it and found it worthy. Then they searched the whole place, leaving nothing un-turned. They came upon my uncle's watch on the night table and inquired: *"Was is dass?"* "What is this?"

"It's Doublee," meaning gold imitation, replied my uncle, trying to sound nonchalant. His attachment to the old watch overcame his fear of punishment.

"Oh well, who wants that?" asked the sergeant of the noncoms.

"Right, we have so many good watches" was the reply, and they left the watch on the night table.

On their way out, the coal box caught their eye.

"Was is in die Kiste?" "What is in that box?"

"Turn it over!" barked the sergeant.

With the coal fell out my *Tephilin.* In sudden rage the German ripped the straps and split apart the two little black boxes by stamping on them, as if expecting to find some hidden treasure.

I watched in horror, expecting the wrath of the Almighty to descend on the violators.

Nothing . . . .

In their bad-temper the soldiers kicked the two containers, the parchments rolling out as if crying out to heaven for justice. I turned my eyes away, unable to bear the sight of the instruments of my God's commandments being violated without the walls of heaven collapsing on the villains.

When the siege of the Jewish quarters had ended everyone tried to find out about the well being of friends and relatives and how they fared during the search. The mention of strangers who lost their lives during the three days of the blockade—news that would have been disturbing before—now evoked only an apathetic response.

NORBERT FRIEDMAN

CHAPTER IX

I remember the winter of 1939-1940 as a cold, cruel period because of the living conditions; the meager food rations allocated to the Jewish population of Krakow, the growing restrictions on movements, the shortage of coal and the looming threat to our lives.

It would get very cold in my aunt's kitchen at night. We tried to save whatever fuel was available for cooking or to heat the large tile-stove in the big room.

My parents would heat a bottle of water and put it into the bed before entering. I was allowed to share their bed occasionally because sleeping on the shelf under the table would leave me cold and awake most of the night. One night when I was prepared to put the hot water bottle into the bed I lifted the down-filled quilt and saw a mouse with a newborn pink litter of several babies. It was so cold in the house that she decided to give her young the warm shelter of our bed.

In the beginning of 1940 when travel on the railroad was still open to the Jews, my mother, I and the wife of a neighbor took a trip to Wielopole-Skszynskie, where my father's family had returned from Zywiec and now resided and where my brother Oskar lived with my grandparents. The reason for the trip was to purchase butter, poultry and any other type of food that might be available.

The lengthy train voyage took us to the town of Dembica, which later played a significant part in the lives of my family. From there we hired a driver to take us on a sled to Wielopole. The driver had several bear skins on the sled to help us keep warm on the 30 klm journey. Still, during the trip we had to dismount frequently and run alongside the sled in order to keep warm. The driver did not like it when we got off; claiming it slowed his progress. Only after we suggested that he stop at a roadside inn for a short while did his surly disposition change. We warmed up at the hearth while he downed a few shots of vodka, courtesy of my mother's purse. We arrived after dusk, paid the driver—my grandfather threw in a bottle of schnapps—and proceeded to greet and embrace each other.

My brother Oskar was at a neighbor's house so Uncle Uniu was sent to fetch him. I watched my brother as he entered; I had not seen him for about six months, and he seemed to have grown a lot. The seven-year-old was dressed in an overcoat too long for him the collar up and the earflaps of his hat upturned carrying a furrow of snow. He tried through the dimly lit room to locate my mother and me, then threw his arms around my mother's neck and firmly clung to her. The two of them stood in the middle of the room in total silence, with only my mother's suppressed sobbing punctuating the scene. After a while he let go of her and ran to me; this time it was he who burst into tears as we kissed and embraced.

His crying spell was very short however, and was soon replaced by a torrent of plans about what we were going to do together and then by a lengthy, proud account of all the things that he had been doing. He bragged of how our grandparents entrusted him with important chores and of all the things that he had learned to do around the house.

The rest of us sat late into night relating news and stories from the outside world and discussing the latest rules and restrictions imposed by the Germans.

We tried to forecast the immediate future based on our available information, which for the most part consisted of unsubstantiated rumors. I tried to share whatever news was available from the radio messages of General Sikorsky from London, broadcast through the BBC.

Oskar finally dozed off in my lap and it was time to go to sleep. I undressed him, careful not to wake him, and put him into the space on the kitchen floor that was reserved for me to sleep on. In his slumber he turned and put his arms around me, and even in his sleep there was blissful contentment in his body language.

In the morning it snowed hard. At breakfast we sat planning how to go about acquiring provisions. Next day was market day, but Jews according to ordinance were not allowed to shop until the Poles had completed their purchases. It was decided that Oskar would intercept the peasants on the way to the market and bring them to the house if they had something to sell. My grandfather assured me that he was good at it.

Meanwhile Oskar suggested that we go outside and play in the snow. He had gotten a sled from the shed and we went sledding on an adjoining hill. We rolled in the snow, threw snowballs, and tried to make up for all the time that we were apart. I was seventeen and he was seven, but ten years of difference in our ages meant nothing. Our love for each other and his recently acquired maturity, brought on by the war conditions, easily bridged that gap.

"Let's go and get the skis," he suggested. "You can use Aunt Netka's and we will go skiing like we used to."

When he was much smaller and only three or four years old, I would let him stand on my skis behind me as we slid down the hill.

"You are to big for that," I tried to convince him. "Let's just keep sledding."

The impracticality of going back to the things that we used to do together in time past made him sad and quiet.

When we were finished sledding, we went back to the house, hung up our wet clothing and sat by the stove. Oskar brought some books that aunt Netka tried to teach him from and insisted that I read to him my favorite poetry, mostly by the celebrated Polish poet, Adam Mickiewicz.

Mother, went visiting with grandmother to some relatives house, cousins of my father whom she had never met before. When she came back her cheeks were red from the frost outside and her eyes shone with the excitement of new acquaintanceship. She was envious of the life in this small shtetl without the immediate presence of the Germans and for once she admitted she was glad that Oskar could be kept out of the perils of the larger city. She paid him special attention that evening, continuously hugging and kissing him, which he in turn coyly enjoyed.

The wooden farmhouse that my grandparents were occupying at that time was well insulated and the stove gave out plenty of heat, so we felt warm and secure. The togetherness of the family: the presence of my grandparents; my uncles Aciek, Tulek, Slomek, and Uniu; Aunt Netka; my mother, her friend, Oskar and I, made it almost cozy, without feeling crowded, and somehow so far removed from the perilous world outside.

The next day was market day and we had to use it to buy whatever victuals we could. It had stopped snowing and Oskar went out on the road, shortly returning to the house with a farmer who had in his wagon most of the things that we wanted to buy.

Grandma bargained briefly with the farmer and sealed the deal when she offered the farmer in addition to money a beautiful headscarf that my mother had brought with her from Krakow just for such a purpose. Grandfather had the two geese slaughtered and dressed that evening and we left the butter between the windows overnight to keep it fresh. We also had the farmer's cheese in wet cheesecloth. We bought several jars of chicken fat in the village but decided not to take any eggs with us for fear of breaking them on the way. Grandma baked two large loaves of bread for us to take along and we engaged a peasant driver with a sled to take us to the railroad.

We had decided after much deliberation not to go to the larger station in Dembica. We knew that the German gendarmes, assisted by the Polish police, searched the travelers and confiscated any food they could find. Instead we opted for a smaller station in a village preceding Dembica in hope of avoiding the dreaded police.

We left the following evening, having spent the day before saying good-bye to neighbors and relatives and packing our bounty in such a way that it would not be conspicuous. I had to promise Oskar that I would come back soon and maybe take him to Krakow for a while, where he had never been. He clung to my neck, pressed his cheek to mine, and whispered his last question to me: "Is Father coming down here sometime soon?"

My mother cried openly when she embraced her younger son, boarded the sled and finally just waved to everyone else, having wrapped herself in a heavy blanket and furs.

The night was clear and the moon was full. The air was crisp and the stars were sparkling the way they do on a very, very cold Polish winter night. The driver snapped the whip and off we went. He removed the customary bells from the horses' harness and we silently glided out of town. We had a long and cold trip ahead of us.

As soon as we had gotten out of the more inhabited area we realized the extent of the snow that had fallen in the last few days. Everything was covered with a thick blanket of white, even the main, frequently traveled road. The horse's hoofs kicked up the stuff into the driver's and my face on the front seat. I pulled up my scarf to cover my face and so did the driver, leaving only his eyes to peer out. We were moving at a brisk pace. After about an hour we had to get off the main highway and proceed to the minor railroad station via a less traveled road.

In the eerie nocturnal bluish whiteness of the countryside where the contour-less landscape and the horizon blended into one, and in the luminescence of the star-filled firmament, the silhouette of the speeding, horse driven sled with its huddled occupants was the only evidence of an earthly presence. We seemed to have been suspended in time and in space, gliding silently toward the full moon, when suddenly the unmistakable, mournful howling of wolves from the nearby woods interrupted the ghostly setting. The horses which up till now had led the sled with sure steps and by sheer instinct found the solid road under their hoofs, roared in fright, reared and pulled the sled off the road.

We found ourselves in a roadside ditch, the sled sidewise, the horses on their side still bellowing. I crawled through the snow looking for my mother, who I found checking the damage to her bundles of food. The first thing she said was: "Thank God we did not take the eggs, what a mess would that be."

I helped the driver to right the horses who kept kicking and whose whole bodies were nervously shivering. The center thill was broken; the sled was on its side, undamaged, but we needed help. The driver unhitched the horses and got them back on the road, and we decided to follow him looking for some signs of habitation. We trudged behind him as he walked between the two horses. I hoped we were following the road. The snow was deep and fluffy; it was bitter cold and after a while the chill penetrated our clothing. Our gloves had gotten wet and now were frozen solid. Despite the fact that we stamped our feet frequently they, too, felt frozen.

We marched for about an hour, covering very little distance without a sign of life; after what seemed like an eternity my mother thought she saw sparks in the distance. We quickened our pace but could see nothing above the line of solid white. Then once again we saw sparks, but could not see any habitat or clearing. Even so, we decided to turn in the direction of the sparks, plunging chest deep into the snow and plowing through it. The horses roared and the driver said that they must have been sensing other animals.

By now dogs started to bark. Once again we saw a display of sparks, this time from close by. We forged ahead and then hit a solid wall of snow. From nearby we were able to distinguish outlines of some structures and we headed toward them. Finally we hit a solid path and saw the dwelling.

The area around the cluster of wooden structures was cleared of snow, which was packed around the house into a solid wall, higher than the roof and even the chimney. The farm was not visible from the road and if we had not noticed the sparks we might had missed it altogether.

The driver tied the horses to a tree. We knocked on the doors of the house, but the people inside had heard the animals and were already expecting visitors.

It was delightfully hot inside. After hearing our story, the peasant woman brought snow from the outside, put it into a pail of water and made us put our hands into it. She knew that we had frostbite and wanted our hands to thaw out gradually. The pain was excruciating. Tears ran down my mother's flushed face but she was more concerned with continuing the journey.

Our driver explained our predicament to the farmer, who agreed to help for a price. The driver turned to my mother and in turn asked her for the money. Clumsily, with her half-frozen fingers she reached into her purse and produced the required sum. It was considerable, including the price for a thill as well as the work. The farmer had awakened two young men to go with him and the driver. I stayed with my mother and her friend who remained totally quiet through the whole ordeal.

They hitched up a sled, tied our two horses to run behind it and took off in the direction where we had left our sled. My mother reminded the driver not to lose our bundles with the food. Meanwhile the farmer's wife heated up some borsht and served it to us with black bread. Circulation slowly returned to our extremities and with it severe pain. Our feet felt as if someone had stuck a knife and needles into them.

The men returned and we bundled up to be on our way. Dawn was breaking and one could see the outline of the road. The farmer advised our driver to keep snapping the whip while driving to scare the wolves away.

Because of the lengthy delay we were sure we would miss the train. God only knows how long we would have to wait for the next one, worried Mom. When we got to the station it was already daytime. Other people were waiting, and to our relief we found out that the train was late and had not arrived.

We paid the driver, thanked him for his efforts and told him how sorry we were for his troubles. He took the agreed fare but seemed very unhappy until mother produced a gold broach from her purse and gave it to him for his wife. He bowed to my mother, bent to kiss her hand and wished her a happy journey. My mother waved to him and after he was gone she turned to me and said: "Thank God, he was an honest *Goy*, an honest gentile. He could have turned around, taken our bundles and left us with the farmer."

The train arrived after some time and we boarded it fighting our way to find a seat. It was full of workers and peasants. We seemed to have been the only Jews aboard. We put our belongings on the overhead shelves but not directly over where we were sitting. We were in the second car from the locomotive and it was warm in the compartment. We arrived in Dembica after a short ride.

Some people were getting off the train and others were boarding it. We were impatient for the train to leave. But before long two German Schutz-Polizei in company of a Polish policeman walked in and our hearts dropped into the pit of our stomachs.

NORBERT FRIEDMAN

"Butter, Eier, Wurst," butter, eggs, sausage? "Who carries those things? Better turn them over, for if we will find them there will be hell to pay"

"Los, Los." Let's go. We looked at each other, my mother got up and in her best German addressed the Schupo: *"Herr Hauptman."*

"Captain, I have some butter and some farmer cheese, I am taking it to my sick sister in Krakow, please may I show it to you?"

"How come you speak German so well?" Asked one of the Schupos.

"I studied German in school."

"Yes, but the Poles do not speak like that."

"I lived in Silesia," answered my mother.

It was an ambiguous reply, for Silesia could mean either Poland or Germany.

I took down one of the bundles, the one with the butter and cheese. "This is my son" pointed out my mother.

"Do you also speak German?" came the question.

"Natürlich," "Naturally."

Meanwhile the Polish policeman, who was inspecting at the other end of the compartment with the other Schupo, approached and watched the goings on. The first Schupo looked into the bundle, took all the crocks of butter except one, shook his head negatively at the farmer's cheese, tied up the bundle and handled it to my mother.

"Hast du was noch?" "Do you have anything else?"

But before my mother had a chance to answer, the Polish policeman called him over and whispered something to him.

"Hast du eine Kennkarte?" "Do you have identification papers?"

Mom showed him her ID.

"Du bist eine Judin," "You are a Jewess," he cried angrily.

"Where is your armband?"

We had put the armbands on the sleeves of our outerwear, once on the train we took the coats off, not wanting to be recognized by other occupants.

We showed it to the *Schupo*, but he was furious, for he felt a Jewess had duped him.

"I could shoot you for breaking the law!" he screamed.

"Take that cheese!" He pointed to the Polish policeman. "And anything else they have"

The Polish policeman climbed on the seat and took down all the other packages and without even inspecting, he carried them out from the train. My mother's tears and her friend's wailing had no effect on him. The Polish policeman barked back as he was stepping down from the compartment. "Shut your mouth, you Jewish whores, you."

We returned home empty-handed. The arduous trip left us deeply disappointed and humbled and so much more aware of the severity of our plight. Shortly after our return, in February of 1940, the Germans issued an edict barring Jews from all rail travel.

The spring of 1940 was like no other spring in my young life. There was no good news to be had. Russia, still at that time Germany's ally, had invaded Finland. Acquaintances and friends were disappearing, supposedly into labor camps. The Jewish population of Krakow was swelled by the influx of some 20,000 people from countryside whom the Germans were relocating to larger cities. Families had to make room in their quarters for strangers. My aunt was spared, for she already claimed us as lodgers. Living space was getting more confined in homes and outside as well.

People were wary of meeting on the street for fear of being apprehended for forced labor. Certain inhibitions and norms of behavior were being abandoned. Young people would openly embrace and kiss in the presence of others. There was urgency in the initiated love relationships; the youthfulness of our lives was in peril.

In April 1940 Hitler invaded Norway, and in May he started his campaign into Belgium and Holland. It seemed as if no one could stop him, and a sense of desperate hopelessness blanketed the occupied countries. The Lodz Ghetto was established and the news from there was also bad. The Jewish population of 160,000 was crammed into an area of two square miles. In Krakow rumors of all sorts circulated: There would be more restrictions, deportations, new ID cards; and a Ghetto might be created.

One morning in June my mother went out on an errand. When she did not return by noon we became concerned. I ran out to find my father and told him about it. We both started looking for my mother at my aunt's homes and at what would be her usual stops. We asked passers-by if they knew about any roundups, to no avail. My father ran to the Judenrat; they knew or would say nothing.

Late in the evening my mother returned, her face grayish, her hair in disarray. Her eyes, red from crying, had a faraway look of despair and resignation. She would not talk to us about her experiences of that day except to say that she was apprehended on the street and taken to the Gestapo headquarters on Pomorska Street and was made to clean their latrines. Any other questions were met with lips squeezed shot and eyes downcast. I sensed that she had been subjected to indignities that she would not or could not talk about.

She insisted on taking a bath, and we had to leave the kitchen. Then she went to bed. I saw my father sitting at the edge of the bed and in a consoling manner bending over her, but all I could hear was my mother sobbing. Next day at breakfast she calmly announced: "We must leave Krakow. Things will not get better here, the German Moloch will master the world, no one will be able to escape or stop it."

She instructed my father to think of a place where we could go to get away from the German presence. A few days later my father came home with the idea of going to the town of Tarnow. He could get a job there, he said, supplying a large jam factory with fruit.

The factory belonged to a wealthy Jew, and although it had the usual German trustee, the man was not averse to employing Jews. He had a contract to supply the German army with preserves and could use all the merchandise that could be supplied. He issued traveling permits to Jews who worked for him and paid above-market prices. Someone that my father knew before the war in the fruit and vegetable business made the contact and supplied him with a travel permit. My father went to Tarnow, rented an apartment off Lwowska Street and my mother and I moved there.

Tarnow was a small town 45 miles from Krakow with a Jewish population of about 25,000. There I found several members of my Zionist organization whom I had met in 1939 at the summer camp. They in turn introduced me to some of their comrades. One of them was a girl of my age who lived with her mother a few blocks from our apartment.

Hanka was tall for a girl. She wore her jet-black hair long and straight and it seemed that her beautiful brown eyes looked right through you. Her widowed mother owned a bakery and Hanka was busy most of the time helping her. When she was free she would come to where we lived and whistle under our window a short tune, a special melody, a signal of recognition for our group. At first my mother was against my fraternizing with a girl who would come and whistle for a boy to come down.

"What kind of a girl is she?" my mother wondered. But when she met Hanka and realized that she was a no-nonsense, straightforward friend who considered herself a future *Halutz*, a pioneer in Palestine, equal in all regards, my mother gained respect for her and encouraged me in our friendship.

Friendship was all that this platonic relationship could be called at the beginning. We would walk together—getting about in Tarnow was much safer at that time than in Krakow—and dreaming of someday being able to find ourselves in Palestine, working on a Kibbutz free from all the constrictions of our life here.

Gradually we confided in each other and shared our experiences, stories about our families and reminiscence of our childhood. We avoided talking about the present situation, so as not to throw shadows on the tranquility of our relationship. Soon we would hold hands when walking and kiss lightly when parting company. We wanted our romance to stay pure and platonic. Although our affection for each other was becoming more pronounced, we wanted to keep it above the carnal experience, an oasis of untainted innocence in a sea of peril, degradation and baseness.

My father meanwhile was traveling in the area of Sandomierz, buying whatever fruit was in season for the jam factory. He had all the necessary papers and was able to commission transportation by rail or truck. I would receive the merchandise at the factory's receiving depot, weigh it, if my father was not present, and have the bill of lading signed. My father would collect the money.

Winter came, the business slowed down, and the Jewish owner of the factory had to stay more in the background. There was talk of a Ghetto to be created in Tarnow.

My father continued to travel and now stayed for prolonged periods in the Sandomierz area, in the village of Zawichost. He would occasionally come to Tarnow with a shipment of winter apples or pears.

Once, after his longer-than-usual absence I went to Zawichost by rail and found my father staying with family Z. A village Jew about my father's age bent from years of hard work, was the head of the family. It included a daughter in her twenties, a son my age and a younger girl of about ten. The mother had died several years before.

The old man knew the Polish landowners in the area and served as broker in buying fruit for my father. From the very first moment I did not like the surprise and embarrassment of my father when I arrived, or the blushing of the older daughter Tova who kept looking away from me, her eyes pointing downward during the introduction.

The family occupied a farmhouse with four spacious bedrooms, a large all-purpose room, a country kitchen, an attic and a cellar. Chicken and geese must have at one time been a part of the household for there was a small wooden poultry house.

I decided to have a serious conversation with my father, for after staying with him for a few days it became apparent to me that he was supporting the family Z. and that there was a relationship beyond business ties, especially with Tova. He vehemently denied my suggestion, protesting that it was strictly business, that the old man was of great help to him finding sources of merchandise and so on.

I was not interested in establishing the truth as much as I was concerned with my mother's welfare amid the worsening situation in Tarnow. We finally agreed to take Mom from Tarnow to Wielopole and have her stay with my father's family and my brother Oskar. I would find lodgings some place in Tarnow and keep helping my father with supplying fruit to the jam factory. I did not want to leave Tarnow because of my attachment to Hanka, but my mother's welfare was paramount to me. I had my father go back with me to Tarnow and we put mother on a train to Dembica.

I found lodgings in Tarnow with a family of a mother and two daughters living on the main square of town. Whenever possible I tried to spent time with Hanka even though her mother objected to my frequent visits because they took Hanka away from her responsibilities. I would sometimes stay late beyond the curfew. One such evening, on my way home, I had taken my armband off because Jews were not allowed on the street after the curfew. As I was walking home I was accosted by an obviously inebriated man, who in broken German asked for my papers. Since I wrongly suspected that the individual was a drunken Pole who was looking for a ransom from a Jew who was violating the curfew, I in turn assailed the man in German calling him a drunken Polish pig and suggesting that he go home to sleep it off.

The commotion on the otherwise deserted street attracted a German Schupo patrol. One of them asked, "*Was is los hier?*" "What is going on here?"

I continued with my line that this drunken Polish swine was bothering me. They turned to the man and asked him for identification. He fumbled for a while in his pockets and finally produced a document. *"Hier!"* He shouted triumphantly. The Schupo examined it carefully and then turned to me: *"Papiere, bitte,"* "papers, please."

I had nothing to show that would justify my being on the street after the curfew, so I claimed that I had no papers. They then escorted us to the Polish police station; there I found that the man who had stopped me was the Labor

Commissar for Tarnow, a *Volksdeutsch*, an ethnic German by the name of Kusnierz.

After the two German gendarmes left he proceeded to beat me, first with his fists and then with a police stick which he took from one of the policemen. I was bleeding profusely and reeling from the assault. One of the Polish policemen, who seemed to feel sorry for me and who obviously resented the action of the turncoat, whispered to me: "Lean on his shoulder next time he hits you." As soon as it was feasible I feinted unconsciousness and fell on Kusnierz's shoulder. He knocked me to the floor, and ordered the police to lock me up so that he could include me in the next transport to a forced labor camp. After one last kick in my kidney area the man left.

The police put me into a cell with four other Jews who were there for various violations. The Polish policeman, who had pity on me and gave me the saving advice locked the cell and quietly informed me, "I will be here tomorrow."

Next day he showed up at noon when we were fed a bit of tea and bread. I gave him some money and Hanka's address and asked him to notify her of my situation. Two days later he returned and told me that the next morning all the male Jewish prisoners, some forty men, would be taken by train to Pustkow, a forced labor camp. He told me to be in the last row, and that he would be one of the guards. When we reached a certain street and turned into it I was to peel away from the line and turn back. Hanka would be waiting for me, he said. "You have some fiancée, what a brave and smart girl!"

Next morning we were marched out, and as promised the policeman was the guard watching the last line of prisoners. Before we reached the designated street I spotted Hanka and another girl with two bicycles. As soon as I peeled of, Hanka gave me one of the bicycles and told me to follow her. We did not go to her house but to her cousin's, where we dismounted and embraced. I tried to thank her but she put her hand on my mouth to silence my gratitude.

"So when are we getting married?" was my first question "The policeman said you were my fiancée."

"I had to tell him that, he was coming on too strong."

"You have to get some safe ID," was her way of returning me to reality.

I discussed it with the two girls in whose house I was staying. They were both in their early thirties, wholesome looking, although one of them had to fight a dark facial growth, she used some kind of a stone which always left her skin red. They were both employed in a place where they sorted goose feathers for a German concern. The working ID cards from that concern did not specify whether the ID holder was Jewish, only that they were employed in defense work for the German army. It had the picture of the employee and the official seal of the German authorities. The girls were able to get me a job in the shop.

I was the only male working there, one man among forty women, ranging from eighteen to fifty years of age. Their job was to sort the feathers into categories for different end uses: The down for officer's quilts, fine feathers for hospitals, feathers for women's hats and dresses, etc. If I remember correctly there were twenty-three different kinds of feathers—eleven right, eleven left and one from the center of the tail. My job was to bring to the women the bags of feathers and put the sorted items into their respective bins.

The women had their fun with me, kidding me about different matters. For the first time I realized how coarse women could be, especially on sex-related conversation. At the beginning I blushed at every allusion to my physical prowess and the mock invitations to display it, but after a while I realized that those were good-natured barbs and maybe an outlet for the tensions that these women were living under.

I worked there a few weeks and stopped after I had gotten my ID. The ID came just in time; a ghetto was being formed and people were being moved to an area around where Hanka lived.

Hanka and I talked about my next step. Hanka insisted that I leave Tarnow and go to Zawichost. I wanted her to go with me but she would not leave her mother and pointed out that they had permission to keep operating the bakery in the ghetto.

We said good-bye, embracing and holding each other, controlling with difficulty our urge to take our relationship a step further. I promised to come back to Tarnow as soon as possible.

CHAPTER X

I arrived in Zawichost, to the discomfort of my father, and started looking for lodgings for myself. Tova, the young woman whom I suspected to have a relationship with my father, introduced me to some young people who used to gather in her house, mostly on Saturday afternoons. They would entertain themselves by singing the melancholy popular hits and Zionist songs of the time, contemplating their future and playing parlor games. One of the girls, named Lola, mentioned that she knew a Polish man who would be willing to share his room with me.

Michal Krawiec was six years older than I, of slim build, about my height. He wore pants tucked into his soft half boots, a fingertip overcoat, a rakishly tilted cap and a smiling, mischievous look in his eyes.

We found each other acceptable from the very beginning, and my share of the cost of the room was affordable. My room was one of three that the landlady, a hunchbacked widowed owner of a bakery, was renting out. Her married daughter and her son-in-law occupied the other side of the house next to the bakery. Her daughter, a scrawny nondescript girl, was married to a husky young man, a baker who had learned the trade while working for her father.

Once after an evening of heavy drinking and inane levity Michal asked the landlady how was she able to conceive with such a deformed back. "On a table," was her jovial reply, "We pulled the drawer out, that's how"

The landlady, in contrast to her daughter, was a friendly woman despite her handicap, always busy, always scurrying around. She liked the company of men and would often drop into our room for a drink and a chat. The other two rooms were rented out to four boys who were attending the vocational school in town.

It soon became apparent why Lola wanted me to move in with Michal: she was carrying on a torrid love affair with him and needed a cover for their tryst. Lola was the perfect specimen of Semitic beauty, full-bodied yet erect, black hair in braids, almond eyes covered by long lashes nestling under thick eyebrows. Her ruby lips were full as a carp's mouth.

I would pick her up at her house, which stood at the end of the Jewish part of the village and walk with her to where I lived at the other end of the non-Jewish section. Sometimes, we would be joined by her girlfriend Sonia, who was in on the secret arrangement. After a while there was talk in the village that I was romantically involved with Lola. Sometimes we would all take a walk into the fields or the nearby woods where we would meet Michal by pre-arranged appointment.

Michal made his living like everyone else—on the black market. He would take extraordinary risks to do a trade. There was a devil-may-care attitude about him. Sometimes I felt that he had a death wish. Michal would invite me in on some deals. Once we bought a lot of Polish pre-war vodka and offered it by the bottle at a very good profit.

We kept the merchandise behind a mirrored dresser in our room and I occasionally checked the inventory. Towards the end of the lot I sold a couple of bottles to a friend and noticed that the seal on the cork looked strange. I opened the bottle and sure enough, it was filled with water. When confronted, Michal admitted having drunk the vodka and having refilled the bottles with water so that I would not notice. Addiction to alcohol was one of Michal's more acceptable vices.

The four boys who occupied the other two rooms were in awe of Michal and seemed always ready to follow his dictates. They attended the Zawichost Vocational School, which had an excellent agricultural department. They all came from farming families. The parents of two of them, Jozek Kowalski and Antek Gora—were wealthy landowners from the area of Radom. The boys would occasionally hold subdued conversations with Michal that would brake up when I approached. Once after we drank more than our share of vodka, Michal confided in me, that he had recruited the boys to an underground political cell, of which there were several in the area.

The only sign of German occupation in Zawichost was an outpost manned by six Luftwaffe soldiers. One of them had three stripes on his uniform sleeve he was the sergeant in charge of the garrison. They kept a motor boat on the Vistula River; otherwise they executed their patrols on bicycles. Sometimes they were accompanied by a Polish policeman from the Polish police station in town. We never knew what their assignment was, for they were inconspicuous and kept to themselves.

Despite the fact that there was a ghetto now in Tarnow we still had the contact with the marmalade factory, and in spring we again started making

SUN RAYS AT MIDNIGHT

deliveries. The first shipment was a load of strawberries for jam, purchased from a prominent Polish landowner located between Zawichost and Sandomierz. The landowner, Mr. Bujak, was known to be an honorable gentleman in the style of Polish nobility, friendly to the Jews with whom he had many dealings. I arrived at his farm early in the morning on the day of loading. He was already up, greeted me cordially, and had one of the women prepare two plates, (one for me and one for himself,) of freshly picked strawberries with fresh sweet cream.

He joined me at an outside table and engaged me in a conversation about the plight of the Jews. He was well informed and knew Michal well; I suspected that he was more than just sympathetic to the underground movement.

At the end of harvesting the strawberries, before the baskets were loaded on the horse-driven wagons, for the journey to the railroad station in Zawichost, Mr. Bujak came over, shook my hand and made me promise that if I should ever be in distress I would come to him for help. He sounded so genuine and sincere—this tall, dignified member of the Polish gentry, shaking the hand of a young Jewish boy on a buying assignment. I said good-bye, impressed and strangely encouraged. This was not to be my last visit to Mr. Bujak's estate.

We loaded the merchandise on a freight car and I tipped the stationmaster generously, expecting to use his services again. I boarded the train to which the freight car with the strawberries was coupled. I was traveling on my identification from Tarnow, with official papers for transporting the fruit issued to that name.

After several hours of travel we arrived in Dembica, the large railroad junction where my mother and I had had the terrible experience of losing all our provisions. We were supposed to stop over for about fifteen minutes but there was so much activity at the station, caused by troop movement and shuffling of box-cars, that it was obvious we would be delayed. I walked out of the compartment asking a young, well-dressed lady to protect my seat from being taken.

I looked toward the rear of the train just in time to see the freight car with my strawberries being unhitched and moved to a siding. I ran toward it and asked the switchman why it was being moved.

"Orders from the stationmaster," was the reply. I ran to the office of the stationmaster, where a short, thinly mustached Polish railroad official was excitedly giving orders over the phone. It was obvious from his conversation that he was under pressure from German supervisors.

NORBERT FRIEDMAN

I decided that the best course of action to save my shipment from rotting on some siding was to pretend to be part of the German establishment and try to exert pressure. I walked over to the stationmaster and, waving the permit under his nose, demanded in German to know what was going on: Why was my car being uncoupled and moved?

He straightened up and in broken German he blurred out: *"Befehl mein Herr,"* "Orders, sir."

In typical German fashion I loudly insisted that the car with the strawberries be attached to the train; and it was the last car.

Once I got back to my compartment, I remained silent during the entire 40-kilometer ride to Tarnow. I tried to assess my actions and the danger that I had put myself in. One blunder or one suspicious official and that would have been the end of me.

Slipping in and out of one identity and then another created for me a tremendous amount of tension. One had to attain completely the characteristics of the person that he was impersonating. It was like entering into someone's shell, and then leaving it again as soon as the task was completed. One moment I was a brash young German, arrogant and authoritative, a master in a conquered country, and then in the next instant I was a Polish youth, weary of the occupying stranger yet confident enough in demeanor not be taken for a Jew.

I had to be constantly aware that I might be watched and my behavior examined by those around me. I must make the habits of the Christians my habits. I must remember to cross myself every time a journey started and every time I passed a church. I had to remember to use all the idiomatic expressions that an average Pole uses, including the frequent invoking of the names of the appropriate saints and deity. I had to appear to be a member of the majority of the population. I could not afford to forget any of the little idiosyncrasies, even if some segments of the population ignored them.

I even had to participate in the frequently expressed satisfaction with the fate of the Jews.

Somehow a part of my own identity got lost in the transformations. By the end of the day of such activity I was spent and numb, craving a drink and a place to sleep.

I arrived in Tarnow and unloaded the strawberries. Then I went to Mr. Shopf's office. To his delight I informed him that there would be shipments of cherries coming soon and other types of fruit to follow. I then asked him how his Jewish workers were going to travel in and out of the ghetto. He said that they were traveling under the supervision of Jewish Ordnungsdienst and the Polish police.

I asked him if I could get in and out of the ghetto before I returned to Zawichost. I said that I had someone I wanted to visit there.

"I will arrange it," he said, "but do not stay too long. It is not safe there."

Hanka was surprised and delighted to see me. I brought some conserves for her mother and we had a very plain dinner together. After dinner she asked me to stay overnight, and this time her mother did not object.

Again I asked Hanka to go with me into the country where things were safer, but she would not leave her mother and her mother would not abandon the bakery. As long as there was bread to be made in the ghetto, they felt needed and safe. I again promised to come back to Tarnow as soon as possible. This time, however, I never did.

After the war I searched for Hanka through various agencies and mutual acquaintances who survived. Finally I was told that she, too, had survived and was in the camp of Bergen-Belsen in the British zone of occupation. However, the Hanka Spanier there, was Hanka's cousin by the same name from Tarnow. Hanka had perished in the Stutthof camp, supposedly while being evacuated on a German boat, sunk by allied bombing on April 28, 1945.

CHAPTER XI

I boarded the train in Tarnow to go back to Zawichost but even before it reached Dembica I decided to get off and see my mother and Oskar. I wanted to leave them money and see how they were doing.

I was able to get a driver right away with a pair of swift horses. He was a talkative fellow who wanted to know too much. I did not want him to know where I was going to stay. After all, I was traveling as a gentile Pole. I had him drop me off at a roadside inn not far from the junction where my mother and I took the road to the smaller railroad station in the winter of 1940. I told him that I was to meet someone there, but he insisted on joining me in a drink and hung around for quite a while. It was only after someone hired him for a ride back to Dembica that he left, his curiosity unsatisfied.

I stayed at the inn overnight and next morning I got a ride to Wielopole. It was springtime in the Polish countryside; the blooming linden and poplar trees lined both sides of the road and peasants were working in the fields. Cattle in the pastures made this scene no different from any peacetime landscape.

When I arrived at my grandparent's house Mom was working in the garden with Oskar. Shrieking she dropped the basket she was carrying and put her arms around me. "My son, my son, my *kaddishel.*"

It was the first time she ever used that word, which meant someone who would recite the Kaddish, the prayer for the dead, for his parents. Oskar was strangely subdued, though, when we embraced.

We went into the house for a glass of sour milk, buttered bread and some fresh radishes from the garden. I sensed some tension in the house. My grandparents greeted me cordially but then left me alone with my mother and Oskar. My uncles were all working with some farmers and my aunt Netka was someplace on an errand.

"Nolek, I have to get out of here," my mother said as soon as we were alone. "Your grandparents and everyone else are trying to be very nice, but things are hard and I am just another mouth to feed. I can't go on being a burden or a charity case. Please take me away; whether I go back to your father or not, it does not matter."

How can, I take her to that house, I thought, with Tova and the whole situation there. My mind though, was made up for me that afternoon when Oskar again brought me some books to read to him. He was sitting in my lap when I happened to read to him a poem about a father who was long overdue in his home and who might have been facing the dangers of a long voyage: flood, wild animals and robbers. All of sudden during the reading Oskar turned to me, slapped my face and broke out crying.

The long months of longing for his father, his perplexing absence and the obvious breakdown of the family structure were all expressed in my little brother's weeping. And he was not so little anymore; suffering matured him beyond his years.

My grandparents did not protest much when I informed them that I was taking mother with me to Zawichost. Grandma, though, insisted that we leave Oskar with them, at least until Mother was settled and satisfied with conditions there.

When we arrived in Zawichost my father was away in the town of Jozefow with Mr. Z., securing fruits to be bought for the jam plant in Tarnow.

I moved my mother temporarily in with me, while Michal went to sleep in his parent's house, some five kilometers away in a village on the banks of the Vistula River. Jozefow was about 40 kilometers from Zawichost. I borrowed a bicycle and went to see my father and to inform him of my mother's arrival. He was very unhappy about the new situation but agreed with me that the only place for my mother was with him and the family Z. we did not discuss the situation with Tova, but it was obvious that the relationship would have to cease. At least that was what I was hoping for.

I moved my mother and her few possessions into my father's room in the Z's house. The person who seemed most resentful of my mother's presence was the old man. He had been comfortable with the previous set-up; it had relieved him from the responsibility of providing for his family.

Tova, in, turn was very cordial to my mother and accepted her presence cheerfully. Maybe she was growing weary of her relationship with an older man, which was robbing her of her youth and the association with her younger peers. Or maybe the commitment had been forced upon her by her father and by economic pressures, and she was glad to have it end.

In the middle of June my father sent me to the village of Zaklikow with which I was familiar from my travel in the first weeks of the war in 1939. I was to stay there with the family of a broker, who was to organize a large shipment of lupine, a soy-like bean used in feed for cattle and fish.

I was taken across the Vistula by Michal who propelled the boat across by a long pole in the fashion of the river people, a skill that he often tried to impart to me. It was a diagonal journey across the current, something I never mastered although I tried it often on our little excursions with Michal, Lola and Sonia. This time it was only the two of us and a bicycle.

I biked the narrow paths through the fields, trying to keep my balance. As I was nearing Zaklikow I started to recognize the area. I asked for and found the house of the broker who lived around the corner from the house where my cousins and I once stayed. It seemed such a long time ago, although it was less than two years.

The broker lived in a small house with his daughter Bella. He showed me where I would be sleeping, in an all-purpose room used for entertaining and eating. I was to sleep in what served during the day as a bench; at night the lid was raised and the coffin-like box was used for sleeping.

I went to see the family with whom my cousins and I stayed in 1939. They did not recognize me until I refreshed their memory. They asked about my cousins, where I was staying, what was the purpose of my visit and so on. The boys in their plain clothing and their ear-locks shorn off seemed so grown-up now. I declined their invitation for supper for I was committed to the broker, who was being paid for his hospitality.

Just as in Zawichost, the only German presence in the village; were some airmen, who went about their life not bothering anyone as long as all their needs were attended to.

The next day I went out with the broker to the farmer who was growing the lupine and gave him some money as a down payment on the whole crop. While we were talking to the farmer and admiring the fields of lupine in bloom—a yellow blanket of flowers as far as the eye could see—we heard rumblings which sounded like thunder, but which I recognized as either bombing or artillery. On our way home, we saw German airplanes flying east. It was June 22, 1941, and unbeknownst to us Germany had attacked Russia, an act that would have severe consequences for the lives of Jews. Not that our lot until now, had not been troublesome enough.

I had to stay one more night, for I had scheduled an appointment with Michal to pick me up the next day on the eastern bank of the river. I concluded the arrangements with the broker for closing the deal with the farmer when the crop of lupine was ready.

In the evening I went for a walk with his daughter Bella. She was inquisitive and flirtatious, trying all the charms of a *Shtetl Belle* on unsuspecting me. When we got home she prepared my bed and I said good night. She planted a long, wet kiss on my mouth and with an amorous look on her face she gathered her skirts and left the room. I put out the kerosene lamp and went to bed.

I was deep in sleep when I realized that there was someone next to me in the narrow box serving as my bed. First there was a hand on my mouth to keep me from making a sound and then a burning kiss replaced it. It was Bella in her nightshirt pressing her body against mine. She was trying to arouse me and when successful she mounted me and made love to me. It was short and passionate, and Bella left as quietly as she came in.

There was no sign of recognition of what had transpired between us at breakfast, except that before my departure she handed me her diary, or "album" as it was called in Poland, which served for friends and acquaintances to register their remarks and declarations of friendship.

I scanned it before leaving my remarks in it, when suddenly a note in familiar handwriting caught my eye: *"To my future daughter in-law,"* signed, *Jozef.*

I read and reread it, trying to absorb its implications, while Bella stood smilingly next to me. Finally, I requested privacy to put in my commentary, and when Bella had left I ripped my father's note from the diary and wrote: "To my dear friend Bella, I shall never forget you, Nolek." I went outside where Bella was standing. I shook hands with her but refused the invitation to go inside the house to say good-bye. Her father had already seen me off when he left early in the morning.

I rode my bike furiously toward Zawichost, mad at my father whom I suspected of making promises involving my freedom in exchange for sexual favors. I pedaled so fast I had to wait a while for Michal to show up.

The first words out of his mouth were: "Have you heard? The Germans had attacked Russia."

"Yes, I know," was my curt reply. "Do you know where my father is?"

"He is playing cards at Finkelstein's house, but what has gotten into you?"

"I will tell you later, first I want to see my father."

I burst into the room where they were playing and without as much as a hello, I angrily called my father out.

"Is that your handwriting?" I shouted, confronting him with the crumbled page from Bella's album.

NORBERT FRIEDMAN

"Yes, so what? You had a good time, didn't you? Grow up son, we all may be dead tomorrow!"

It was the first time that my father spoke to me like that, and it did shed a new shocking light on his thinking and actions. He turned and without another word returned to his card game.

We made a few more deliveries to Tarnow, but because traveling had become more perilous, especially for Jews in disguise; we had Michal make the deliveries. Then even that had to stop. For whatever reasons, the German trustee was no longer able to issue permits for purchasing and transporting merchandise.

The war against Russia intensified the punitive actions against Jews and Poles and it was becoming increasingly difficult to get around. Jews were being herded into ghettos and transported to unknown destinations. At the same time, Michal and the four boys would disappear frequently and then return from meetings that I was not privy to.

One day, before the boys were to go home for a holiday break, when we were reminiscing about our past and our family life before the war, Jozek Kowalski approached me and offered to take my brother Oskar to his parents' estate. He would be safe there, he promised, among the many children of the farm workers. Judging from the pictures that I had of Oskar, he said, Oskar did not look Jewish and I did tell him that he spoke Polish well. He said that there were things going on with the Jews in and around Radom, Jozefow and other communities and that it was not safe for children.

Although my father and I were inclined to accept my friend's offer, the final decision rested with my mother. I went with his offer to my mother who categorically refused. "They will make a *Goy*, a gentile out of him," she protested, her eyes swelling with tears. "No! Thank Jozek for me, but no" There was no visible reaction from my father. "She says no, its no," was all he said, and we left it at that.

A few months later my mother and my little brother were on their way to the extermination camp of Belzec where they perished with the other members of my father's family. My father's pain was of such intensity that in the following twenty years he never would mention the name of his younger son, my beloved younger brother.

In 1963, when I named my middle son Yehoshua, after my brother Oskar, the floodgates of tears finally opened up for my father and for me.

But what about my mother's tears? What about her anguish and the torment of self-reproach as she was led to her death with her beloved child, whom she refused to part with?

Still, closure of the mourning for my brother Oskar did not come to my father or me till 1967 when we buried my son Yehoshua/Oskar. By some strange osmosis my ailing child took with him to his premature resting-place the scarred memory of the uncle he never knew.

The fall of 1941 was a harbinger of things to come. The German army was advancing in Russia, Kiev had fallen and there were no good tidings to be had. Traveling gentiles brought us news of atrocities against Jewish communities and ghettos.

My family was dipping into the capital that we had saved from the profits of the fruit business, and we felt the need to make some more money to survive. Michal and I decided to take some meat to the Warsaw ghetto for sale on the black market. We slaughtered and dressed some calves on the estate of Mr. Bujak from whom we bought the animals. We packed them in wooden crates such as were used to transport eggs and apples. We put two layers of apples on the top and bottom of the boxes and straw between the apples and the boxes.

Michal got a permit for a shipment of apples from a German fruit concern in Warsaw. The business was located on *Plac Mirowsky*, the Mirovsky Square, adjacent to the ghetto boundary. Michal felt that the safest way to go was by a steamboat, which traveled up and down the Vistula River. We got on the boat in Zawichost and had reached *Kazimierz/Wisla*, Kazimierz on the Vistula, when the German police boarded the boat.

"*Ah, Eier,*" "Oh, eggs," shouted the German triumphantly. (Eggs seemed to be the produce most coveted by the Germans.)

"*Nein, nein, dass sind Apfeln,*" "No, no, these are apples," I protested, showing him the permit.

"We will see," was the German's reply, and he took his bayonet from it sheet and plunged it through the space between the boards of the crate.

I was frozen with fear: If the dagger came out bloody, so would I. But it went through one of the apples and came out with only apple juice on it.

"*In Ordnung,*" "In order," shouted the policeman to his companion as they continued their search among other passengers.

NORBERT FRIEDMAN

In Warsaw we got a steward at the boat landing to take the crates to the German warehouse, concerned that in the heat of the day the meat might betray itself. The black marketers from the ghetto paid us handsomely, and we shared the profit with the German trustee.

We had some time on our hands before we could get back so we let the smugglers, in the company of a Jewish policeman who was being paid off, take us into the ghetto. The one hour that we spent there did not give us a total picture, but what we saw as we walked the streets—the death and devastation, the walking corpses, the abandoned urchins begging for bread—made me aware again of the hopelessness of the lot of the Jews.

We went back by rail, changing trains in Radom and waiting for a connection. It was late and I was tired. I took part of the newspaper Michal was reading and laid my head on it and went to sleep. Michal awoke me a few hours later when our connecting train arrived.

"You don't know how lucky you are," he said. There was an identification check by the German police. When they came to where you were sleeping, one of them said: "Let him sleep. He must be legitimate, judging by the innocent way that he is sleeping, like an angel." And they went on. "Be grateful to your Guardian Angel, Nolek, you may need him."

There was a note of tender, almost brotherly affection in the tone of his voice and it accurately reflected my own feelings toward this man. At the beginning I had judged him to be a lone wolf walking his own path and satisfying his own appetite and needs. I had discovered that hiding behind that devil-may-care façade was an engaging and gallant man in the best tradition of the heroic, swashbuckling Polish romantics so admiringly described by the Polish poets and writers. I felt a swell of warmth and gratitude to Michal, and the only way that I could demonstrate my feelings and my total trust in him was by a lusty hug and, for the benefit of those within earshot, a loud, *"Niech bedzie blogoslawiony Jesus Christus,"* "Blessed be Jesus Christ," accompanied by a knowing wink of an eye.

CHAPTER XII

My mother was able to communicate with her brother and sisters before the formation of the ghetto in Krakow in March of 1941, but since then she had gotten only one postcard, from her youngest sister Hela. She was distraught by the lack of news, and that on top of her other worries made her very depressed. I had promised her that I would try to go to Krakow to check on our relatives, but she was reluctant to let me go because of the increasing dangers of travel.

I tried to make some arrangements for entering the ghetto in Krakow through Michal's connections. Finally in September I was told how to go, through which gate and at what time to enter. There was to be a Polish policeman on duty, easy to recognize, big and blond with a large mustache and a red nose. He would accept a bribe and let me in.

The trip by train was uneventful. In Krakow I took the streetcar across the bridge and got off near the entrance to the ghetto. I slipped the armband on and proceeded to the gate. The designated Polish policeman was on duty as scheduled. I showed him the ID, he took the two 100 zloty notes in it and I went trough.

It was a typical fall evening, warm and pleasant. But there were few people on the streets even though it was well before the curfew. Only the uniformed Jewish *Ordnungsdienst* roamed the streets, mostly in pairs. I walked quickly toward the address were my aunt Hela was living.

This I thought was what was left of my city: A few streets encompassing about 300 buildings, housing some 15,000 people. A fraction of what it once was. A gray, silent, lifeless area, like the bare trunk of a tree stripped of its foliage, its truncated limbs crying out to heaven for mercy. My Krakow, the lovely vibrant city of my childhood, reduced to an unrecognizable stranger.

I walked up to my aunt's apartment. The person who opened the door was my aunt Hela, but this was not the young, neat, handsome woman with a whimsical smile I had left only a year ago. In her place a gaunt, haggard, worn-out matron let out a shriek, both of delight and anxiety. She hugged and kissed me, trying through tears to ask the question, "What are you doing here?"

My uncle got up to greet me; oh, how he had aged! This always happy man with a sunny disposition, with a terrific sense of satiric humor, had developed a nervous twitch, his head jerking backward with disturbing regularity.

And my cousin Nusia, my lovely sprite of 12 years, who had said good-bye to me only a year ago, weeping with her head on my neck, extracting the promise: "Nolek you will come back, won't you? I love you." She stood there silently, a transformed youngster, pale, the sparkle gone from her eyes. She slowly approached, put her arms around me and quietly sobbed.

My aunt lived with two other families in this two-room, sparsely furnished apartment. That evening over a glass of tea brewed from dried strawberry leaves I was briefed on the events of the last year: the formation of the ghetto, the deportations, the continuously shrinking Jewish population; the daily atrocities decimating the families. My aunts and uncles, my cousins and other relatives were scattered in different directions, to small villages and communities, wherever they thought to have safe contacts, only to become a part of the tragic fate that every community experienced.

After my uncle had told me of the daily brutalities and the extreme difficulties of the life in the ghetto, I understood the physical and mental transformation of him and his family. My aunt told me of her efforts to land a job in a safe place, such as the Emalia factory (the Schindler's workshop portrayed in the picture "Schindler's List"), but it took clout or money to obtain those jobs, and she had neither.

The next day, which was *Erev Yom Kippur*, the eve of the Day of Atonement, I searched out few of my friends who still lived in the ghetto to get news about the whereabouts of our other comrades.

I listened to the accounts of their fate. Some had gone east before Germany attacked Russia to the Russian-occupied part of Poland. Some had left on various transports to unknown destinations, some had died during the atrocities, and some lived on the Aryan side of the city and were active in the resistance.

Most disturbing were the accounts of some of our friends who had turned to serve the Germans as *Ordnungsdienst,* the Jewish police, and others who had become informers or collaborators for the Nazis. The rationale for their behavior was their desperate desire to save their families, but this did little to soften the pain and the sense of betrayal and shame that I felt.

I extracted a promise from one of my friends to look out for my family especially, for cousin Nusia and to try to get a safe job for my aunt. I spent *Erev Yom Kippur* with my aunt and uncle. The pre-fast meal consisted of a slice of black bread dipped in oil that had been cooked with garlic to resemble the taste of goose fat, washed down with a glass of ersatz tea.

Yom Kippur day I spent with my friends again, arranging for a way to leave the ghetto the next day, a task more complicated than entering it.

In the early dawn of the day after Yom Kippur I said good-by to my relatives, sensing that this was a final parting. I walked out of the ghetto with a work detail and peeled off at a corner as prearranged with the group leader. I took my armband off and boarded a streetcar that would take me to the railroad station. To my horror, next to the motorman stood a familiar figure, that of Leibek A. who had been my group leader in the Shomer Hatzair Zionist organization and who was now one of those my friends had told me was working for the Gestapo.

There he stood in a black leather coat; riding boots and leather cap, making him look tall and formidable. I froze in fear, expecting him to finger me to the next German or Polish policeman, but he showed no sign of recognition. It was as if all those hours of shared experiences, as if though those lengthy lectures and friendly games in the summer camp had never happened. He simply looked right trough me as if I did not exist.

Frightened and shaking, I got out at the next stop from the other end of the streetcar and walked briskly across town to the other line that went to the railroad station.

I left my hometown, the cradle of my youth, without really looking back at it, never to see it again, except in my dreams and nightmares.

We heard once more from my Aunt Hela, and then my family was swallowed up by the brutal events that overcame the remnants of the Krakow Jewry.

CHAPTER XIII

In the winter of 1941 I heard that someone had a lot of pre-war soap for sale in the town of Opatow. Michal volunteered to go there and try to purchase the lot. The price that the broker quoted was attractive enough to warrant the trip, but while in Opatow, Michal was apprehended by the Germans. We never found out whether it was a trap set up by the Jewish broker who came to Zawichost or just bad luck.

The merchandise was confiscated; Michal was arrested and was to be brought to trial by the military. The colonel of the German garrison there was judge and jury, and there were only two possible verdicts: Guilty, with an automatic death penalty, or innocent and free to go.

The same broker who had brought us the deal then informed us of a chance to intervene. He said that the colonel had a Jewish mistress and that an appropriate gift might persuade her to intercede on Michal's behalf. Otherwise, he said, Michal's chances were slim.

Lola and I put our resources together and purchased a large diamond ring from a woman in Zawichost. Then we went to the town of Opatow to see the mistress of the colonel. A beautiful young woman in her late twenties greeted us and served us tea and German cookies. She sympathetically listened to our story, and although she made no concrete promises, she accepted the ring as a conditional gift for the colonel. I felt that she was going to try hard to have Michal released because she seemed to have been moved by Lola's emotional plea on behalf of a non-Jewish lover, a parallel to her own situation.

Sure enough, three days later Michal was released without trial and we took him home to Zawichost. Everyone agreed that this miracle called for a celebration, and we had a party in the home of one of Michal's friends. We roasted a lamb and drank warm *warzonka,* home-made vodka mixed with honey. It went down so smoothly that I did not feel its impact until I got up to go home. It was extremely cold outside but I didn't feel the cold. I walked, or rather staggered, to where I lived; Michal stayed on at the party with Lola.

The wooden wicket to my yard opened outward, but I, under the influence of the alcohol, tried to push it inward. Of course I was unsuccessful, so feeling warm and peaceful, I gave up and lay down on the ground beside the gate. The landlady, alerted by the noise of the gate luckily found me where I lay, half-frozen. With the help of her son-in-law she brought me in and restored my extremities—and me—to life.

When things become critical, one usually falls back on his most reliable skills. So it was with my father who, cornered by circumstances, unable to move around to do business in the countryside anymore, unable to earn the necessary resources, resorted to his original trade of kosher butcher. He disregarded the risks and the capital penalty that went with being in the dangerous enterprise of buying and slaughtering cattle.

There was a new resolve and a new maturity of action in his conduct. All the insecurities and frustrations of a young husband and father, burdened by the responsibilities of a head of a household; all the scars and the sense of inadequacy resulting from the mostly unsuccessful fight for a livelihood which had marked his prewar behavior had been replaced by the realization that circumstances had leveled the playing field, that everyone was equally vulnerable. The common denominator was that everyone's life was now in danger. When warned by friends of the perils associated with the outlawed butchering, he replied: *"Tak mogila i tak mogila,"* "Graveyard, one way or another."

He now became more concerned with my mother's needs, more interested in my life and more prone to seek my advice and help. I accompanied him on the trips into the neighboring villages to purchase cattle and helped to bring them in under the cover of darkness.

On one occasion we had to fight off a gang of three Polish thugs who lay in wait for us as we crossed the Vistula with the animal. My father's head was bloodied by a blow with a wooden stake, but he fought fiercely, wielding his long butcher knife. I, in turn, protected his back using the long rowing pole. This experience strengthened the bond between us, which we sealed by sharing a bottle of vodka at the house.

The slaughtering was done by the ritual *Shohet*, in the small shed next to the house, usually at dusk. After inspecting the animal the *Shochet* would leave. My father and I, by the light of a candle would skin and quarter the animal and clean up scrupulously so as not leave a trace. The blood and unusable parts had to be buried deep in the woods, and there was always the fear that dogs might snuff it out and dig up the site. The meat was sold to the people in town, the hind-part to some Polish black marketers. A Jewish man in the village would buy meat from us and deliver it to Jews who lived outside the town. The whole enterprise was very tense and fraught with danger, but it was the only available means of income and rather profitable.

In May of 1942, shortly after the holiday of *Shavuoth,* we slaughtered a young heifer and proceeded to dispose of it the usual way. Some of it was sold in town and delivered to the people who had placed the orders in advance and some of it was picked up by the man who would deliver it to his customers out-of-town on his bicycle. My father and I were in the house when someone came running to tell us that the vendor, who picked up the meat for the neighboring villages, had been sighted from the hill outside the town in the company of two German gendarmes and the Polish chimney sweeper, who was suspected of being an informant for the Germans. They were riding on bicycles in the direction of our house.

The road to the house was winding and uphill but still there was very little time before they would get here. We sent the women out of the house and started to check for any telltale signs of butchering. Mr. Z. was to go with his son Mottel to the basement and remove whatever meat was there.

My father and I went to the shed to make sure it was clean, and as we were about to go back into the house, the two German gendarmes, the chimney-sweep and the delivery carrier showed up. The man was chalky with fright and started to say something to my father when the German policeman whacked him with the butt of the carbine, bloodying his face.

They lined us up against the side of the house. One gendarme watched us while the other went into the house with the chimney-sweep to search for evidence. The deliveryman sensed a chance and took off, running around the house. The gendarme ran after him, cocked his rifle and shot twice. We heard a scream and then another shot. I pulled my father by his arm and we ran in the other direction, down the hill through an orchard toward the Vistula River. My father was some six inches shorter then I, but with short powerful legs, he soon was running ahead of me.

"Where to?" he was yelling as we ran for our lives through the thicket.

"To Michal's boat," I yelled back, looking behind me to check how close was our pursuit. I was determined to stop them somehow and to give my father time to escape should they be closing in on us. I could hear shouts in German but I did not see anyone.

We reached the bank of the river out of breath. I found Michal's boat and untied it from its mooring. We lay down in the bottom of the boat and I tried to guide it with my hands with the current, keeping close to the bank. We drifted down-stream for a couple of kilometers, listening for the sound of a motorboat from the Luftwaffe outpost.

Later I found that Michal and his boys had some time ago put sand into the gasoline tank of the seldom-used craft, rendering it useless. I stopped the boat from drifting and tied it to some willow branches at the riverbank. I sat up in the boat and looked for the first time at my father. He was shaken his face ashen. His eyes had the look of a frightened animal.

"What will we do now?" were his first words, and he said them in Yiddish, an indication that he was shaken to the core. He and I usually communicated in Polish.

"I will take you across the river and hide you. Then I'll go back to Zawichost to find out what is the story and where is Mama. I will come for you at night and we will decide then what to do."

He nodded his head in agreement and looked at me in a very strange way, as if he had not seen me in a long time.

I picked up the long pole for navigating and started to push off in the direction of the eastern bank. I did not realize how strong the current was, until I got near the middle of the river. I was unable to hold the course and found myself drifting down-stream.

When we arrived on the other side we walked a little ways and found a small clearing with a large old poplar tree. I assured my father that I would be back sometime after dark and begged him not to be impatient. "I will try to have some light with me," I told him, but in any case he should listen for the sound of my voice, singing an old Polish drinking ditty: *"Umarl Maciek, umarl . . ."* "Maciek croaked, he croaked . . ."

We hugged and kissed as I got ready to go back. He had some cigarettes with him and a pack of matches. It was almost noon by now and he should be all right until I got back. If I did not show up by morning, I told him, he should start in the direction of the village of Zaklikow and wait there for news.

I started back and again I encountered the problem of steering upstream. When I reached the other bank of the river I realized that I was just a little above Michal's parents' village, some five kilometers downstream from where I started. I tied up the boat and made my way to their house.

To my great relief Michal was there. He told me that when he had heard what happened at my father's house he had ridden to his parent's home where he expected me to bring my father to hide. His mother served us some food and his father put a bottle of homemade vodka on the table. We considered different courses of action, and finally Michal said: "You stay here. I will go to town and I will be back in a couple of hours. We will have a plan by then."

I lay down on his bed. As the excitement and the tension of the experience passed and the gravity of the situation settled in I began to shake uncontrollably. Michal's younger sister Zosia tried to calm me, covered me with some blankets and finally lulled me to sleep with soothing words and sympathy kisses.

When Michal came in and woke me up, it was dusk already. "Here is what we will do," he started out, "we will go for your father as soon as it gets dark. Then we will take him back to Zawichost. Marysia, who works for the Polish police and lives above the police station, will hide him in her room. No one will look for him there."

"Did you find out where my mother is?" I interrupted him.

"She is staying with Sonia, she will be all right there for a while. We will find a different place soon." He continued: "I am not going back to our place, for the police were there already looking for you."

As soon as darkness set in, we started for the other side of the river. Michal deftly steered the boat upstream and laughingly commented on how far downstream I had drifted. It took us a while in the dark to find the clearing where I had left my father. Michal waved a lantern while I sang at the top of my voice *"Umarl Maciek, umarl . . ."* finally we heard his cry: "Nolek, Nolek, here."

We told my father about our plan to hide him with Marysia above the Police station. Despite his anxiety he appreciated the irony of this scheme.

Halfway through the crossing in direction of Zawichost, Michal changed his mind and turned the boat down-stream in the direction of his parent's house. There he hitched a wagon, covered my father and me with hay and drove to town. We got out of the wagon a few hundred feet from the police station. The moon was out and we had to get to the back of the police station without being detected. Michal took my father to the bottom of the steps leading to Marysia's room, while I stayed hidden in the shadow of a house. I watched my father gingerly climb the outside wooden stairway and then disappear through the door to her apartment.

Michal wanted to go back to his parent's house but I wanted to see my mother first.

Despite the late hour, my mother was up expecting some news from me. Her eyes were red from crying. We briefed her on what had transpired and she sadly shook her head in acknowledgment.

"What will we do now?" was her query, just what my father had asked earlier in the day. She took me aside and in an agitated whisper confided: "All our money and my jewelry is in that tin can holding those dried flowers on the night table in my bedroom."

Then she said "They have a guard in front of the house, what are we going to do?"

She was obviously very troubled; the dreamy romantic demeanor that had marked her earlier life was gone. Now that mortal danger was facing her family, she was the pragmatic realist, concerned with the earthy problems.

"Do not worry, Mom," was all I could come up with, "I will see you tomorrow." I comforted her not sure that I would be able to keep my promise.

On the way to Michal's house I kept thinking of schemes that could get us out of our predicament. Next day Michal went to town again to find out what was happening. I had told him that I had to get into the house to fetch some things for mother. He came back after lunch and it was obvious that he was concerned. "They are printing a wanted poster for your father, with a price on his head," he informed me. "We have to get him out of Zawichost, you cannot trust people once it becomes a matter of money," he concluded.

"Listen," he continued, "this evening there will be a Polish policeman standing guard in front of the house. Marysia is going to bring him supper and keep him busy. This is your chance to get in, can you do it?"

"I will have to," was all I could reply.

"We also have to get some Aryan ID for your father. Do you have a picture of him?" Michal was thinking fast. "But first we will take your mother to a friend in Sandomierz. He owns an abandoned store, she can hide there."

"Wait until I get her stuff and a picture of my father from the house," I interrupted. "By the way, do you know where is the Z. family?"

"They all went to a village across the river. They have relatives there. Don't worry about them, they will be all right" Michal dismissed my concern: "Worry about your own." I thought I noticed a note of irritation in his voice.

In the afternoon we rode to Zawichost, to Sonia's house. This time I sat with Michal in the front of the wagon, a cap drawn deep over my eyes. Mother had nothing to pack. She had left all her clothing in the house when she made her hurried departure. Sonia gave her some underwear, a skirt, a peasant blouse and a "babushka."

In the evening I walked through the back alleys toward the house and cautiously approached it through the rear. After a while, when I heard Marysia's voice talking with the policeman to whom she brought supper, I inched toward the house and entered it through an unlocked window in my parents' bedroom.

I had no problem finding the tin can serving as a vase for the dried flowers and removing the contents, but it took me longer to find my father's old permit from the jam factory which had his picture on it. My heart beat so loud that I actually thought the policeman outside might hear it. Looking at the room it was obvious to me that someone had rummaged through it looking for valuables. I grabbed my mother's coat and ran out of the house without bothering to close the window.

Breathless, I approached Sonia's house. Michal was outside, nervously waiting for me. "How did it go?" were his first words.

"In order," I replied, "I have the picture." Michal took the old permit from me without looking at it; it was getting dark by now. Before we entered the house, he informed me that we would take my mother to Sandomierz early the next morning so as not to violate the curfew there.

We started at sunrise; it was market day in Sandomierz, so our wagon did not arouse any suspicion. The empty store owned by Michal's "friend" was on the outskirts of town. There was a cot, a chair and a desk in the store and a privy outside. It seemed as if the place was used recently. The floor was swept and there were blankets on the cot. We left Mom with some food. Michal's friend, whom I did not get to see, promised Michal that he would look out for Mom until I got there.

We went back to Michal's parents' house. Three days later Michal brought me an ID for my father in the name of Jozek Kowalski, born in Pszysucha. It was an ID issued to Jozek Kowalski's father. Jozek Kowalski Jr. was the fellow who offered to hide my brother Oskar, and who apparently was connected to Michal's underground activities.

We picked up my father early next morning, hid him in the wagon, and took him to Sandomierz. The wanted posters were on all the walls in the public places in Zawichost, offering two thousand zloties for turning my father in.

I had said good-by to Lola and Sonia, to Zosia and to Michal's parents, but I never had a chance to thank Marysia for all the risks she had taken. I suspected that she also was a part of Michal's clandestine ring.

In Sandomierz Michal went to see his contact, who this time came with Michal to speak to me and my father. He was a tall man with a large gentry-like mustache who looked vaguely familiar. He gave us the key to the store and told us where to put it when departing. He wished us luck and left. After he was gone I realized that I had seen him in the house of Mr. Bujak on my visits there. Michal would not confirm this.

Michal stayed with us to discuss our next step and to offer advice. My mother and my father thought it would be most prudent to go to Wielopole Skrzynskie where my brother was staying with my grandparents. It was decided that it would be safest if my father went first by himself and waited for us in Dembica. My mother and I would go the next day and we would meet in the large waiting room at the station. Then we would proceed together to Wielopole.

Michal went out and checked the railroad schedule. There was one train leaving in the morning and one late in the day.

We all had a drink together and said good-by to Michal. As I hugged Michal he said, "Don't you get sentimental on me. Keep your eyes and ears open and keep in touch. In case of danger write to me at Mr. Bujak's address. If you need shelter, go there and they will get in touch with me." He shook hands with my father, kissed my mother on both cheeks and we embraced again.

I thanked him for all that he had done for my father; my mother and myself saying; "You are one in a million, Michal."

He dismissed my gratitude with a wave of his hand. "There is good in every man. Look for it and it will find you my brother, I can feel that angel of yours watching over you." His voice cracked, and without looking back he left the store.

CHAPTER XIV

I walked with my father to the station, watched him board the train and went back to our hideout. Next morning my mother and I walked to the station and boarded the same train my father took. I again instructed my mother, as on the previous train trip, to watch me and repeat the same movements of crossing one's self when the train was taking off and to speak only when necessary and then not in the manner of town people.

I watched her when the train started to move and I had crossed myself. Her hand started toward her forehead but she did not complete the crossing cycle. She only pushed some hair under her kerchief and let her hand drop in her lap. She looked at me as if saying: "I can not do it, what do you want from me?"

Her religious convictions would not let her to make the sign of the cross.

We ate some bread and cheese, washed it down with water, which we brought with us. After a while my mother rested her head on my shoulder and fell asleep. I looked at her hands folded in her lap: Callused and wrinkled from all the house chores and the tasks she had to perform helping my father before the war and now. Those hands that in her young years seemed to be designed for turning the pages of romantic novels, crocheting goblins and playing melancholy melodies on her mandolin; those hands that lovingly took care of me in my childhood. Now they were folded as if given over to my care.

We got off the train in Dembica and went into the waiting room looking for my father; he was nowhere to be seen. I went to the counter and got two glasses of beer, one for me and one for my mother; it was common for peasant women to drink in public. We drank slowly, waiting for my father to appear. I went to the counter for a second glass of beer and started a conversation with the man behind the bar.

I remarked that there were very few people in the waiting room although shortly a train would be arriving. I was informed that there had been a round up by the Germans yesterday and most of the men were hauled away, probably to farm labor in Germany.

My heart sank to the bottom of my stomach.

My father, what had happened to him? But I could not ask that and I could not show my anguish. I walked over to my mother and asked her to go outside, where I told her what had transpired. Shaken, all she could say was: *"Yossel, Yossel, wie bist-du?"* "Josef, Josef, where are you?"

I told her that it was possible that my father took a driver yesterday and went by himself to Wielopole, not waiting for us because of the situation. I did not believe in that theory but I was trying to reassure her.

We were looking for a driver ourselves when from behind a building the figure of my father appeared. His clothing was wrinkled and disheveled, his face unshaved and frightened. We walked to a little park outside the railroad station where we sat down on a bench and my father told us what had happened. There was a round up by uniformed and secret German police, and my father was one of those netted. They were being counted and registered when a German in civilian clothes recognized my father. He was an ethnic German from Bielsko, who played cards and shared many a drink with my father. The man pulled my father away from the group under the pretext of having him do some work, led him outside the area and told him to disappear.

My father was still shaken from that experience and suggested that we go to Wielopole as soon as possible. There were no drivers around the railroad station but the man at the bar told me where I would be able to find one. We had to walk a couple of kilometers to the outskirts of town, where we found the man who agreed to take us to Wielopole for an exorbitant sum.

We arrived in Wielopole late in the afternoon, got off in the square of the town and paid the driver. We walked to my grandparents' house only to find out that they did not live there anymore. They had rented two houses outside the village on a small hill overlooking a side road. The reason for the move was that my Uncle Henry had returned from Lvov with his wife, his two children and a son in-law and more space was needed to accommodate them all.

After quickly exchanging greetings with everyone, I left my parents telling the family about our escape from Zawichost and ran to the fields where my grandmother had told me that my brother was watching some animals.

"Oskar, Oskar!" I yelled at the top of my voice. He came running, dragging with him two obstinate goats. We walked the goats toward the house and I tried to tell him quickly what had happened. He asked about Mom first and then wanted to know if Dad was all right.

I inquired about Uncle Henry and his family. Oskar said he loved my cousin Lusia, and that her brother Zev, her mother Idka and her husband Edie were all right. But he said nothing about my Uncle Henry, which did not surprise me.

My mother met us on the path before we reached the house; my father was still inside talking to his parents and his siblings. Only Uncle Tulek, Aunt Netka and Uncle Henry with his family were present. Uncle Slomek, Uniu and even Uncle Aciek were out of the house working, Slomek and Uniu with some farmers and Aciek at some kind of a job with the Judenrat in the village. Oskar ran into my father's arms. My father got down on his knees to kiss and hug his seldom-seen son.

Meanwhile I tried to get acquainted with my cousins Lusia and Zev, both of whom I met for the first time, and with Lusia's husband Edie. Lusia was four days older than I was, Zev was fourteen and Edie seemed a lot older then I. We, all went outside for a walk and left the parents and grandparents to themselves. Oskar stayed with my father, or rather sat on my father's knee.

Zev did most of the talking, while Lusia and Edie walked ahead of us holding hands. It was the beginning of June, the fields smelled of freshly worked earth. The oats and rye were already knee high, with poppy and cornflowers adorning their domain. Nature was going through its normal cycle as if there was no upheaval in its laws and as if it was not aware of all the blood already spilled upon its earth.

Zev spoke mostly about himself, about his life in the Russian-occupied Lvov, before the Germans overran it. He boasted about his accomplishments in school and mostly about his crowning achievement, that of appearing in a Russian *Consomole* propaganda film. He was the star of that short reel, he told me, and had pictures to show me.

At one point during the walk Lusia turned around and said to me: "Do not listen to him, he is a braggart, just like his father." I was startled by that pronouncement, although it ran parallel with my mother's opinion of her brother in-law.

In the evening my other uncles came home and there were more greetings and more retelling about our perils. Grandma put us up in one of the houses after some reshuffling. I was to sleep with my favored Uncle Tulek and my brother Oskar and my parents moved in with Uncle Henry and his family.

At breakfast before Uncle Henry had joined us I had gotten the story of his arrival. After the Germans conquered the Ukraine, where Lvov is located and instituted severe restrictions on the Jews, and after several incidents of carnage by both the Ukrainians and the Germans, Uncle Henry left Lvov in December of 1941 and arrived in Wielopole. He stopped in Jaslo, the town where he had lived before the war, but his house and his wife's photo studio had been ransacked and he was advised to move on.

I asked Uncle Tulek whether Uncle Henry was paying for the rented house where they were staying. I was told that he said that he did not bring any money but would pay after he sold some of his shares in oil wells in Boryslaw and Drochobycz. Meanwhile the Germans controlled those wells and there were no takers for the shares.

Uncle Tulek told me that he, too, had had to resort to butchering in order to support the family. When I made a face in response to his statement, he asked me, "Do you have any other ideas?"

I had asked my grandmother to see if anyone could find a job for me with a farmer or a locksmith—any job. Meanwhile, I spent most of my time with Oskar sharing his chores with him and with my newly acquainted cousin Lusia to whom I felt an immediate affinity. We confided to each other our most intimate youthful dreams and emotions. She talked to me at length about her husband of one year.

Edie Danzinger came from the town of Bielsko, where I had lived. He graduated from a conservatory in Czechoslovakia and held a degree in engineering from a technological institute there. His parents owned a textile dye-house in Bielsko and he played an expert violin, giving recitals with his sister at the piano.

Lusia was tall and beautiful. She wore her black braids around her head like a garland. Her skin was of dark complexion and her brown eyes spoke of wisdom and soft loveliness.

She fell in love with Edie in Lvov when she met him in 1940 at the university at a philosophy class. She took the courses to get out of the house and away from the constant quarrels between her parents, caused by her father's bombastic and imperious behavior. Edie, by contrast was gentle and understanding, able to take her on a flight of fancy away from the reality and the peril of existence in a city run by Communist Russia.

Now they were stuck in the village of Wielopole, surrounded by members of one family, not all of them equal. They could not see what lay ahead, but only the specter of trying to get through one day at the time.

In reality, we were all vassals of the German Empire, which was spreading its shadow over all of Europe. The news from the various battlefields was not encouraging; it seemed that Germany was being victorious on all fronts. Even their allies the Japanese and the Italians claimed victories. No one believed that England was going to last for long, and America was so far away.

NORBERT FRIEDMAN

We spent the next few days settling into a routine of existence. But on the fifth day of our stay a tragedy struck our family. The day started routinely enough, until in the afternoon someone noticed a black limousine coming along the road in the direction of our enclave.

"Quick, out of the house," yelled grandma. "All the men out of the house, its the Gestapo!"

Uncle Henry was the first to run; he did not even bother to check whether Zev and Edie were with him. My father and I followed, thinking that the Gestapo was after us as a result of the events in Zawichost. Uncle Tulek would not leave his mother and neither would my grandfather; the other men were out working.

We were already in the rye field when I realized that Oskar was not with us. Zev told me that he refused to leave my grandparents. The car was nearing the house and it was too late to run back to get him.

Uncle Henry suddenly decided that there were too many of us in the same field and suggested that some of us should leave. My father looked at him in anger and growled: "Then why don't you leave."

We were more than a quarter-mile from the house but we spoke in whispers. I could see Uncle Henry trembling and his words were coming out in a stuttering manner. I concluded just then that my Uncle Henry was not only a braggart but also a coward.

We sat hidden among the young rye stalks wondering about the goings-on in the house when suddenly two shots rang out, followed shortly by another shot. Startled and shocked we looked at each other, not knowing what to do. Who were the victims of that shooting? What was the cause of it?

Time stood still and so did we, paralyzed into inaction. I was about ready to run to the house when three men exited, reentered the car and drove away.

I rose and ran as fast as I could, fearing the worst. On the floor sat my grandmother lamenting and rocking back and forth, her hair over her eyes, my mother and aunt Idka trying to console her.

My grandfather stood by the wall hitting his head against it and moaning *"Vy is mier, vy is mier,"* "Woe is me, woe is me." My Aunt Netka held him by the shoulders, trying to keep him from falling. She, too, was wailing: "My Tulus, my Tulus."

"Where is Oskar?" Was all I could get out of my throat, my mother motioned with her head towards the steps leading to the attic. I ran up three steps at a time and there was Oskar sitting on the attic floor holding the motionless body of my Uncle Tulek.

"What happened?" I asked as if the facts were not self-evident.

"They shot him, they shot him," was Oskar's reply, also an obvious statement.

"How did it happen?" I started again.

"They took him upstairs looking for meat. When they could not find any, they shot him. They shot him twice through his heart, and when he put his hand on his chest, they shot him through his head."

"Where were you, how do you know all this?"

"I was on the steps watching, I wanted to see what they were going to do."

"Come on downstairs," I begged, trying to take the youngster from the scene of murder and the pool of blood.

"We have to bury him today, don't we?" was his only response. The young child's acceptance and comprehension of the situation startled me. I finally made him come downstairs. My father and Edie had returned from the fields. Uncle Henry and his son Zev were still hiding, waiting for a report of what had happened. Lusia finally ran out into the field to tell them.

Oskar was told to run out and find uncles Uniu and Slomek. My father went into the village to make funeral arrangements and to fetch Uncle Aciek.

When Lusia came back from the fields she briefed us on what had happened. Two Gestapo officials came in the company of a Polish man, again a case of an informer, who served as a mailman in the area. They asked for Uncle Tulek by name. They requested that he show them where he did the butchering. When he denied it, they started to search the house. They apparently did not know about the other house, where Uncle Henry lived, for it was in the basement of that house that the meat was butchered and stored. When they went to the attic and could not find anything they shot Uncle Tulek anyhow.

My favorite Uncle and my grandmother's most loyal son was a victim of pursuing his trade, the same as my father, a casualty of his occupation.

The burial ceremony was simple and brief. Many relatives and friends did not attend for fear that the Gestapo would raid the funeral. They came to visit a few days later when the family was observing *Shivah,* the seven-day period of mourning.

The period of mourning was hardly over when on the night before June 16 German trucks and army vehicles surrounded the village of Wielopole. Soldiers poured out of them, creating an un-penetrable ring. Flood lights and loudspeakers were erected, and on the morning of June 16 a blaring message was delivered in German: "If all the able—bodied men will volunteer to go to work in a labor camp, the older men, women and children will be guaranteed to be spared resettlement. Otherwise the whole Jewish Community will be put on the trucks and hauled away, right now."

We had until ten o'clock in the morning to decide.

Is it true, what do we do?

What are the others doing?

Uncle Aciek ran into the village; it was permitted for Jews to circulate within the surrounded area. He came back after a while and reported that the rabbi, the renowned and respected Rabbi Lipschutz of Wielopole, was sending his grandson and that the Judenrat's Eldest Mr. Kleinman said that he was also sending his son, and so were many others.

Now it was for us to decide which, if any of us would go. Edie was the first to declare himself. He had a German mentality and he believed in what was being promised. "They do not have to do that unless they are sincere," he argued. "They could simply take whom they want and ship the others away."

Uncle Slomek was next. "I believe that Edie is right. What is the difference where I work, at least this way I can help my mother and father to stay here." My father looked at me for guidance. I had somehow felt that we were un-invited guests at my grandparents' home and I sincerely wanted to contribute to my mother's and Oskar's safety.

I looked in turn at my mother. There she was, facing the gravest decision of her life. Should she part with her husband for whom her love and loyalty had never ceased, despite their stormy marital relationship? She was always able to ascribe his escapades to his youth and to the pressure of finding ways to provide for his family.

Should she ask him to volunteer for an unknown fate for the promise of securing safety for herself, for her younger son and other members of the family.

And should she part again with her firstborn, who had lately become the provider and the decision-maker, in whom once she placed all her dreams and aspirations.

"Do what you think will be best for you and us," she said, "for you have to make it, so that we might have a chance at all."

"I will go," I declared. "So will I," added my father. The violent death of Uncle Tulek and our recent migration must have influenced our thinking. Aciek, Uniu and Uncle Henry, each for their own reasons, decided to stay with the rest of the family.

There was little for me to pack, for I owned little: a comb, a toothbrush and some pictures. My mother took me aside and handed me some money; she then reached into her bosom, took out a knotted handkerchief, untied it and handed me a five-dollar American gold coin.

"Hide it and keep it, your father does not know about it," she whispered. "It came in a letter from relatives in America. Guard it! It might buy you, life and freedom some day." She hugged and kissed me. "May G`d be with you. We might never see each other again," she prophetically declared. "Here Oskar," she cried, "kiss your brother good-bye." We were about to go to the village square, where everyone was to assemble, when Uncle Henry after a short and animated discussion with Aunt Idka suddenly declared, "I am also going."

I had said good-by to everyone in the house. I felt a real sadness that my relationship with my newly found Cousin Lusia was being terminated. I had missed lately the company of my peers, such as Hanka, Lola, Sonia and Michal. Lusia was now my only coeval and we had to part.

My father and my mother were saying good-bye in one corner of the room, while Uncle Henry and Aunt Idka were talking in another corner.

Lusia and Edie were unabashedly kissing and embracing in the middle of the room when Uncle Sol yelled: "What is going on, we are not going to the gallows, we are only going to work, let's go." the spell was broken and we started out.

The scene at the village square was chaotic to say the least; so many were saying good-bye while the SS tried to load the volunteers on the trucks. I watched my mother as she stood there with her hands on my little brother's shoulders. Lovingly and yet with so much resigned sadness, with tears in her eyes, she seemed to say: "Farewell my son I will always love you."

The two trucks with about 100 men in them took off, followed by a staff car with two SS officers whom we had not seen till now. I looked around the group in the truck, but except for the members of my family I did not know any of them.

As we bounced along the rough Polish country road, I thought about my life, my childhood and my un-lived adolescence. I felt that, sadly, it consisted of series of incomplete associations. I never had a continuous relationship with my little brother whom I loved so. When he was four I left the house to go to school in Krakow. After that he went to my grandparents' home. Since 1939 I had had only a few brief occasions to be with him, and there was so much I did not know about him. I had to complete my mental picture of him from what grandmother and Aunt Netka told me.

For instance: The time when the whole family was leaving Zywiec on a train when the war broke out; the train was strafed by German machine-gun fire from attacking planes and he covered grandmother's body with his own to protect her.

And then when he kept all-night vigils when grandfather was sick and ran a high fever for a whole week.

And then I thought about his bravery when Uncle Tulek was shot.

Now he had Mom to take care of, a ten-year-old saddled with adult responsibilities.

I thought about my relationship with Hanka, of our young love so abruptly interrupted, of moments of adolescent happiness so cruelly denied.

I thought of my friendship with Michal Krawiec, such a strong bond of unquestioning fealty between two so very different friends.

And then I thought of my mother, her lovely face wrinkled from all the hardships and worries of her long forty-two years. I searched my memory for the happy moments in her life. They were very few—maybe only those when she rejoiced in my scholastic achievements, or maybe earlier at the time she was courted by my father.

And I looked at my father who was deep in his own thoughts, standing next to me, not realizing how much our lives were going to be intertwined from now on.

What was awaiting us in our new situation? What kind of environment were we entering? When would we see our loved ones again?

MIDNIGHT

"These things will I remember,
and pour out my soul in me."
Psalm 42

The following chapters will be the most difficult for me to write, for they will deal with events and circumstances unlike anything that I had ever encountered. None of us had a point of reference or a precedent to compare with the situations that we were to find ourselves in. None of us had ever heard or read, in fact or fiction, of a world so awry, so disfigured, so cruel, or a people so heartlessly barbarous as those who controlled our lives.

In fact, humanity has never had the need to develop a language capable of describing the events, conduct, emotions, suffering or degradation that we were about to experience.

CHAPTER XV

We entered the Mielec facility through an iron gate guarded by two armed plant guards. As we were to find out later, our camp was an adjunct to the *Heinkel-Werke*, a large aircraft manufacturing facility. It was once a part of the Polish defense industrial complex known as COP.

Ironically, before the war ethnic Germans were allowed to be employed there, but Jews were not. When the war broke out, acts of sabotage by the ethnic German workers resulted in many malfunctions of military equipment that had been built in that complex.

Now over a thousand Polish workers and several hundred of German supervisory personnel were employed in manufacturing the fuselage for the Heinkel aircraft, mostly for the Heinkel 111 model.

After a couple of hundred yards our convoy turned right, into a cluster of barracks. The staff car with the two SS officers continued into a large complex of office and factory buildings and we did not see them again. We were told to get off the trucks and line up in two rows. Inmates stared at us from the windows of the surrounding barracks.

A husky man in civilian clothes faced us, flanked by a tall lanky man, also in civvies, and an uniformed plant guard. The husky man introduced himself in Polish as the camp director, by the name of Falerowski. He then introduced the lanky civilian as Herr Stein, head of security for the facility, and the uniformed man as *Wachmeister* Drozd, who would be in charge of the guards.

He told us: that we had come here to work and that if we obeyed the rules we would be treated well.

"Any questions and requests are to be channeled through these two men, who are in charge of camp's internal affairs," he said, pointing at two camp inmates standing at the entrance to the main barracks. One was tall, skinny and lose-limbed, the other heavy-set and jovial-looking. The heavy-set man's name was Yosiu-Mayer, the other's Mendel. In Yiddish the two men directed us to the barracks where we were to live; in front of the barracks stood a kettle with hot coffee dispensed by an inmate. He also handed each of us, a portion of bread with a spoonful of jam as we walked in.

Each section of the barracks had rooms with wooden tables and benches. Two-tiered bunks with straw-sac mattresses covered by a blanket were lined up against the walls.

As we sat down to eat, most of us unpacked whatever provisions we had brought along. We tried to assess our situation, but all our guesswork was just that. After a while, when the officials had left the premises, inmates from other barracks started to filter in. After short greetings, we gave in to our curiosity and anxiety and plied them with an unending stream of questions.

Before our transport had arrived, the camp already had several hundred inmates, mainly from the adjacent town of Mielec. They had been chosen for labor in the plant after the execution and subsequent deportation of most of the remaining Jewish population to various camps, most of them to the extermination camp called Belzec.

The two Jewish men in charge of the camp were past officials of the *Judenrat* in Mielec. Some of the inmates were either related to or acquainted with some of the men who came from the Wielopole-Skrzynskie transport and volunteered information on how we were to conduct ourselves and on the conditions in the camp. The camp had been in existence for a couple of months before we arrived. Most of the inmates of the camp had been erecting barracks and installing the facilities. In terms of how to behave, we were warned to conceal our valuables, for Mr. Falerowski, who was an ethnic German, would occasionally conduct searches of the inmates and confiscate whatever he found.

Yosiu-Mayer and the other man, Mendel, were in charge of distributing the food rations and assigning jobs. The inmates complained that these two would favor some prisoners whom they knew and assign them the easier tasks.

We were told that the German security chief Mr. Stein was a *Kalter Gazler,* a cold-hearted killer who always carried a handgun and did not hesitate to use it when he thought an inmate was lazy or useless for labor.

Werkschutz Wachmeister Drozd made a lot of noise, especially when Mr. Stein was present. He used a long, dried-out oxtail or a two-by-four, which he called a "lolly," to prod inmates into order, but was otherwise benign.

We were advised that when asked about our professional skills, we should say that we were mechanics, carpenters, electricians or that we knew some other trade that would get us jobs in the plant. Those who happened to be chosen to a job outside the camp, on what they called the "Garden" detail, might have a better opportunity for contact with civilian Polish workers and therefore an avenue for connection with the outside world and its sources of food.

The following days were spent getting acquainted with the routine and the layout of the camp. We were called on to perform tasks in the camp itself, mostly connected with construction of new barracks. Occasionally some inmates would be assigned to help fetch the food from the plant's kitchen.

We soon concluded that going out to bring the coffee and bread rations in the morning was less profitable then helping out at noon when the once-a-day ration of soup was brought into the camp. That was when the various meals for the Werkschutz guards and the German personnel were prepared. Scraps and leftovers from those meals were sometimes dispensed to the begging inmates, poured into the tin cans, which the inmates always carried for that purpose. How quickly did hunger and the fear of it transform once-proud men into mooching beggars!

Within a week people were assigned to various details in the plant itself. Very soon it became apparent that some jobs were easier to perform than others. The severity of each task depended on the temperament of the German supervisors and the nature of the job. It also became apparent that the better jobs were being assigned to the cronies of the two men who were in charge of the camp, both of them ex-members of the *Judenrat* in the town of Mielec: Josiu-Mayer and Mendel.

Meanwhile another transport of about one hundred people from Wielopole-Skrzynskie, one from the town of Radomysl, and transports from other localities had arrived in the camp. We anxiously begged the new arrivals for news about our families, and many of us received letters through them.

I received a note from my mother and my brother Oskar, with a small picture of my mother taken in happier times. It was a strictly informative note, giving details of the family situation in Wielopole, where Uncle Aciek joined a group of young men in the forest, and about aunt Netka and cousin Lusia's new jobs in the village. Even in the everyday language, though, I sensed an undertone of gloom and despair. "Stay with your father, I love you my son, Mom," the note concluded.

It was the last note that I was to receive from my mother or anyone else in the family. The picture of my mother included with the note accompanied me all the way to Dachau.

My father had attached himself to a kitchen detail by declaring that he had served as a mess-sergeant in the Austro-Hungarian army. His expertise in butchering soon elevated him to the head of the detail. The head meat-cutter in the German kitchen soon recognized my father's butchering skills and used him to help out in dressing and cutting up the meat rations. At the end of the day he always rewarded him with an extra ration or two of leftover *Eintopf*, a sort of German stew. My father always shared it with the members of his family and sometimes, when there was enough, with my friends.

I joined a group of young people, who occupied a room in barrack #4, which soon became a model of order and cleanliness. The room leader was a fellow from the city of Tarnow named Hamek Schildkraut. A few years older than most of us, he had been married, but his wife had been killed during the deportation from Tarnow. She had refused to part with their infant son, who was then shot and killed in her arms.

Often we would find Hamek brooding or staring at the picture of his young wife, or playing a melancholy tune on his *Mundharmonika*, a little mouth organ. At other times he was full of energy, coordinating things in our room, always attentive to those who needed moral support. He was a talented cartoonist and decorated the walls of our room with caricatures of camp life. He used stolen crayons of different colors, used in the plant to mark sheets of aluminum. At first we were apprehensive that we might be questioned about the origin of the crayons, but the visiting Germans were so amused and impressed with his work that our room became the model to be shown to the Red Cross personnel or any other visitors. This emboldened us to the point that we even built a stove in our room from stolen materials, insulated all around with asbestos panels. Soon our room became an envied example, a status often resented by other inmates.

I was assigned to a night-shift job in the "L-Bau-Halle," so-called for its L shape. It was a large, hangar-like structure where the parts for the fuselage of the Heinkel aircraft, model # 111, were manufactured. The heat-treating department, the machine shop and the cyanide baths were also located in that giant building.

Because of my knowledge of mechanical drawings acquired in the Jewish Vocational School in Krakow, I was assigned to operate a giant brake where sheets of metal were bent into their designated shapes. The job was interesting and challenging. Most of the difficulties occurred when large sheets of eight-foot widths had to be shaped into a washboard-like configuration for use on the outside of the large *Junkers* transport planes which came to us for repair when they were damaged by anti-aircraft fire on the Russian front. The Polish day-shift operator and I were the only ones qualified to handle that task.

Around my workstation were various milling machines, drill presses, and giant power presses. The German foreman of our workstation was a young man by the name of Schmidt. A mean individual with a cruel and even sadistic disposition, he delighted in making our lives miserable. He would hide our work orders, then come and inquire about them, using their absence as an excuse for administering severe beatings. He knew that we were aware of his trick, and the sardonic smile on his face added insult to our injuries. He clearly took pleasure in our discomfort and suffering.

I noticed one particularly cruel joke of Schmidt's when a young inmate suffering from a lung ailment, who was working on a drill press next to me, begged him to be assigned to another job. (Inhaling the fine aluminum scrap was literally killing him.) Schmidt agreed to do so, but he put him to work on a milling machine that produced a very fine and lethal aluminum dust. Shortly the young fellow started to cough up blood and eventually collapsed. He later died in the camp.

My traumatic fear and hatred of the young German, Schmidt, was the cause of many nightmares featuring chases and other terrifying scenes. Even today in my worst dreams I am running after him, just as I am about to close my hands on his throat, I am yanked back into consciousness. For years after my time in the camps, while living in Germany, I would search the faces of passers-by, looking for the all-too-familiar features of Schmidt's face, forever seared into my memory.

In July, one of the men from Wielopole received a note from his family, delivered by one of the Polish workers. It was postmarked at Dembica, and went as follows: "The whole village of Wielopole was rounded up and marched out to Dembica. Many perished on the road. We are desperate, waiting for something to happen with us, we do not know what."

The message was dated July 21st; a little more then four weeks after the Germans had promised that if the men of the village would volunteer for work, their families would be spared deportation.

Despair and self-blame for being so gullible, coupled with the frustration of impotence and the guilt for resigning ourselves to the situation, surged through the two hundred inmates from Wielopole.

Some time later a transport was brought to the camp from Dembica itself. The camp inmates anxiously surrounded the new arrivals trying to find out what they knew about the fate of the transport from Wielopole and other villages. Dembica, because it was a railroad junction, had become a gathering point for transports going to other destinations in the East. When the transport arrived I was awakened from my sleep by the commotion in the barracks. I was about to get ready for the night shift anyhow and I listened to a young man, whom someone had brought into our room. He was telling us that the transport from Wielopole was kept in the town for a couple of days. He was a pharmacist, and in Dembica people from the transport kept coming to him, begging for medication for various ailments. On the second day of their stay, he said, a beautiful dark-haired girl who wore long braids around her head came to him and begged for some quinine in order to abort her pregnancy.

I jumped off my bunk and ran to Edie's room, grabbed the picture of his wife Lusia and showed it to the man outside the barrack.

"Yes that is her, how did you know?" he asked. "That is my cousin," I told him. "Her father and her husband are here in the camp with us. Please do not tell them," I begged. "It would only aggravate their distress."

The man must have been a very decent individual, for he never to my knowledge broke his promise. I, in turn, kept the secret from the rest of my family.

The man also told me that the whole Wielopole transport was put on a train going east on July 22nd.

Shortly after liberation in 1945, my father sought out a rabbi to consult about the date of the Yarzeit, the anniversary of mourning to be observed for one's family. According to the best information available, our family, which was transported from Dembica to the extermination camp Belzec, had perished on or about the 23rd of July 1942.—This corresponded to the date of the 9th of Av, a day of mourning for the Jews that commemorates the date of the destruction of the first and second Temples—But since there were no witnesses to verify the precise time, the rabbi set the date for the Yarzeit observance for Av 13th in order not to detract from the religious observance and the fast that accompanies that day. Many years later, after the opening of the Holocaust Memorial Museum in Washington DC, I found documentation substantiating the date of July 23rd, 1942, as the date that those aboard the transport from Wielopole were murdered. Again, there were no known witnesses.

NORBERT FRIEDMAN

About 50 members of my father's family were on the transport: my grandparents, uncles, aunts, cousins, both the unborn and the living. My father's aunts, uncles and cousins, my mother and my brother, went up in smoke in the crematories of Belzec, sharing the fate of 600,000 other Jewish men, women and children who perished there. In one year of evil madness, in this infamous place amongst the screams of inconceivable anguish, they perished, creating a black hole of emptiness and silence in my life and in the existence of mankind.

After the arrival of the second transport from Wielopole-Skrzynskie, the inmates realized that they would need someone to represent their interests, for many reasons: to have their interests protected, to be assigned jobs based on qualifications and not favoritism, and to receive the allocated food rations without someone shaving the sizes of the bread ration or stealing the thicker part of the soup. They went to the camp supervisor, Mr. Falerowski, and suggested that a Judenrat-like committee, composed of deputies from the various communities, should be appointed. They pointed out the advantages of such a set-up: less discontent, better job performance and an instrument for maintaining order. The model for it was already present in the ghettos and communities of occupied territories. Mr. Falerowski agreed only too happily. From now on he could delegate the jobs of searching and inspection of the inmates as well as keeping internal order to this committee.

And so the Camp Council was created (later to be converted into the *Ordnungsdienst*, the internal police of our camp.) Uncle Henry and a couple of other individuals from the village of Wielopole were chosen, together with representatives from other communities. Uncle Henry was made the head of the unit because of his knowledge of German and because of his claimed rank of non-commissioned officer in the Austro-Hungarian army.

With time, it became obvious that these O.D.-men, as they were called, enjoyed considerable advantages: special quarters, better food rations, a uniform, the exercise of authority over other inmates. My Uncle Henry offered me a chance to join the *Ordnungsdienst*.

Although the stigma that later was associated with that institution was not yet obvious, I declined. I could not see myself in a position of superiority over my suffering co-religionists whose lot was thrown in with mine. There was something odious about shouting orders at other Jews and making them perform tasks required by the Germans. I confronted Uncle Henry with my perception of his position and suggested that he steps down and takes his chances with the rest of us.

He then presented his reasoning. "You never know who would take my job. You never know what kind a person he would be. He might be inclined to harm the inmates in order to ingratiate himself with the Germans, something I would never do. I am going to be square and fair to all the inmates; I am going to protect them the best I can. I will never forget that I am a Jew like everyone else in here. Come join with me and you will be able to help me to do things justly."

He sounded well meaning and sincere and I left him in the hopes that I would not be disappointed in him in the future. That evening I shared the content of our conversation with his son-in-law Edie. Edie listened to me and then threw out his arms in a gesture of desperation.

"Norbert," he said, "he is a vain man. He likes the power, the uniform, and the opportunity to address the whole camp at the morning roll call. Under all his shouting and bravado, though, he is a weak and cowardly man. I do not want to have anything to do with him."

So of all the members of our family that came to Mielec, Uncle Henry became the head of the *Ordnungsdienst*. My father became head of the kitchen detail, and as such was incorporated into the O.D. as well and wore a uniform. I continued to work on the L-Bau and uncle Sol worked in the "Repa" building where the final assembly of the fuselages was performed. Edie, because of his superior knowledge of the German language and his academic background, got a job in the accounting department, the only Jewish inmate working there. As a result he was allowed to walk to work and back to camp by himself. The *Werkschutz* had gotten to know him, and his slightly limping, muscular figure could often be seen coming back to camp late in the evening, waving to the patrolling guards as they passed him on their bicycles.

Edie Danzinger was something of an enigma. Those who did not know him well and did not know that he was Uncle Henry's son-in-law suspected that he was being helped on the job by some merciful German working with him, because he always looked well groomed and well fed. He refused to accept any food rations that Uncle Henry offered him and instead would notify Uncle Sol that Henry had some extra food available. The only time that he would accept any assistance from the Friedmans was when I offered to share with him some of the food that my father would bring in.

He seemed to thrive on the camp rations, however, and he devoured the bread and the often-tasteless soup with gusto. He stated—and I believed him— that he very seldom got anything from his German co-workers. He had only contempt for the professional skills of the German personnel in the accounting department. He believed that the men there were simply hiding from active duty at the front and that the women were nothing but fat camp followers. His own Germanic cultural upbringing revolted against what he considered an unprofessional and disorderly waste of manpower.

Before Edie went abroad to study, he was a swimming champion in the state of Silesia. He still had the body of a swimmer, and he and I would occasionally sneak away on a Sunday, supposedly to do some work in his office (which on occasion we did). We would also go beyond the plant, which stood almost at the opposite end of the facility behind the delousing station and the laundry were located, to the large basin where the water from the cooling systems was being recycled. There we would swim for hours. Edie would do countless laps while I could only wonder at his stamina. He then would try to teach me how to breathe so that I could extend my own endurance. Later, exhausted, we would sit around and Edie would share with me some of his knowledge. He would talk about philosophy, piquing my interest with quotations from Plato, Kant, Nietsche or Schopenhauer. My head would swirl with what I sometimes considered conflicting philosophies. According to Edie, the great philosophers had the answers to every question in the universe, including human behavior.

And here all this time I was trying to get answers from my own God, my Savior, my Redeemer, and none were forthcoming.

My primary difficulty with Edie stemmed from trying to understand his sympathies for the German Aryan philosophy and his preoccupation with physical attributes.

"In mens sano, corpora sano," a healthy spirit in a healthy body, he would quote. And then he would say, "We Jews are a dead race. There is a New World Order arising and there will be room in it only for those who can think progressively and adapt to it both physically and intellectually. There will be room for the likes of us, you will see. They will need bright minds who will be willing to follow."

Often Edie would lapse into melancholy recollections of his home life in Bielsko before the war. His parents had been wealthy owners of a textile dye house and could afford to send him abroad for studies in chemical engineering and to a conservatory. He had one sister whom he loved dearly and with whom he would play duets—she on the piano, he on the violin. He would lovingly recall the evenings when they would perform together for their friends, or just for themselves. There was such a harmony in their playing, he said; it was as if the two of them were one instrument of the muses. There was ecstasy in those moments and he longed for the day when he would be able to play with Herta again.

His love for my cousin Lusia was more physical of course, but not less sensual. He loved her for her intellect as well as for her beauty. Sometimes I felt that he loved her so much because he could love in her the things that he could not love in his sister Herta.

Edie struck up an acquaintanceship with some of the Werkschutz guards, and occasionally in the evening, several of them would come to the outside of the barracks and hand Edie a violin. He would stand in one of the barrack windows without any sheet music, giving an impromptu concert of serious compositions for the violin, such as sonatas by Beethoven, Mozart or Paganini as well as some entertaining humoresques. The Werkschutz, aware of his dedication to serious music, nevertheless would sometimes request a light folk song or a popular selection from a German musical operetta. Edie happily obliged, for after the Germans loudly applauded and left, there would always be a package of *Wurst*, German sausage, and some pipe tobacco under the window.

"Herta would die if she heard the '*quatch*,' the trash that I play for them," he would say.

I had learned to like Edie very much even though he was so different from all the young Jews I knew, or maybe because of it. We made plans to stay together if this war ever ended.

In July of 1944, when our camp was moved to Wieliczka for a few weeks and then from there to Germany, Edie was separated from us. I think he consciously made an effort to be left behind because he did not want to be part of the Friedman clan any more.

In 1946 while a student at the University in Frankurt-am-Main, I received a communication from Edie. He was back in Bielsko, Poland.

He wrote to me: Would I please join him. We would have no financial worries; he had sold his parents' dye-house and had lots of money. He knew that my cousin Lusia was dead, and that his sister also had perished. There was no one left that he had loved in the world, except me; would I please come.

I sent him a letter immediately. "Edie, come to Frankfurt, we will make a new life for ourselves as we planned. There is a New World out there, but not amongst the old ruins. It is called America." Only a few weeks before his letter arrived I had filled out my application for a permanent visa to the United States of America. "Come," I wrote "we will grow new wings together, and soar with those who invite us to be free. Come Edie, please!" It took nearly six months before I was able to learn that Edie, my master who tried to educate me in the thoughts of the giants of philosophy, had shot himself after getting my letter, there amidst all the confusion of his introspection. He did not even leave a note with his thoughts for me. I was wracked by guilt for a while; after all, had I heeded his suggestion and at least gone back to Poland to see him I might have been able to change the course of events. I felt that the loss of the two women he loved, his sister Herta and my cousin Lusia were the main reasons for his suicide. The eventual reunification with them was the raison d'être for his struggle to survive, his dream of what his life would be, his vision, his goal to achieve, something that he needed to find strength and motivation against the overwhelming odds of wartime. I tried to convince myself that if he had cared for me as much as he had claimed he would have come to Frankfurt to join me. I also suspected that his disappointment in the New World Order, in which he had, once believed so strongly in his Germanic way, was a factor in his decision to kill himself. After all, it was this New World Order that had destroyed his world and the lives of his loved ones. I was also saddened that all his knowledge of the great philosophers and their theories was of no solace to him; the world apparently was in need of a new moral imperative.

Poor Edie never had a chance to know the New World and its hope-instilling overture; instead he became the tragic case of a "casualty after the storm." His knowledge of philosophy did not shield him from his end and may have even given him the reason to cease his struggle before he could learn a new libretto.

CHAPTER XVI

As time went on we became accustomed to a certain routine. The events outside the camp were full of savage dying. Inside, only occasional executions and beatings interrupted the rhythm of existence that the inmates tried to create for themselves. There was a thread of hope, that maybe the usefulness and skills of the prisoners, employed on behalf of the war effort, would insure our safety and spare our lives. In comparison, the tales of horror brought from the outside made the camp seem like an asylum of safety.

We were learning what conduct was more or less dangerous to survival: Infractions of work rules, ruining of equipment or spoiling of material were all considered acts of sabotage. One's number would be taken down and once a week or so the Gestapo from the town of Mielec would come and execute the guilty ones at a place outside the campgrounds. This place was in the village of Berdychow, whose land served to grow agricultural products for the plant's kitchen and for the German personnel. In addition to the fields, the village held an airport and our killing fields.

We knew when the executions would take place because on the day before, Menashe the grave-digger could be seen leaving the camp on his gimpy legs, swaying from side to side, the tin can that served as his mess-kit hanging at his side. He would never disclose the number of graves that he dug. He would grow silent and keep to himself while greedily slurping his soup, which he would pick up in the German kitchen before coming back to camp.

The day after the executions he would tell us what had happened at the killing fields, how the victims behaved what the execution squad was like. After a while we stopped asking him what happened. We knew the scenario: undress, kneel, and bend your head, the shot and a kick in the back, hurling the victim into the common grave.

The same procedure was used for Jews who were brought in from hiding in the nearby forest. In most instances those were Jews who were denounced by the Polish peasants, either for a reward or just out of hostility to the Jews.

At the beginning, some camp inmates, especially the scheduled victims, would try to escape, sometimes with success. But the cunning system of group responsibility that the Germans enforced virtually stopped the escapes. For every escapee, ten to twenty inmates would be chosen to be shot. Of course, any blood relatives of the escaped man would be the first victims of retaliation. Other unfortunate victims would be chosen from the place where the man had escaped, from the work detail that the man worked on or from the barrack where he lived. That system caused the prisoners to be constantly on guard, watching each other, serving the German purpose, so that they themselves would not become the next victims. Still, the occasional prisoner would still try to run, leaving brothers or in one instance a father to be executed in payment for their dash for freedom. Those who had young wives or children in hiding were the greatest threat to run. Unfortunately, Menashe would report the news afterward; these men were almost always caught and brought back for execution, having been betrayed by Polish informants.

The Gestapo chief from Mielec and his assistant, an ethnic German, by the name of Zimmerman, usually carried out the executions. Rudie Zimmerman had lived in Mielec, a son of poor parents. He had made extra money by doing chores for Jewish people: lighting the fire on the Sabbath, chopping wood, and cleaning yards. One day Menashe told us of an incident illustrating this man's callousness. A family for whom Zimmerman used to work was brought in from the forest for execution. The daughter, a beautiful Orthodox teenager who had been kind to young Rudolph Zimmerman, showed a glimpse of hope when she recognized him. When he in turn saw who the intended victims were, he approached the girl and said to her, smiling: "Hannelle, for always having been so nice to me, I will personally shoot you so no one else will have the pleasure."

He made the stunned girls undress, turn around several times, and then expressed his regrets: "It's a shame I could not be your lover, you are so beautiful." He made her kneel down in front of her parents and then shot her.

One day in the winter of 1942, Hamek Schildkraut came back from work very dejected; he refused to talk to anybody. We attributed his behavior to one of his mood swings. But we soon found out what had happened from one of his co-workers in the power-press department. It seems that after he had set up a new job and tested it to the inspector's satisfaction, someone had moved the matrix in the power press. The die crashed, and, according to standard procedure, Hamek's number was taken down and reported to the plant security.

The inmates in our room were terrified. We knew this meant that we would have to watch him closely. Surely he was not going to wait for his execution. He would try to run a sure death sentence for all of us.

He had been our role model, our leader. Did we have any right to prevent him from trying to save his life? We did not speak to him about it but it bore heavily on everybody. We could only imagine what he was going through.

A decision was made to approach the one German foreman in his department who had a reputation of being a decent and compassionate sort. We asked the foreman to go to the German *Meister*—the head of the department who reported Hamek to the Security—with an offer of a bribe. I knew that my father was hiding a diamond ring that he had worn on his pinkie before the war. I was determined to ask for it, and if he refused, even to steal it.

It was too late; the German *Meister* was indignant, and besides, we knew that the head of security, Mr. Stein, who kept the records of the reported inmates, would never change his mind.

The ensuing couple of days were torturous for the group in our room. We expected Hamek to make a move at any time, so someone was always assigned to stay with him while in the camp. Whether he went to the latrine or wash up or line up for food, at least one of the boys from our room followed him—not that we knew what we would do if he tried to go over the fence. It was sometimes possible to make an escape if you were lucky enough to climb over the barbed wire on top of the cement wall and to escape the notice of the Werkschutz patrol outside the camp periphery and his German shepherd guard dog.

Eventually the day came when Menashe the gravedigger left the camp for Berdychow. We knew that the execution was going to take place the following morning.

We went to bed that night knowing that Hamek was aware that we knew, but no conversation about the predicament took place. We could not muster enough courage to face the situation. We lay in bed trying to act normal, but no one closed an eye. We expected him to get up at any minute and make his break, but he, too, lay motionless on his bed.

Finally, a few hours after midnight; Josiu, the youngest inmate in our room, who also came from Hamek's town of Tarnow and was Hamek's special protégé, blurted out: "Hamek, run, don't wait. We will be all right, we will follow you."

"Hamek," he cried, "please save yourself!"

And now the rest of us followed, urging Hamek to save himself, some convincingly, some only meekly parroting the others. Finally Hamek spoke out: "Do not worry, I will not run. I would never jeopardize your lives to save myself. We will say good-by like men."

There his voice broke a little. "One thing I promise to you. I will never give them the satisfaction of cowering before them. I will die like my wife, on my feet. Those of you who might make it and live when all this is over, I want those of you to be able to stand up straight and say. Some of us never lost their dignity. I am all right, my comrades, I am not afraid anymore!"

Even before the roll call at the *Appelplatz* that morning, Hamek and eight others who were on the list were escorted by the Werkschutz and accompanied by Menashe to Berdychow. We anxiously awaited Menashe's return from Berdychow, hoping to hear that somehow Hamek made a run for it and escaped.

The cart on which the clothes of the victims from Berdychow were brought in carried nine sets of clothing. Only one set, Hamek's, carried bloodstains.

Later we found out from Menashe what had happened. When the order was given to undress, Hamek refused and simply started to walk away. The infuriated Gestapo yelled after him to stop: "*Halt! Du Schweinhund, Halt!*" But Hamek just gave them the sign, "Up yours," and kept walking. They shot him in the back; it took four bullets to bring him down.

We were disappointed that Hamek did not get away, but we were also so proud that he kept his word and did not meekly submit.

"Up yours," to the Germans. What a man, Hamek.

The next Sunday evening, before going to sleep, little Josiu surprised us all when he took out the *Mundharmonika*, the little mouth organ that Hamek left him, and played Hamek's favorite melody "*Tehezakna Yedeynu.*"

The most painful and yet the most frequently asked question that a survivor had to face after the war, in the USA or Israel, was: "Why did you allow yourself to be led like sheep to the slaughter?"

This question always seemed to reflect insensitivity, ignorance of conditions, pre-judgment, inability to comprehend and, worst of all, the sense that our co-religionists, be it in Israel, United States or elsewhere, were disappointed that we did not resist and were ashamed of our conduct.

Those who watched the extermination of the European Jewry from positions of safety and comfort; doing little to help our plight; adding to our sense of having been abandoned and forgotten; it now seemed that they would have preferred for us to go down in the glory of armed resistance, giving them cause for pride in our kinship rather than shame.

We could only shut up in horror, saddened to our depths by the realization that our case will never be understood. We closed our lips and drew a dark curtain across our minds, not to be lifted for many years.

In 1969, when I gave witness publicly for the first time, I chose to speak about my friend Hamek Schildkraut and his heroic stance; about his disregard for his own life; his sensitivity to the danger to his comrades; his ultimate resistance to the orders of his executioners and his resolve to die on his feet. I used his example to rescue the honor of his memory and the honor of the memory of all who perished.

It took years of research, of listening to other survivors (who eventually opened their lips and parted the curtain of silence) to erase the shameful stigma created by erroneous perceptions of the common Man as well as by the misguided conclusions of scholars.

NORBERT FRIEDMAN

CHAPTER XVII

In the winter of 1942 conditions in the camp and at the work stations were steadily deteriorating. The news from the outside was not good. The process of transferring the Jews from small towns and ghettos to the camps, most of which were extermination centers, was being accelerated. We tried to keep up our spirits by creating habits of normality, by trying to keep ourselves as clean and neat as possible.

There was a tailor and a shoemaker shop on the camp premises. To have something fixed you had to be a "somebody" in the camp hierarchy—or be willing to offer something materially. For the sake of self-respect, many were willing. The camp barber was also kept very busy.

Evenings after work, men would gather in the barracks to play cards, sing songs, and hold study groups. There were learned Talmudists and secular scholars in the camp, so that those study groups were conducted at a high level.

The most common diversion, however, was to talk about the past, about life at home, about one's family—and mostly about the food we used to eat. We daydreamed about the meals our mothers once prepared for us, especially at holiday times. Some of us dreamed of having a whole loaf of bread from which they could cut as many slices as they wanted. Some fantasized about drinking tea again from a thin glass with a handle, as we used to do on Sabbath afternoons.

My vision was to be in an all-white room with tables under white tablecloths, drinking a glass of milk and eating a piece of white bread. A craving, a vision of cleanliness and purity, conditions totally absent from our existence.

In 1969, while visiting California, I was walking through the town of Carmel late in the morning with my wife, who knew about my vision in the camps. We were looking for a place for brunch when suddenly I did a double take. We had just passed a restaurant with white lacquered walls, white chairs, white tables covered with white tablecloths, even a white floor. Straight from my dream! They were just getting ready for lunch traffic, but not ready for customers.

Nonetheless, I walked in, sat down and asked the waiter to please bring me a glass of milk and a piece of white bread.

The waiter had told me that they wouldn't be open for half an hour. When I insisted, he stared at me suspiciously, then looked questioningly at my wife, as if to say, "What's with him?" My wife took him aside and explained the source of my odd behavior. He quickly nodded as he understood and filled my order, refusing to charge me. He stood silently watching me from a distance as I experienced that vision from long ago, in real life now; streams of tears flowing down my face.

Sometimes the men would talk about their jobs and about their German supervisors. My own job had become routine, Schmidt would leave me alone most of the time, so that usually I would see him only at the beginning and the end of my shifts. My performance had brought him praise from his supervisors, so he mostly left me alone. Then he was removed from my shift so that he could supervise the day shift.

One morning, though, as I was about to join the rest of the inmates from the night shift on their return to the camp, Schmidt stopped me and informed me that the Polish operator from the day shift would not be in that day. Because there was urgent work to be finished, I would have to stay on.

"Have your food sent in, we must finish the assignment!" Schmidt barked at me.

Some *Yunkers* transport planes, it seems, had been shot up on the Russian front and we had to make the corrugated aluminum sheets to repair them. A twelve-hour shift was tiring, but 24 hours in a row would be totally exhausting. I could barely stand up, and Schmidt kept stopping by every so often to prod me on: *"Los, los!"* I could not wait for the shift to end. My arms were weary and my eyes bleary and felt like they were full of sand.

When the day shift was over and we were getting ready to leave, I started to clear my station and join them when Schmidt showed up in a fury. "Where do you think you are going?" he screamed. "You pitched in for the Polish operator, but that does not excuse you from your own job. You go back to the camp in the morning when your own shift is finished." He flashed his satanic grin as he yelled at me.

"Please let me go back to the camp for a couple of hours of sleep," I pleaded. "I will come back refreshed, and I will work that much harder."

"Go to the latrine and wash up, you will be refreshed," he offered. "And you better work harder anyhow, because we have to finish all these before tomorrow," he shouted, pointing to a stack of work orders.

NORBERT FRIEDMAN

"We?" I said to myself. He was going back to his quarters, to his wife or whomever, where there surely was a bed and a beer. But I took his offer and went to the latrine. In order to leave your work post and go to a latrine you had to have permission from your foreman or supervisor. But first I told Dolek Z. the Jewish foreman for the day shift, to tell my father in camp not to worry, that I had to work the night shift and that I would be all right.

"All right?" he said doubtfully.

By ten o'clock that night the figures on the prints were swirling before my eyes; my head would fall down on the desk and my eyes would close. Every half-hour I would ask permission from the German supervisor in the mechanical department for permission to go to the bathroom. He was aware of my plight and the reason for it. His remarks were not complimentary to Schmidt, but he had no authority to send me back to the camp.

I was petrified that I might spoil some work and be charged with sabotage, or that I would not complete my quota of work. Every work order had a certain amount of time allocated to perform it, and failure to meet the deadline would bring charges of sabotage. I put my head against the frame of the machine to cool off and to stop the semi-conscious hallucinations. I was sure that Schmidt had set this whole thing up to get rid of me.

When the midnight break came I ran to the latrine, stuck my head under the cold water and let it run till my neck felt stiff. The coffee that was issued during the break was of little help. It was *ersatz* coffee, made of chicory and void of caffeine. Some Germans who had connections would get real coffee, *Bohne Cafe* as they called it, but certainly not the inmates who were working in the plant.

"Only six more hours," I tried to tell myself. I had been on my feet for thirty hours. "Keep going. You can do it. If you don't, you're *kaput*," finished.

By three AM. I could not go on any longer. I told myself that I had to get some sleep if only a half an hour or so, and then I would be all right.

The windows of the machine shop, as well as all the other windows, had long blackout curtains hanging over them and all the way to the floor. At the base of each window was a sill maybe twenty centimeters wide. I had to find a way to sneak behind one of those curtains and get some sleep. I waited until I was sure that no one in the machine shop could see me and slid behind a curtain, lay on my side and flattened myself against the window. Immediately I sank into a stupor.

I don't know how long I lay there, because the whole incident remains a dim, groggy, disconnected nightmare. Suddenly a large paw grabbed me by the collar and dragged me inside. Blows started falling on my head, which I tried instinctively to protect, and on my arms. I could distinguish only a giant figure of a Werkschutz and an unusually large head with an albino-blond mane of hair under the Werkschutz hat.

Oh my God! Podolny! I am dead.

Werkschutz Podolny was of Ukrainian ancestry and known for his cruelty even amongst his fellow guards. The other Werkschutz would warn us whenever they were guarding us on the outside: "*Achtung*, attention, here comes Podolny."

He had spotted me from the outside while making his rounds around the facility. When I lay down on the windowsill it was still dark and I did not realize that I would be clearly visible to anyone outside the building.

So now Podolny was living up to his reputation. The blows from his giant fists were coming from all sides. I had spit out a couple of teeth and was reeling when my knees buckled and I fell against one of the machines.

Podolny in his rage took his rifle and swung at me, hitting the heavy machine and breaking the butt-end. He probably would have beaten me to death if not for the German foreman of the machine department, who came running and stopped him, pleading my case.

"We need the man to finish very important work; he has not slept for over thirty hours. Besides, you have punished him enough. Leave your gun here and I will have the butt-end fixed."

Thankful but unable to speak, I dragged myself back to my work-station and tried the best I could to continue.

In the morning when Schmidt arrived there was a long discussion between him, the foreman from the mechanical department and the supervisor. The quality of my work was checked and I was sent back into the camp without being charged with sabotage.

When I came back into the camp my father was anxiously waiting for me. "Go into my room," he suggested. He shared one room with Uncle Henry at that time. Soon he came in with cold compresses and some food. "You cannot go back to this job," he said. "This son-of-a-bitch Schmidt will kill you."

"But he will ask for me," I replied. "He needs me and will not give up."

"We will tell them that you are sick, and then we will think of something."

I had visions of Schmidt going to the administration to request punishment for my absence and the Security Chief Stein coming into the camp to take care of me. Once again my nights were full of anguish and terror.

NORBERT FRIEDMAN

After a couple of days a new job was found for me. Schmidt, oddly, found a replacement for me from the ranks of inmates who worked for him.

I was to start working on the outside in the German settlement located some three kilometers from the plant. Ours was the garbage detail. Two of us dumped the garbage cans into a cart while four others pushed or pulled the cart. We had one Jewish foreman and no Werkschutz with us. Each of us had family in the camp who were the guarantors that we would not run away. Besides picking up the garbage we were not to refuse any work that any German asked us to perform: clean attics, move furniture, carry packages, paint fences, etc. This was a welcome change from my previous job: no worries about reading technical prints, radiuses and angles, no worries about committing sabotage. The job was physically demanding, but after a while I got the knack of using leverage and motion energy to lift and dump the garbage cans. Besides, we rotated our duties and helped each other. We had a small basement room in one of the buildings with a stove where we could heat up a beverage or even cook a meal during breaks.

Before the war this settlement had housed Polish engineers and office workers from the industrial complex. Now the German plant personnel occupied it. The buildings were mostly two-story houses of two apartments, one on each floor, with a little garden surrounding each house. Most of those employed in the plant commuted on bicycles, so as we were marching to work in the morning we passed a stream of Germans on bicycles going to work in the opposite direction, with the reverse happening in the evenings. The Germans of course knew who we were, with the letters KL painted in bright yellow on the backs of our jackets. We were their vassals, on the way to clean up their garbage. They were our sovereigns, our masters of life and death, lords of our dignity and self-esteem. We chose to march as erect as possible, heads high, defiantly singing whatever marching songs we knew. Evidently that did not sit well with some of the bigwigs from the plant, for shortly we were informed that our detail would not sing while on the way to work (other details, however, were encouraged to sing). The Polish workers who traveled the same road as the Germans to the plant were aware of our little by-play. We heard numerous comments about our in-your-face courage that was relayed to other inmates at the plant. Although we had to march on the opposite side of the road we could hear the encouraging comments of the Poles.

When the order was issued to stop singing, Uncle Henry devoted a lecture at morning roll call to proper behavior of prisoners vis-à-vis our oppressors and the necessity to avoid antagonizing them. His tirade was resented and discounted as usual, for it was tiresome and not thoughtfully delivered. Even if it was justified (and it well might have been, because the rate of executions and shooting of prisoners had increased sharply), its tone of delivery did not sit well with the inmates and did not gain any friends for my uncle.

The job at the *Osiedle,* the housing settlement, was a welcome departure from camp routine and an exposure to a life of normalcy, even if it was only the normalcy of the Germans. Occasionally we would find scraps of newspaper in the garbage and had a chance to find out what was going on in the outside world. Even if the information was in the form of propaganda and censored communiqués, we were able to read between the lines. We cheered when we read such disingenuous notes as, "The victorious German Army for strategic reasons withdrew from such and such a strip of land."

One day while dumping a garbage can we noticed a neatly folded package on top of the garbage. When we opened it, we found some fresh bread and sausage, evidently put there by some merciful soul. We tried to determine which of the German *House-Frauen* along our route might be our benefactor. One day we again found a paper bag filled with food and fruit, and a heavyset woman with a noticeable limp quietly asked in German as she passed: "Have you found the package?"

We answered "Yes," without lifting our heads, so as not to give her away.

We started to anticipate those parcels, not only because they were welcome for their nutritious value but also because this gesture of human kindness lifted our depleted spirits. One day the lady came out openly to us and asked for two men to come in and do some work in the attic, pointing to another prisoner and me. Upstairs in the attic we found a tray with food on one of the boxes. We were invited to sit down and eat.

The lady must have either taken a liking to me or pitied me as the youngest of the group, for she started to find chores for me to do by myself. One day she started asking me questions about my background and the whereabouts of my family and then volunteered some details about herself. She came from Yugoslavia, of Croatian parentage. Her husband was German; he worked in the plant and held a very important position as an engineer. Their name was Pusch.

There were also Polish girls employed as house helpers in the compound. We would see them pass by and sometimes engage them in short exchanges.

NORBERT FRIEDMAN

There was one pretty, dark-haired, petite girl who would glance and smile at me when passing by.

One day when I was putting up curtains in Mrs. Pusch's apartment she called the girl in and introduced her. Her name was Jasia and she blushed a lot. From that time on, every time I was working in Mrs. Pusch's house, Jasia was also there doing some chores. Mrs. Pusch would frequently go out, leaving Jasia and myself alone. The pretty blushing girl soon became a good friend, eager to talk and to learn about my lot but offering very little information about herself. Her diction was that of an educated city creature and not of a country bumpkin, which is how Mrs. Pusch introduced her.

One day when I was relaying to her the goings-on in the camp and the details of recent executions conducted by the Gestapo, Jasia broke into tears. While she was sobbing bitterly, she blurted out: *"Ja sama jestem Zydowka."* "I myself am a Jewess."

She came from a well-to-do family, either from the town of Rzeszow or Przemysl, I do not recall. Her whole family was deported eastward, never to be heard from again. They had the foresight to obtain a Christian birth certificate for Jasia (her real name was Rachel) and provide her with money and some jewelry to sustain herself. She eventually found employment as a housemaid in the German compound in Mielec. She guessed that Mrs. Pusch suspected her origin, and that that was why she introduced me to her. She felt that Mrs. Pusch could be trusted completely and even suggested that Mrs. Pusch herself might have had Jewish blood. A deep friendship, enforced by my knowledge of her secret, developed between us, and at times I had to restrain myself to keep it from going beyond brotherly affection.

The winter of 1942-43 was very bitter. Working outside, now in the snow and cold rain, started to take its toll on my health. I was repeatedly coming down with severe colds and sore throats. Jasia was transferred to a job as a personal housemaid to some top brass from the plant and could not visit my workstation. Mrs. Pusch tried to find more chores for me to do in her house, where she continued to ply me with hot tea with honey and biscuits.

She became seriously concerned about my poor health. One day when I was nursing a vicious cold, she suggested that I might be better off working inside the plant, under a roof. Her maternal concern for my welfare was very moving and Jasia's suspicion about the possibility of Jewish blood did not sound so outlandish.

She offered to ask her husband to find a job for me in his department. She gave him my ID number, and a few days later I was called into the camp's secretary office. The secretary Chaim D. sat me down and told me that because he came from the same village as my father and because he respected my father so much, and because he had noticed my worsening health, he had decided to find a better job for me. How would I like to work in the *Werkstoffprüfung*, the materials-testing laboratory.

Of course it was all humbug. He had received a request from engineer Pusch and was following orders, but he could not, true to his character, miss an opportunity to have someone beholden to him. Certainly a degree of gratitude from the nephew of the head of the O.D. was useful capital in politics of the camp.

CHAPTER XVIII

The *Werkstoffprüfung* department under engineer Pusch encompassed some of the most vital responsibilities of the *Heinkel Werke* in the Mielec plant. Engineer Pusch was in charge of the Physical Material Testing Department, which included the x-ray facility, the chemical laboratory, the heat-treating room and the cyanide bath facility. The last two were used to make the aluminum alloy components malleable so they could be shaped into parts for the wings and fuselage of the Heinkel aircraft.

Mr. Pusch was of medium height, with smiling blue eyes and an occasional impish grin. He wore a Tyrolian hat with a colorful feather stuck in it; much like my Uncle Lipek used to wear.

On my first day of work he greeted me with a thorough look-over and remarked, "So you are my wife's *Libeling,* my wife's pet. Come on, I will give you a nice sit-down job." He proceeded to take me into a bright, large room filled with strange machinery and several desks manned by neatly dressed Polish personnel.

"This is Norbert," he introduced me. "Treat him right." He left me in the hands of a Mr. Jankowski who invited me to sit down at his desk.

"What do you know about this kind of work?" Mr. Jankowski asked me.

"Very little," was my reply, although I did have some knowledge of physics and metallurgy from my days at the Jewish Vocational school in Krakow.

Mr. Jankowski proceeded to explain the kind of work they were doing. They conducted sheering and hardness tests on samples made of strips of aluminum, which had to be machined to a given shape. After the stress test they calculated the pounds per square inch (or kilograms per square centimeter, in European terms) that the strips could withstand. They also cut through samples of welded parts, polished them to a high micro finish, applied acid and examined them for any flaws in the welding.

In contrast to other departments in the plant, the working conditions in materials testing department were very relaxed; no one seemed to overwork himself, although everyone tried to look busy. This was especially true when Nazi dignitaries were visiting.

Adjacent to the physical lab was the x-ray facility. Zoltan Rosner, an inmate who bunked with me in barrack #4, operated it. Upstairs, was a chemical lab manned by a Polish chemist assisted by another inmate, one Ernest Noble.

Engineer Pusch would occasionally drop into our department, always inquiring about my work "How is he doing, my wife's *Libeling*?"

Soon he, too, started to bring in little food packages, which he said were sent by his wife. I always shared the goodies with Earnest and Zoltan. When the package contained eggs or sausage, Zoltan and I, would lock ourselves in the x-ray room and fry the food there. We would turn on the red light outside the sliding heavy lead door, indicating that x-ray examination of parts was in progress. When Mr. Pusch was about to bring someone on a tour of his department, he would alert us by buzzing the x-ray room with two short and two long rings and we would open the windows and turn on the fan. The smell of fried eggs and sausage in a x-ray lab would certainly invite questions from visitors.

On one occasion, when a group of high-ranking SS officers were inspecting the plant, Engineer Pusch found himself in front of the x-ray room without a chance of forewarning Zoltan and myself. The red light was on, and despite the insistence of the SS officers, Mr. Pusch refused to open the heavy, lead-reinforced door. Finally, as he later relayed to us, the insistence of the SS officers became forceful, all cordiality gone, and he said: "All right, all right, I will let you in but I will not be responsible for all of you becoming sterile because of the heavy radiation." The gamble paid off; the group agreed to tour other installations and come back to the x-ray facility later. Mr. Pusch proved to be a reckless bluffer and a lucky gambler when it came to saving the lives of inmates who worked for him.

In the summer of 1943 a young German boy, obviously related to some influential figure, was assigned as a summer intern to the chemical lab. Once, while pretending to be cleaning his revolver, he shot Ernest Noble in the thigh above his knee. When Ernest was being attended to, the young German coolly remarked: "*Ein Jude weniger.*"

"One less Jew." He obviously knew that a wounded inmate unable to work was useless chattel who would quickly be slated for execution.

Mr. Pusch was livid over the shooting and took Ernest to the German dispensary, where he had the German plant doctor remove the bullet and place Ernest in the camp's sick bay. He impressed upon the German doctor that Ernest was absolutely essential in running the chemical laboratory and had to be saved. Whenever it was necessary to save one of his people and he had to justify it to the head of plant security, the dreaded Mr. Stein, the inmate in question always turned out to be the most indispensable cog in the machinery of the plant's operation.

On one occasion an elderly Orthodox Jew, a Mr. Reichman who was interned with his three sons and who was working in the cyanide baths, because of some infraction, was taken to the killing grounds in Berdychow to be executed by the Gestapo. When we got the word of it we ran frantically to locate Mr. Pusch, who immediately jumped on his bicycle and rode to Berdychow. When Zimmerman, who was to be the executioner, refused to hand over the prisoner to Engineer Pusch, Mr. Pusch told Zimmerman he would report him to Berlin for sabotaging the war effort. Mr. Reichman, according to Engineer Pusch, was the only man capable of running the cyanide baths.

Mr. Reichman's life was saved, at least for the time being. Mr. Pusch detested the Nazis and would do whatever he could to undermine them. The German authorities must have sensed it, for in the winter of 1943 he was relocated to Rostock, a facility that was frequently being bombed by the allies.

After the war Ernest Noble, whose life Mr. Pusch saved, opened a factory to produce tooth powder in Schweinfurt, Germany and made Engineer Pusch his partner. I have often wondered how it was possible, amid that malignant sea of cruelty, for one man's decency to create an island of humanity. Mr. Pusch simply refused to join the orgy of destruction and tried, often successfully, to thwart its design. Was it something in his upbringing? He did not seem to be a practicing Christian. Was it some other ethical imperative that prompted him to behave this way or was it simply a mysterious predisposition to do the right thing?

Why were there so few like him, especially those whose moral training should have equipped them with the knowledge and proper attitude to step forward?

Having a job in Mr. Pusch's department certainly made my life easier. The opportunity to interact with Polish employees gave me a chance to help other inmates and enabled me to communicate with the outside world by exchanging mail with Michal. I was even able to buy food on occasions.

One day Mr. Jankowski, with whom I had developed a mildly friendly relationship (he was always tight-lipped about the situation outside the camp's walls) sat me down at his desk. While pretending to go over a set of figures from the last series of tests, and without lifting his head, he addressed me in a somber tone.

"I have some bad news for you," he said, and then haltingly proceeded: "Your friend Michal Krawiec is dead. I am to give you this message. Do not ask any questions! Just remember, he died like a true Polish patriot, cut down by machine-gun fire while attacking a German troop transport on a train that he helped to blow up" And then he added: *"Niech mu ziemia letka bedzie."* "May the earth weigh lightly on him. That is all! Now go back to work." He must have seen the tears welling up in my eyes; I instantly went to the x-ray room where I could cry unobserved.

In the course of the previous four years I had become hardened. I had witnessed many killings and faced the threat of death daily. I knew that my life and the lives of my dear ones hung by a thread and I felt choking fear every time the black limousine of the Gestapo chief entered the plant.

Every time there was bad news from the war front I expected the drunken Gestapo henchmen, joined by some of the camp guards, to take out their anger on the inmates. Screams for mercy and shots would ring out through the camp at night and someone I knew would be no more. Getting through those vicious forays was like waiting out a fierce storm, praying not to be the one hit by lightning, or sitting out a bombing raid, not knowing who would be the next target.

Still, the news of the death of my friend, my partner and in many things my mentor shook me deeply. That night I thought of all the things we had done together, the risks we had taken, his love for Lola and his bravery in saving my father. In a time when the value of individual lives was almost nil, he demonstrated extraordinary conduct, disregarding mortal danger and risks, spurred to honorable action only by the simple needs of another human being.

I had lost a comrade with whom I had shared a precious friendship, a friendship of total trust and acceptance, one without recriminations, without judgmental views of each other's actions. He was a Christian and I a Jew, but we shared a brotherhood that transcended all the reprehensible conduct of my other Polish compatriots. It nurtured hope at a time when there was so little of it.

My dad was equally saddened by the news, although his reaction was different than mine: "At least he died like a hero," he said, "with a weapon in his hand."

From the day he relayed to me the news of Michal's death, Mr. Jankowski seemed to regard me in a different light. He started to share facts and rumors from the outside world and to engage in quiet conversations about resistance activities. Eventually he disclosed that the news about Michal's death had come from Mr. Bujak.

NORBERT FRIEDMAN

Meanwhile the conditions in the camp were growing worse. In the beginning of 1943 a typhus epidemic broke out and claimed the lives of hundreds of prisoners. The Gestapo would visit more frequently and seize inmates who were recuperating and still alive, put them on wagons, and take them to Berdychow for execution.

Sanitary conditions deteriorated, as did the quality of the food. Both changes were due partly to general shortages in the occupied territories and partly to the fact that the camp population was increasing with new inmates from camps that were being closed out. One new group from the camps included a man named Max from the town of Bielsko, where we had lived before the war. My father knew him well, for they frequented the same coffeehouses, the two of them gambling together until the early morning hours. He was from a well-respected, assimilated, German-Jewish family in town, but his family regarded him as a black sheep. He had no trade and would not work in his family's business.

He was good-looking, with a swarthy complexion, and before the war he had been an elegant dresser, always wearing a flower in his boutonniere. He was considered an available bachelor and a good catch, but his family did not consider the women he hung out with suitable. Finally a match was made with the heiress of a chain of department stores. She was not considered the most beautiful girl in town, but still was pursued by other eligible bachelors. Max and his bride honeymooned at all the fancy spas of Europe, especially those with a casino. But the marriage did not work out. It was rumored that one night Max gambled away the key to his wife's bedroom. They were separated and he continued to frequent the old coffeehouses, where now he was seen in the company of girls of lesser repute.

So this man Max arrived in our camp from a smaller labor camp where the prisoners had been building roads for the German army. His knowledge of German culture and language had helped him get somewhat better treatment from his German overseers. Now, however, in the larger compound of Mielec, he had trouble adjusting. His gambling addiction soon got the better of him. He started to gamble with whatever valuables he had brought with him. When those were gone, Max wagered his bread or soup ration on a cut of the deck of cards.

When I brought his plunge to my father's attention, his reply was, "Let him be, he wants to lose." Max's health started to fail, and when the typhoid epidemic struck, he was one of the firsts to succumb. When he was being

SUN RAYS AT MIDNIGHT

prepared for the burial, my father put a deck of cards in his pants pocket and a joker in his hand to be buried with him. For my father, Max's death marked the last hand in his former life, the gambling times in the Bielsko coffeehouses.

For the others in the camp, except for his gambling partners, Max's passing went unnoticed. The sad fact was that death was not a major event. It was our daily companion and sometimes even a welcome liberator.

One day the camp received a carload of shoes and clothing from an unknown source; they were simply dumped in the warehouse barrack. As they were being sorted it became apparent that this was the clothing of other inmates from the camps of Treblinka and Majdanek, whose fate we could only guess. None of us yet knew what was happening in those places. The people assigned to sort the clothes started looking for hidden valuables. They also found messages, however, most of them written in Yiddish, informing the finders of impending doom and imploring them to try to save themselves.

One Sunday I was assigned to work in the warehouse sorting shoes. The Werkschutz Drozd who wanted to find a matching pair of boots for himself supervised us. I was fortunate enough to find two boots that formed a virtual pair and fitted him well. As a reward I was permitted to find a pair for myself. I found a pair made of soft leather, and except for the height of the heels they looked like a matching pair of riding boots. Somehow I never even stopped to consider who the previous owners might have been or what was their fate.

CHAPTER XIX

In the spring of 1943 a remarkable incident occurred in our camp, one that left an indelible imprint on me. I have described it in presentations I gave after the war to highlight the deep impact of religious upbringing and Jewish values, which became forever imbedded in our psyche. These values governed the actions of the faithful, sometimes under the most appalling circumstances.

Until that fateful day, the Gestapo had always chosen the victims for killing both inside and outside the camp, with the henchman Zimmerman doing most of the shooting. Occasionally the director of security, Stein, would shoot somebody, or the Werkschutz Drozd would participate in a drunken binge with the Gestapo and kill some inmates.

On this day the chief of the Mielec Gestapo, in the company of Zimmerman, arrived in the camp. He strode to the offices, called in Uncle Henry and Chaim D., the secretary, and administered several lashes to them with his riding whip to set the tone. Then the Gestapo Chief proceeded with his uncommon request. He demanded that the camp leadership deliver, by the next morning, twenty prisoners for execution. It was a most unusual order. It was the first time the Gestapo had demanded that the camp leadership do the selecting.

The Gestapo chief informed Uncle Henry and Chaim D. that unless they complied with his request, many more would die. He himself would conduct a selection in the morning, taking every tenth person, including Uncle Henry and Chaim D. as examples. Before taking leave, he emphasized his point by cursing and striking them both again.

After he left, the news spread and a sense of doom and despair filled the camp. A meeting of the camp's council was called that evening and a heated discussion began. Different kinds of prisoners were recommended for selection: the hopelessly sick, the convalescent, the old, those too weak to work, the troublemakers. Everyone had his own reasons for the various suggestions. The leadership, however, felt that it was too grave a matter to be decided exclusively by the inmate administration, and they sent out for additional people who had been respected leaders in their home communities. Strangely enough, similar suggestions were offered by these leaders as well, although the reasoning was a little more subtle and sophisticated.

It was now early 1943. The Jews of Poland have been under the Nazi yoke for nearly three and a half years. Twelve hundred days of terror and twelve hundred nights of sleepless apprehension.

Auschwitz was by then a known reality. Everyone was either aware of or suspected the fate of their dear ones, and had reason to expect the worst for himself.

The heroic uprising of the Warsaw Ghetto was over and the fate of the fighters was common knowledge. In the used clothing that was shipped to the camp from Majdanek Lubelski and Treblinka, we had found the letters stained with tears of despair. These letters contained messages of tragedies befalling whole communities and notes of warning: *"Yidden ratovetz sech, es brent"*— "Jews, try to save yourselves, anyway you can."

The process of degradation and dehumanization was in full force; all of Europe was engulfed in the night of the Hun. The laws of man and God had been cast out; decency had become an act of naive heroism. Whip, bullet, gas and fire replaced love, compassion, kindness and devotion to God. The law of the day was survival of the fittest, but even that law guaranteed nothing.

The leaders assembled in that room—knowing all this—were drained of what once had been their ethical convictions. The fiber of their being had been shredded by hunger, deprivation and the constant threat of annihilation. On the shoulders of such men was now heaped the additional burden of choosing life or death for their co-sufferers, a dilemma contrived by the diabolical mind of the oppressor.

I was in and out of the room, for my father was one of those assembled and he continued to send me out for fresh coffee from his camp kitchen. And when it came time for the decision to be made, my father rose and instructed me to fetch Rabbi Schenken from his barrack. He felt that they needed some rabbinic wisdom to guide them in their decision.

Rabbi Schenken and I do hope I remember his name correctly, came from a small town in eastern Galicia called Gorlice. He came to our camp late in 1942 and was housed in a barrack with some other intellectuals, including another Rabbi, whose name I do not recall with whom he was very friendly. From their demeanor I would have judged that Rabbi Schenken was an

NORBERT FRIEDMAN

Orthodox man while the other Rabbi came from a more progressive background, for he held the title of Dr. Rabbiner, which was granted in theological seminaries.

The two of them were always engaged in animated discussions, mostly on Talmudic dicta regarding ethics and the application of certain laws to the environment of camp life. They both worked in the tool crib of the mechanical department. Rabbi Schenken was often called upon by the traditionalists to solve difficult *Halachic*, legal questions, created by the abnormal conditions of the camp.

Rabbi Schenken entered the room, which was by now filled with smoke and the odor of human perspiration. He looked around, assessing the individuals gathered there, and then asked why he was called. Chaim D. explained the situation and asked for advice.

The Rabbi thought for a while and then quoted Halacha, the Jewish Law, which most of the gathered were familiar with. "The law states," he began, quoting the maxim and the place that it can be found: "that you are not allowed to try to save your life by substituting some one's else. 'How do you know that your blood is redder then your brother's?' says the Talmud in the tractate *Sanhedrin.*"

Silent disbelief and then excited voices greeted the Rabbi's words.

"Whose laws are you quoting? Where is our God, who has abandoned us?"

"How can he demand this of us now?"

The Rabbi then spoke slowly in a trembling voice of our history, of the destruction of the Holy Temple, of our struggles in exile and about the martyrdom of our sages under the Roman occupation in the first and second centuries AD. In a halting tone he noted our responsibilities not only to live as Jews but also to take particular care to die with honor as Jews.

He spoke for a long time, and when towards the end he referred to the grave responsibility he had assumed in instructing us about our laws in this situation, his voice broke and tears ran down his cheeks. Then he offered his own life to be the first to be taken by the Germans.

I was sobbing in the corner of the room and so were many others. The elders nodded in agreement, got up and silently began to leave the meeting muttering under their breath, "May God help us all!"

Were they merely convinced by Rabbi Schenken's Talmudic argument? Or, as I suspected, moved by his inspiring example of courage?

SUN RAYS AT MIDNIGHT

Early the next morning we all lined up at the *Appel Platz*, the reveille square, to face our tormentors. Once again it was *Yom Ha Din*, the Day of Judgment. We stood there in fear and terror, praying in the depths of our hearts.

"Dear G-d! Do not let it be me, not me!" We put out our chests, as if saying: "Look I am still young, I am strong, I can still work. Dear G-d, do not let it be me."

The Gestapo chief's riding whip pointed at one man after another in short, impatient jerks. His face showed the disappointment and annoyance that the damned Jews, *Die ferecten Juden*, had denied him the pleasure of reducing them to vassals without a soul. Their death was to be his revenge.

"*Raus . . . du raus!*" "Out, you out!" he barked angrily at each victim, as from the midst of our trembling yet erect rows he selected his fill. Out they went to their deaths, as varied a group as they were in the microcosm called *Zwangs-Arbeit Lager Mielec*, forced labor camp Mielec. Thirty-some of the faithful and the faithless, the pious and the defiant, the learned and the ignorant, all giving their lives for *Kiddush Hashem*, the sanctification of His holy name.

Never again were the inmates asked to choose the victims for slaughter in our camp.

Debates and discussions about the ordeal of this selection process began almost immediately and continued among some people into the years after the war. Those, whose friends or relatives were victims of the selection, along with many others, held that it was imprudent not to deliver the requested number of people, in the face of the threat that refusal would lead to a larger loss of life, a threat that was in fact carried out. Others argued that there was no way of knowing whether the threat would be carried out, in view of the labor needs for the German war effort. There was also some disagreement about the correctness of Rabbi Schenken's interpretation of Halacha, the Jewish law.

In the course of the Jewish history of persecution, there were many instances that could be compared to certain aspects of the Holocaust, with similar problems of interpretation and application of Jewish law. After the war ended, various authorities with conflicting conclusions discussed those instances. It is still being debated, for example, whether it was morally correct for the leader of the Judenrat in the Lodz Ghetto, Chairman Chaim Rumkowski, to deliver to the Germans thousands of ghetto dwellers, including children, in the hope of saving at least some of the Jews. It is estimated that out of the 200,000 ghetto inhabitants in Lodz, only 10,000 to 20,000 were still alive when the ghetto was liquidated.

Yet even many of the survivors have argued that Chairman Rumkowski deserves some credit for the fact that of all the ghettos, only the Lodz ghetto counted as many survivors at the time of its liquidation.

Was it more prudent or heroic to refuse to cooperate with the Germans by committing suicide? This was the choice of the chairman of the Warsaw Judenrat, Adam Czerniakow, when he was asked to participate in the first deportation from the Warsaw Ghetto in June of 1942.

But when on October 26, 1941, the Germans in the Kovno ghetto posted notices that all Jews should assemble for a selection, the chief Rabbi of Kovno, Rabbi Shapira, determined: "If the decree to destroy the entire Jewish community has been determined by the enemy, and through some means or other it is possible to save part of the community, its leaders are obliged to summon up their spiritual strength and take upon themselves the responsibility of doing whatever needs to be done to save a part of the community."

On the other hand, Maimonides, the great codifier of Jewish law of the Middle Ages, ruled the opposite: ". . . if pagans should tell them [the Jews], 'Give us one of yours and we shall kill him, otherwise we shall kill all of you,' they all should be killed and not a single Jewish soul should be delivered."

After the creation of the State of Israel, the Israeli legislature followed Maimonides in formulating the canon of behavior, tested in the Israeli courts, under which "the delivery of a persecuted person to an enemy administration" was declared a punishable crime (Art. 5 of the Nazi and Nazi Collaborators Law 5710-1950).

The position of Rabbi Schenken and the decision by the elders of the Zwangs-Arbeitlager Mielec to follow his leadership must then be considered a sacrifice of human lives for the Sanctification of His Holy Name, an act of Kiddush Hashem.

Rabbi Schenken, his friend and a group of other men were executed a few months later, following a charge of sabotage.

CHAPTER XX

Soon after the selection incident, Werkschutz Drozd informed the camp leadership that important changes in the supervision of the camp were about to take place. No longer would the security of the camp be the responsibility of the plant's administration. The camp's classification would be changed from *Zwangs-Arbeit Lager,* a forced labor camp, to *Konzentratzion Lager,* or concentration camp. It would be guarded by a contingency of Ukrainian SS under the command of an SS officer.

SS Hauptscharfuhrer Herring was an imposing figure, of rough, darkly handsome features, taller then anyone in the camp. His first request upon entering the camp for an inspection, before his installation as Commandant, was for a barber. He wanted a shave.

Several men in their pre-camp lives had worked as barbers, but it was generally accepted that one man, I will call him Simcha, excelled. Simcha was a product of a small shtetl, some place in Galicia. In order to eke out a living, besides serving as a barber, he had doubled as the village entertainer who had mastered the ability to simulate several musical instruments. With the aid of an ordinary comb, he could imitate a whole orchestra, preferably a jazz ensemble, which in the thirties was the *cri dernier* for the young. He would also perform at weddings as a *Batchen,* a sort of bard or minstrel. He had the gift of improvising and composing little ditties about the principals in the affair.

Hauptscharfuhrer Herring's request for a barber threw Uncle Henry into a state of panic. He hoped in his simple-minded thinking that Simcha somehow might be able to loosen up the Hauptscharfuhrer with his repertoire of jokes and picked him to give the shave. Simcha could not speak German, but like many others he had always felt that the knowledge of Yiddish could somehow bridge the language barrier. Uncle Henry ran to his quarters and handed Simcha all his shaving paraphernalia, which he had requisitioned from the property of other inmates. He gave the barber all his after-shave lotion and his rare perfumes as well as a tube of what he thought was shaving cream.

Uncle Henry and Chaim D., the camp's secretary, anxiously waited in the office, expecting to be summoned by the *Hauptscharfuhrer*, hoping that Simcha's services would be able to put Herring in a good mood. Suddenly Simcha came running into the office, red in the face with fright and crying: "The stuff in the tube that you gave me will not lather! The German is getting mad, what do I do?"

Uncle Henry ran back to his room, looked at his assortment of toiletries and realized that in his state of panic he had given the barber a tube of toothpaste instead of shaving cream. He quickly corrected his mistake and ran out with Simcha to apologize to Herring. Red-faced, grinning sheepishly, he bowed and asked forgiveness. The man obviously had some sense of humor, for he broke out laughing and absolved the barber of any guilt; he even rewarded him at the end with some cigarettes. But he also made up his mind about Uncle Henry, who he decided was a buffoon and a subservient coward.

That first impression became a source of many difficulties for Uncle Henry in his future dealings with Herring. And for all practical purposes, it marked the beginning of the decline of his influence in camp affairs.

Hauptscharfuhrer Herring liked to drink, and *Werkschutz* Drozd, who was concerned about his position as the camp's security overseer, was a good drinking companion. He would brief Herring about the details of running the camp and about the individuals of influence in the camp's internal administration, as well as about the men inside the camp that could be relied on to be of service.

I do not know under what circumstances *Hauptscharfuhrer* Herring made the acquaintance of engineer Pusch, for Pusch to the best of my knowledge was not a drinking man and did not share the political sentiments of *Hauptscharfuhrer* Herring. But one day before the end of the shift Engineer Pusch called me into his office, pulled a gun from his desk drawer and, with the impish smile that meant mischief, said to me: "Take this gun to the camp and give it to Hauptscharfuhrer Herring."

"What?" I stuttered. "How can I? He is sure to shoot me if I do."

"Do not worry," laughed Mr. Pusch. "I have called him and he knows you are coming. Just make sure that the barrel is pointed at you when you hand him the gun."

"But why? What is his gun doing here?"

"The firing pin broke and we fixed it for him. Do not worry," insisted Mr. Push "It may be a way for you to get into his good graces. Just don't tell anyone about it." He wrapped the gun in some newspaper and instructed me to put it inside my shirt.

As our work detail marched into the camp and we were counted at the entrance ramp, Herring appeared at the window of his office, asked for me and instructed one of the Ukrainian guards to bring me inside. Everyone in the small work detail wondered what I had done and what kind of punishment I was going to get. The guard led me to the door of the office and let me enter.

Herring sat behind his desk with his feared German shepherd at his feet. I snapped to attention and reported who I was and the purpose of my visit. Then very gingerly I unwrapped the newspaper with the gun in it. Pusch had assured me that the gun was not loaded. I handed it to H.H., butt first. He took the gun, pointed it at me and pulled the trigger, all the time watching my reaction. The blood from my face must have run to my toes, but I managed to stand motionless.

"You knew it wasn't loaded?' Herring broke out laughing. "Didn't you?"

"Yes, but I was not quite sure," I answered truthfully.

"You are the Ordnungsdienst Commandant's son, aren't you?"

"No," I answered emphatically. "I am his nephew."

"Ah, so Joseph, the kitchen supervisor is your father?"

"Yes, *Herr Obersturmfuhrer*"

"Do not try to flatter me. You know that I am only a *Hauptscharfuhrer*."

"Yes I do," I answered, regretting my attempt to ingratiate myself.

"I was going to give you some sausage, but I do not like false flattery. I will give it to my dog."

Then he seemed to have another thought. "Rolph, los!" he said to the dog, siccing the beast on me.

I wore at that time a pair of riding pants made of coarse canvas, tucked into a pair of riding boots. As the German shepherd jumped to snap at me, I instinctively bent my right leg and stuck out my knee to protect myself. It hit the dog in the teeth and it ran howling under the table.

Hauptscharfuhrer Herring was furious, more at the dog than at me, and ordered me out of the office. "*Los . . . Los*"—"Get out of here, before I shoot you."

I needed no encouragement, I ran out as fast as I could, straight into the arms of my father who was waiting outside, anxious to find out what my summons to Herring was all about. I went with my father to his room and I told him the whole story.

NORBERT FRIEDMAN

Since our time in the camp, my relationship with my father as well as my perception of him had undergone a drastic change. He had been consistently helpful to others, especially to my friends, singling them out for chores in the camp's kitchen or, when necessary, in the plant's kitchen, tasks that guaranteed them some leftover scraps of food. He also lectured Uncle Henry on his actions, scolding him for his stupid tirades, which Uncle Henry continued to deliver at the morning roll call. These were becoming more scornful along with the growing pressure of running the camp under H.H., and the demands for cleanliness and order were growing more difficult to meet. The difficulty of maintaining order was further aggravated by the integration of the inmates from smaller labor camps into our facility. These new inmates were always men.

One day, however, a forced labor camp several miles away from Mielec was closed. The inmates in that camp performed work for a large German construction company called Baum & Lesh. The camp's several hundred prisoners were brought into our compound, and among them were approximately one hundred females. The camp's Jewish leadership was in the hands of a certain Mr. Bitkower, a tall, athletic-looking man whose wife was the camp's doctor.

After the arrival of the people from the Baum & Lesh camp, the hierarchy of our camp's functionaries changed drastically. Mr. Bitkower, it was reported, went to Herring and told him about his own military rank in the Polish army, about his expertise in running a camp facility and asked to have a hand in running our camp. To prove his willingness to cooperate, he proceeded to inform on those from his camp who had any valuables that might be of interest to H.H.

Hauptscharfuhrer Herring, who until then had not encouraged informers, shown interest in any one's property, or taken any bribes, nevertheless accepted Mr. Bitkower's offer and installed him as the O.D. Co-Commandant. The people from the B&L camp were encouraged to part with some of their treasures, with promises of favoritism, better jobs and better accommodations.

Others, hoping for a place of influence, also offered Hauptscharfuhrer Herring their services. The one who was most successful, besides Mr. Bitkower, was one Mrs. Presser, a good-looking, statuesque woman in her thirties. In her previous camp she had been in charge of the women's barracks, her husband and brother had had easy jobs.

Her husband was a short, bald-headed man who was obviously much older then her. She seemed to hold him in contempt for not being more aggressive and for being unsuited to camp environment.

She must have impressed *Hauptscharfuhrer* Herring for he made her a member of a harem of women whom he sexually exploited. As a reward, she retained her position as the "Elder" of the women's barrack. Her husband got a job in the camp's office and her brother served as a roving informant. The brother would occasionally go into the countryside for a day or so with *Hauptscharfuhrer* Herring and some camp inmate. We knew that those trips were taken to the inmate's homes to retrieve their hidden property. Sometimes the inmate did not come back. Meanwhile Mrs. Presser would strut around the camp in her fine clothing, always made up, painted and ready to be summoned to Herring's office while her cuckold husband pretended he did know what was going on.

A new element had been introduced into the camp's life, previously almost unheard of: that of informing on fellow inmates in order to better one's fortunes. Forever marred was the common bond of sense of trust and loyalty created by our common misery, common adversary and common interest. Up till now, despite Uncle Henry's clumsy and pompous tirades and despite his inability to control the actions of the O.D. the men under his charge, informing was rare and discouraged by the tacit threat of ostracism.

Uncle Henry envisioned himself as a buffer between the German authorities and the inmates, a man who held the inmates' welfare at heart. Sometimes he would step in when a prisoner was caught smuggling food into the camp or found violating some rule. He would seize the inmate from the hands of the guards and threaten him in the earshot of the Germans or Ukrainians with the worst punishment. He meted out the punishment himself to protect them from more severe and sometimes deadly consequences at the hands of the authorities.

"I will kill you, I will put you to worst torture," he would scream, "With my own hands I will beat you to death." In the heat of his diatribe he would call the prisoner most demeaning names.

Perhaps he meant well, but the indignity of receiving such harsh insults from another Jew sometimes lasted longer in their memories and was resented more bitterly than the physical punishment itself.

With those changes in Herring's behavior and in the climate in the camp itself, an incident took place that until today has stood out for me as the most improbable, almost unbelievable, example of the complexity of human nature that could be encountered in the furnace of hell.

One day we were brought to the camp for the usual noon feeding. As soon as we entered the campgrounds an O.D. man informed me, "Herring has your father in his office and is killing him!"

I rushed into the first barrack where Herring's office was located and shoved aside the Ukrainian who stood guard in the hall and who tried to stop me from entering. I pushed the door open and there lay my father, naked from the waist, bent down over a chair. Herring was hitting him on the back with the dreaded dried ox-tail crop while his German shepherd Rolph was snapping at my father's naked body and tearing bleeding pieces of flesh from his buttocks. Every time the ox-tail rod came down an inhuman scream emerged from my father's throat. *Werkschutz* Drozd was holding my father's head down while Herring administered the punishment.

Later I found out what the beating was all about. The plant administration drew food rations for the camp inmates from the German government. Although meager, the rations were standardized at a specific number of calories per prisoner and contained some margarine, beans, potatoes, pasta and occasional scraps of meat. The SS drew their ration from the same commissary and often appropriated the choicest part of our rations for themselves. Consequently the quality of the soup that was being sent to the camp as the main fare for the prisoners steadily deteriorated.

It seems that my father, whose job was to heat the soup in special camp kettles before it was served, made arrangements with some Polish farmers on the outside to sell him potatoes to boil and add them to our soup. He devised a plan for the potatoes to be thrown over the electrified barbed-wire fence from a passing wagon. This practice went undiscovered for some days, until someone reported it to *Hauptscharführer* Herring.

My father was caught receiving the potatoes and brought in for questioning. He was threatened with corporal punishment unless he disclosed the identity of the Poles on the outside who were involved. He stubbornly pleaded ignorance, claiming that he only picked up what some benevolent Pole was willing to throw over the fence.

I walked in during the corporal punishment itself, not knowing the reason for my father's ordeal. The only emotion that I remember is one of horror. I was bewildered by the drama of the situation and the peril that it posed to my father. Instinctively, I stretched out my arm to block the next blow and cried out: "Please stop, please! This is my father, don't hit him anymore. Please!" I begged them: "Take me instead and punish me instead. Please, let my father loose, please!"

Dumbfounded, Hauptscharfuhrer Herring stopped in mid-air, looked down at me and screamed: "Get the hell out of here before I kill you!"

"Go ahead," I yelled back, "do whatever you want, but please let my father go." I held onto his arm as I pleaded with him.

"You must be crazy boy, are you?"

"No," I blurted out. "This is my father."

With a look of amazement Herring turned to Drozd and, pointing at my father, said: "Take him out of here!"

Then he turned back to me, showed me the chair on which he was administering the punishment to my father and ordered: "Sit down."

My father hastily pulled up his trousers and, bowing to Herring, backed out of the office, saying, "Thank you, thank you, *Herr Hauptscharfuhrer,*" while at the same time stealing grateful glances at me, his son, and now his savior.

My father and Drozd left the room, Drozd taking the still excited dog with him. Herring looked at me and asked: "Why did you do that? You know that I could have shot you? What made you do that?" He spoke in a tone of genuine perplexity. "Are you that brave or just crazy? Why?"

I looked up at him, sensing a moment of human contact and responded to what I thought could be a meeting of filial emotions: "If it was you in my place, you would have done the same thing for your father."

There was a moment of charged silence. An SS officer, who wore the blood of many Jewish inmates on his hands, was having his humanity challenged by a young and insignificant Jewish serf.

He turned around, opened the door to his cabinet and, with his back to me, asked: "What was that again that you said?"

"I said that if it was you in my place, you would have done the same thing for your father."

He took out two glasses and a bottle of brandy, poured a drink for me and for him. He handed me my drink, looked me straight in the face and gravely replied: "I never had a father."

We drank heavily that afternoon, an SS officer and a nonentity of a Jewish youngster, a concentration camp inmate without hope or future—A life hanging on to a thin thread of sentimentality, dancing precariously on a predacious spider's web, expecting at every moment to be devoured.

NORBERT FRIEDMAN

After a few drinks Hauptscharfuhrer Herring began to speak of his childhood: A bastard born to a poor girl, put into an orphanage, recruited later by the Nazis, as a faithful and unquestioning cog in the killing machine of the SS. He rose quickly in the ranks; the only fealty he knew was to his benefactors, the German National Socialist Party.

He wanted to know the nature of my loyalty to my father, the extent of my love for him. He probed the emotional ties between us and insisted that I describe to him the times that I spent with my father in my childhood. Even though I was feeling the effects of the alcohol I realized that I must paint my relationship with my father in the most laudatory terms and not mention the tensions that once existed between us. To Herring I described my father as the most loving parent for whom I would gladly give my life. As I spoke I realized that, yes, I would.

The brandy and my emotional recitation triggered a most unexpected trace of a tear from Herring. And when the conversation turned to the perils of existence in the camps, Herring offered a solemn promise that as long as he, *Hauptscharfuhrer* Herring, was in charge, no harm would come to me or to my father. He then sealed his promise with a handshake.

I left his office two bottles of brandy and several hours later. With his arm on my shoulder he escorted me out the door of his barrack—to the astonishment of all those in the vicinity.

No one, not even my father, ever learned the totality of what transpired behind the door of Herring's office after my father's release. From that time on, a mysterious aura of importance accompanied my person as long as Herring was in charge of the camp.

CHAPTER XXI

The conditions in the camp continued to change for the worse as more transports arrived from smaller camps and caused more congestion. Order was more difficult to keep and the O.D. became more irritable and more violent toward the inmates. The lines at food distribution became difficult to control, and getting people off to work on time in the morning became a real task.

H.H. and Werkschutz Drozd were getting drunk more frequently and would, in the company of other SS men, roam the camp at night and pick victims for beatings and occasional shootings.

Mr. Bitkower, who was a calm, well-organized individual, took almost total control of the logistics of running the camp, making changes that helped to keep order. He would not consult Uncle Henry, whom he treated with disdain and whom he used mostly to make unpopular announcements and relay his orders to the O.D. men.

Mrs. Bitkower, a physician who was several years older then Mr. Bitkower, set up a dispensary in her quarters were she administered to inmates' minor wounds and ailments. She had also served as physician in her previous camp. One day when I visited her to get something taken care off she engaged me in a conversation and invited me to have some tea with her. We became friendly in a strange sort of way. I liked her, but I was also wary of her; she, on the other hand, seemed to have total confidence in me. She seemed to regard me as a younger brother with whom she liked to discuss people and literature.

She had a sizable library, at least by camp standards, which she had brought with her from the other camp. We would read poetry together, there in the camp—a most incongruous picture. She was particularly fond of two classic Polish poets, Mickiewicz and Slowacki, and of Tuwim, a contemporary Jewish poet. She favored poems with romantic and erotic themes.

She would query me about the politics in the camp and its power brokers. She wanted to know if I had found a girl friend from among the women who came with her, and even offered to choose one for me, as if they were chattels.

I was entertained by her rough sense of humor. "Go have a good time, stupid," she would say. "We're all slated for death anyhow."

Werkschutz Drozd was Dr. Bitkower's frequent patient. He suffered from ulcers, and after his drunken binges he would come to her for medication. She would mix some opium for him, which seemed to help him, but to me it looked as though he was becoming addicted.

Among the transports that came to us, a group of about one hundred former prisoners of war arrived from a POW camp in Budzyn. They were a cohesive, well-disciplined group of Jewish men of similar age who had served in the Polish army. A few of them came from the Russian army, who were taken as prisoners of war by the Germans and interned in Budzyn.

As soon as they arrived they presented themselves to *Hauptscharfuhrer* Herring and offered to assume key discipline-enforcing positions in the camp. Bitkower had to exert his influence with Herring to keep them from taking over control of the camp.

Their failure to gain authority disappointed the leadership of the group. Most of their ire, however, was directed toward Uncle Henry, probably because he was very vocal and they perceived him as the weaker member of our leadership.

Bitkower was also effective in wielding power in other ways. For example, he considered a number of inmates troublesome and apparently he decided to get rid of them. He compiled a list of about forty men and arranged with *Hauptscharfuhrer* Herring to have them shipped out to the camp in Plaszow.

One evening I happened to be in Mrs. Bitkower's quarters at a propitious time. We were playing checkers, I remember; I had made the checkerboard and the pieces for her as a gift. She confided in me that that very night a transport with some of our men was being shipped out to another destination and that my father and Uncle Henry were to be on it. Apparently she thought that this was an irreversible situation, and that was why she shared it with me. Or maybe, as I later thought about it, she was trying in a subtle way to thwart her husband's underhanded scheme.

I ran out, leaving her wide-eyed and startled, looking for Herring. I was hoping, in all my youthful innocence, to reverse his decision to ship my father out. I found him outside the entrance to his office. He was slightly inebriated, talking to Drozd.

SUN RAYS AT MIDNIGHT

"How could you?" Were my first words to him, "You promised, you gave me your word!" He knew what I meant, but he was not about to be pushed around.

"Scheisse, Man."—"Shit, man, you again?" He glared at me with all the awareness of his absolute power over life and death, with all the authority bolstered by his drunken state. Annoyed at my presence, he concluded: "I do what I do, *Schluss*, finished!" And then, as if an afterthought, he said, "What are you? My conscience? Get out!"

But I grabbed him by both his sleeves, almost sinking to my knees, and pleaded with him. "You cannot break your word, you will destroy what is left of my faith in Man. If you do not keep your promise there will be no honor left in this shitty world. You are a better man than that, I know!"

"Lass mich los;" "Let me be, I cannot change my orders."

"You can do anything that you want," I said, and sensing a slight wavering, I played my last card: "If you let my father down, you will be letting your own father down too!"

His hand slashed across my face, knocking me to my knees.

"You do not give up, do you? Where do you live? *In ein Märschen Land?* In a fairy-tale world?"

"That is the only world that we have left, to keep us human, *Herr Hauptscharfuhrer.*"

The struggle between keeping a promise given in a moment of drunken weakness and between his commitment to his authority, the fight between pity for a wretched vassal and between exercising his power was surging through his conscience, and he must have hated himself for his indecision.

Finally he blurted out to Drozd: "Take Friedman of the truck and keep him away from Bitkower! I am still the boss here."

"Both the Friedmans," I added meekly, and since Herring did not object, Drozd choose to interpret his silence in the affirmative.

Next morning after the truck with the transport left, Uncle Henry sought me out and profusely thanked me for my intervention. "You are like my son to me," he sobbed. "I always knew I could count on you."

My own father said nothing, simply embracing me in his powerful arms, letting the touch of his cheek on mine and the quiver of his body express his emotions.

Mr. Bitkower, cool customer that he was, never said anything to me, although he must have known the reason why his plan was not carried out. However, I was said to discover that Mrs. Bitkower would never invite me to her quarters again.

NORBERT FRIEDMAN

In the fall of 1943 Herring was notified that he would be relieved of his post and would be transferred to the Russian front. One night during one of his drunken binges he shot Mr. Bitkower to death and *Werkschutzfuhrer* Drozd executed Mrs. Bitkower. It was rumored that the Gestapo was investigating relationships between various camp commandants and their Jewish confidants and that Herring did not want his dealings with Bitkower to be disclosed to the Gestapo or the next camp Commandant.

Mielec, which was a satellite entity of the concentration camp in Plaszow—prominently featured in Steven Spielberg's widely acclaimed picture "Schindler's List"—was evidently the subject of the same Gestapo intelligence portrayed in the picture, investigating the relationship between Mr. Schindler and Commandant Goetz who later executed his camp's head of the Ordnungsdienst, Wilek Hilewicz, whom he originally recruited from our camp in Mielec.

I could never understand though how Drozd could have shot Mrs. Bitkower, who took such good care of his ailment and whom he seemed to favor so much.

Later, on his only visit to our camp from the front, H.H. wanted to see his German shepherd, Rolph. When it became obvious that the dog has lost his vicious edge by having been fed and cared for by one of the prisoners, Herring shot the animal.

I did not see Herring on his visit to the camp and he did not ask about me. So ended the strangest association, a relationship held together by the thinnest of threads—his faint filial loyalty to an unknown parent, or maybe a longing for the kind of loyalty he had seen in me for my own father.

According to the best information I could find, Hauptscharfuhrer Herring was killed after the war by one of the inmates from Mielec whose sister Herring had violated.

CHAPTER XXII

A new camp commandant—a new king and master of life and death—was coming to us, and no one knew what to expect. Six new Ukrainian black guards (so called because of the color of their uniforms) appeared in the camp to prepare his lodgings and a stable for his horses; they even brought a carriage for the horses to pull him in.

The inmates assigned to work on the new commandant's quarters started bringing bits of information which they gleaned from the Ukrainian guards. The name of the new commandant was *Hauptscharfuhrer* Schwammberger. He would have a wife with him and a six-year-old son. He was known as a fearless terror, the guards proudly informed us. He had overseen the liquidation of the Przemysl and Rzeszow ghettos, where 3,500 Jews were murdered, and he was said to have personally gunned down at least 600 Jewish men and women. The guards bragged that he had handed his pistol to his six-year-old son to shoot the children.

(The inmates said that he *"supposedly"* did that, because even in our numbed callousness, we could not imagine that anyone could be so cruel.)

"*Vy is tzy inser Yoren*," we cried. Woe's unto us if the rumors were even partly true.

The *Hauptscharfuhrer* arrived late one evening with his entourage, and the next morning he announced a general roll call. He was of average height; an autocratic looking man dressed in the SS uniform. His well-polished boots and his gun holster shone in the morning sun; in his hand he held a riding whip.

Without any visible emotion he took the roll from fear-stricken Uncle Henry, then slowly walked around the rows of erect prisoners, inspecting these frightened, pitiful forms of human beings, most of them doomed by fate to perish soon.

Without a word, this silent, fearsome apparition turned around and with his peculiar stroll literally glided out of the campgrounds. Not a threat was uttered, not a shot was fired, but for us, based on his appearance and reputation, the forecast was unmistakable: doom!

We dubbed him the *"Malach ha-mavoth,"* the Angel of Death.

In the months to come he would fully earn his nickname. He silently strolled through the camp with his killer-dog Prince, a German shepherd trained to go for the jugular when a prisoner was late in taking his cap off, or to rip the testicles from the prisoner walking by with his hands in his pockets.

Executions became numerous for any minor infraction, or when there was word of German misfortune at the Russian front.

On two occasions, though, *Hauptscharfuhrer* Schwammberger traded life for material ransom.

The horses which drew his carriage on the leisurely Sunday drives into the country with his family, were a perfectly matched pair of white thoroughbreds. Someone left the gate of the stable open one night. One of the horses walked out, and in its attempt to leave the camp it stepped on a recently installed electrified wire and was killed. We were given forty-eight hours to produce an identical match or sacrifice at least 50 people.

Through frantic efforts and through contacts with the underground we located on some Polish farm a close match of the horse that was killed. The owner was willing to part with it for a high sum, paid in gold and paper American dollars. With an effort of forceful persuasion the camp's Jewish authorities convinced some inmates to part with their hidden treasures to satisfy the demands of *Hauptscharfuhrer* Schwammberger. They managed to obtain the necessary payment before the deadline and to save the threatened lives.

The second occasions came in the spring or early summer of 1944, when *Hauptscharfuhrer* Schwammberger informed the camp's Jewish authorities that a tattooing of the inmates was going to take place. The letters KL, until now painted on our jackets (striped uniforms were not issued to us yet), would be tattooed on our foreheads. If we supplied a substantial ransom—entire prize worthy possessions the inmates were still hiding (and he warned that he had accurate information from the in-camp informers and favor seekers)—the tattoo would be done on the wrist. He also threatened to order inspections and body searches if he was not satisfied with the results from gathering the ransom.

Again a forceful appeal for all that was of any value was conducted by the camp *Ordnungsdienst*, the Jewish camp police. If any of them were not hated by then, they surely invited the wrath of the prisoners now. This was the time when inmates had to part with their last safety nets, treasures that might prove to be the last chance to save them in an emergency. Now they had to part with the diamonds which some had hidden in the crevices of their bodies; with their American currency in gold or paper; with family heirlooms deeply hidden in every nook and cranny of the camp with considerable ingenuity.

They turned in more than expected, because the Jewish camp police had bluffed that they knew of what everyone had hidden, and they threatened that if every item was not produced, the culprits would be turned over to the "Angel of Death." But of course when the diamonds, gold jewelry, and American and British currency was turned over to Schwammberger, his response was that it was not enough.

"Where is the gold from their teeth?" he screamed. "Unless you produce it promptly, I will get it from their dead bodies!"

Mr. Kleinman, the camp dentist, got very busy. His brother, a dim-witted camp policeman, came to me and threatened, "Nolek, I know that you have a gold piece hidden in your jacket, you have to hand it over."

And so I came to part with what was my last, precious, tangible link to my mother's love and her ultimate sacrifice for me.

In March of 1980 my father of blessed memory lay dying in a small hospital in New Jersey. During his stay in the hospital I would drive early every morning to Irvington, New Jersey, go straight to his side, stay a few hours, then go to work and then again leave in the afternoon to stay with him until late at night.

My father was suffering from heart failure. He would occasionally drift into unconsciousness and then again be lucid for a period of time. One morning when I walked into his hospital room I found him tied to the bed, lying in a spread-eagle position. Shocked and furious, I ran to ask the resident physician why this had been done. He told me that my father had sat up in his bed at night, became incoherent and hallucinated in what sounded like Hebrew and German. It was for his safety that they tied him up.

I untied my father, sponged him off and gently tried to soothe him, for he still seemed to be terribly agitated. He finally calmed down and drew me to his face to feebly kiss me. I asked him then, What happened? He was silent for a moment, a faraway look in his sunken eyes, and slowly he told me in Yiddish: "Der Maloch ha-moveth is do gevein," "The angel of death was here."

Understanding that he meant the angel of death in its popular sense, I tried to reassure him, and told him that he had many happy years ahead of him. I even gently scolded him for his thoughts.

He impatiently shook his head. "Nein, nein, my kind, Der SS maloch hamoveth is do gevehn, er is gestanen do in die Tiehr," "The SS angel of death was here, he stood in the doorway." "Mit sein revolver," he added, "With his gun."

NORBERT FRIEDMAN

It finally dawned on me: "Weim meinst die, die meinst Schwammberger?" "Whom do you mean, you mean Schwammberger?"

"Yo, yo mein kind," he nodded. "Er is du gevehn . . . zei vellen ins keinmul nish nuchlosen." "Yes, yes my child, he was here, they will never let go of us." And then he went off into unconsciousness again.

My father died two days later. I will never know if he took the horror of his past to his grave with him. But I know that I shall always live with the memory of the terror in his eyes.

CHAPTER XXIII

In the spring and summer of 1944 the fortunes of war were turning badly against Germany, but even then the fate of their prisoners dominated their agenda. We were hearing reports that ghettos and camps were being liquidated.

Through the grapevine we heard about the atrocities that were taking place in Plaszow, the escapades of the Commandant Goetz and other incidents. We knew about Auschwitz and believed that the soap rations we received were made from human fat.

So the apathetic, the callous and cynical, the numbed and hopeless dealt with it through gallows humor: *"Jak sie twoja babcia mydli?"* they would ask, when using the soap. "How does your grandma lather?"

Or they would react to the incident in Plaszow, where Camp Commandant Goetz killed someone for smuggling in a chicken: *"Hob moch azoy gebeten, koif nish dos Hindle!"* "I begged you so, do not buy that chicken!" This became the standard sarcastic plea whenever someone committed a costly, deadly mistake.

Laughter was not uncommon, but the jokes were sad and fatalistic. Still, they were a sign that we were not willing to accept the inevitable, and were trying with all our resources—physical, intellectual and spiritual—to maintain our hope and the vestiges of humanity. It was getting tougher all the time to hang on to our moral uprightness.

The supervisory personnel who ran the camp changed often. A new SS officer by the name of Landsdorfer took over as commandant. From his previous post he brought to the camp several members of his own camp police, mostly German Jews. They were very strict men and not very accessible.

We were getting news about the military situation from our Polish contacts and were wondering what the SS would do when the Russian army got closer. A group of young people even dug a tunnel under the surrounding wall, to be used for escape in case the Germans decided eventually to exterminate the camp.

On the night of July 22nd, 1944, a long train of railroad cars moved onto the railroad siding. The next day we were ordered to prepare for evacuation of the camp. On July 24th, nearly three thousand inmates of the Mielec Concentration Camp boarded the cars to be moved.

Of course we did not know why. We heard rumors that the Russian partisans were already in the neighboring forest. The group that dug the tunnel decided not to use it, however. They felt that it would be wrong to risk certain retribution by the SS and to endanger the lives of hundreds of fellow inmates. Later on, in retrospect, they regretted their decision, for they felt that in the confusion of liquidating of the camp they could have slipped away unnoticed and would not have been missed. I discussed it later after the war with the leader of the group who felt responsible for his mistake. Most of the group of the twenty conspirators eventually perished anyway.

So now I was about to leave Mielec where for over two years I had managed to avoid the terrible fate that had eliminated most of Polish Jewry. Despite all the butchery and misery, despite the hunger, lice and typhoid, Mielec had been a place where the chances of survival were better than outside the camp or in other camps. (In the course of its two-year existence, over a thousand prisoners had perished in the Mielec camp: some from the typhoid epidemic some murdered by the Gestapo or the SS.) The routine and protection of holding a job vital to the German defense effort offered some relative, albeit conditional, security. It was a place where, for reasons I have tried to describe, I enjoyed an advantage over most of my fellow inmates. But now it was on to some new place where I did not know what to expect. I would encounter a series of these moves, every one of them a new and frightening experience with its own particular dangers.

Wieliczka, the first new camp for me, where we arrived after several hours of traveling, was an adjunct to the Plaszow facility. Most of the inmates from Mielec had to work in the salt mines next to the facility.

This time the camp was run by the leadership of the POWs from the Budzyn camp, part of the group who had wanted to run Mielec. Sure enough, except for the women, who were placed in the women's facility, our transport was allocated the worst barracks, at the outer perimeter of the camp. The sanitary conditions, the barracks, and the road leading to them were the poorest in the camp; the farthest removed from the center and the distribution points for food. The group of ex-POWs got accommodations close to the center of the camp. They made it clear to us that they would get even for the lack of preference shown to them in Mielec.

The head of the camp police was a Mr. Stockman, an officer in the Polish army, the same man who was in charge in Budzyn. He seemed to look out for his POWs, who held all the controlling positions in the camp administration. His brother-in-law, Mr. Szczypiacki, was the next in command. It was clear that cronyism and nepotism were the norms for running a camp wherever we went.

It was difficult for me to adjust to the fact that I would not enjoy any of the advantages, small though they were that I had in Mielec. On the contrary, I would be the target of resentment because of my relatives and their positions. I quickly saw the first evidence of this. Upon our arrival we were ordered to turn in our leather boots in exchange for wooden clogs. It was clear that the order was aimed at those who enjoyed some distinction in Mielec, like the O.D. men, foremen and block elders, for they and very few others owned high leather boots.

I decided to cut down mine to the height of a regular shoe and disguise it by smearing it with mud. It worked for some but not for me. Someone, for whatever reason, reported me to the camp elder. I was called to the center of the camp, ordered to drop my pants and lie over a chair. An inmate from Mielec, an ex-POW who was now an O.D., held my head down while the brother-in-law of the camp elder, Mr. Szczypiacki, administered the flogging with a rubber truncheon, making me count the lashes aloud.

"Who do you think you are? This is not Mielec, here you do what we tell you to," he yelled at me. After twenty-five strikes he let me get up, applying a boot to my derriere, adding the pain of insult to my injury. I dragged myself to the barracks, whimpering from ache, discomfort, and shame, and for the forecast of things to come.

Here is a typical incident of random cruelty. The latrines were steel drums set outside the barracks. One night a friend of mine, one Moniek Pinkas— "*Lonczyker,*" as we called him, for he came from the hamlet of Lonczyk— went outside to use the makeshift sanitary facility. We heard a gunshot and a scream, and as we peeked out the window we saw Moniek writhing in pain and calling out for help. None of us moved until my father ran out, slung Moniek over his shoulder and brought him in. The guard from the watchtower who shot Moniek—apparently for his own amusement—fired one more shot somewhere and then it was quiet. We bandaged Moniek's hip the best we could and decided not to report the incident unless his condition got worse. We felt that his best chance for survival would be to report him sick and keep him in the barrack.

The wound eventualy healed, Moniek lived with the bullet in his hip and survived the war. He had the bullet removed, while in the United States. He died in the nineties from unrelated causes.

. . . A few weeks later, most of the inmates from Mielec were assembled for a transport to another unknown destination. Anxiety and uncertainty prevailed in the gathered crowd. We were marched to the railroad siding where closed cattle cars awaited us.

In the course of a life of constant danger, one develops an uncanny sense of being able to assess other people's trustworthiness and foresee to a degree their behavior under stress. When new and unpredictable circumstances presented themselves, one tried to surround himself with dependable people. The cattle cars, into which we were being loaded, helped along by a torrent of shouts and blows, held 120 men each. Our car carried some of the unstable element, but it also contained some of my trusted friends, some intellectuals and, most importantly, Reb Mayer.

Reb Mayer Katz came to our camp in the summer of 1942 from the village of Pszeslow. Though he was small in size, an aura of sweet, quiet strength radiated from him. His gestures were deliberate, his manner of speech, soft and reassuring. It did not take long for the other inmates to take note of him. He would, in the face of the most depressing events, offer hope and moral support; he would quote from the Talmud, mostly from the psalmists, lending strength to others. He could often be seen in silent, solitary prayer: a vulnerable silhouette in the shadows of darkened barracks, a lonely testimony of man's faith in God against the background of Satan's landscape.

Somehow he was able to get a job working in the fields from where he would smuggle in, at the risk of being shot, vegetables or fruit for the sick. Even when a typhoid epidemic swept through the camp he would walk among the dying, unafraid of infection, reciting with the patients the *vidui*, the confessional. He was able to bring news from the outside world to us, always promising the defeat of our tormentors and the eventual arrival of redemption.

The wagons were shut up tight, and we tried to assess our new habitat. There was hardly any room to move around, so we expected a short journey.

SUN RAYS AT MIDNIGHT

It was not to be, however; and we couldn't even determine the direction in which we were traveling. When night fell we were already exhausted from standing in the heat. Everyone tried to find a place to lay down but there was no room for 120 people to do so. The tired men were irritable and fights were breaking out. Someone suggested sitting down between each other's legs, and in this way we settled as best we could for the night. There were no sanitary facilities, so with our fingers and spoons (knives were forbidden) we had to tear a hole in the floor.

Next morning we expected to stop and to be fed, or at least to be given some water. The train slowed down several times for the convenience of the SS guards, but there was no relief for the prisoners. The heat of the August sun started to take its toll. Men were fainting and cries for water punctuated the air—what air there was.

The cattle cars had four small, steel-barred windows, one in each corner, hardly enough to provide ventilation. Desperate men were licking the salty condensation from the walls. At our end of the car we designed a system of rotation, so that each one could at least for a brief period of time stand by the window to revive himself.

The second night was chaotic. Hopeless, despondent men directed their frustration at each other. Two men took poison and their corpses were propped against the wall so as to take up less space. The third day of our voyage took us through German countryside where we could see people working in the fields, but no one paid heed to our anguished cries. The thirst and stench, the heat and lack of air were becoming unbearable. Our lips were parched and our spirits totally deflated.

That afternoon the train stopped at the railroad station of a larger town. Wermacht and SS troops were patrolling the station, and we also saw some army nurses. Feverish pleas of "*Wasser, Wasser,*" "Water, water," could be heard from all 24 cattle cars. Fate so willed that at our end of the car it was Reb Mayer Katz's turn to stand at the window, facing the station. Miraculously, one of the nurses heeded Reb Mayer's plea and handed him a bottle of water. The men in the wagon all surged toward Reb Mayer. Before he could drink from the bottle to quench his torturous thirst, he turned slowly toward the inside of the cattle car, considering the unruly mob for a moment while still holding the bottle outside the window. Then, without bringing the bottle close to his own face, he moved it to the mouth of the man next to him, and in his caring voice implored him: "*Drink, drink mein Kind, nor a klein bissel.*" "Take only a little sip, my child." And then he went on to the next person, and so on. As if

NORBERT FRIEDMAN

mesmerized, the men stopped pushing. Those close by obediently took one swallow or two. Even when the bottle was empty it was still being passed around.

Human dignity and sanity slowly returned, as if by a miracle. There were no complaints, only weeping and sobbing. We hung our heads in shame for our animalism and also in quiet tribute to Reb Mayer's personal restraint and sacrifice.

We arrived at the *Konzentration Lager, Flossenburg* 24 hours later. The four days and three nights on the train seemed like a lifetime, a descent into Dantean depths, ending in a victorious ascend back into Man's dignity. All of our victory was the result of Reb Mayer's limitless love of his God, expressed by his caring for his fellow men.

Was Reb Mayer Katz *Ha'kohain*, one of the *Lamed vov tzadikim?* One of the thirty-six legendary saintly men whose righteous deeds sustain the universe?

His blessed soul was extinguished in the winter of 1944 in the Flossenburg camp. But the memory of him, of his faith and his piety, served me as a beacon of hope in a then hopeless world and saw me through the abyss of despair. "God's rays of sunlight"—he showed me—"shining through the midnight of mankind."

CHAPTER XXIV

The doors of the cattle car were opened and we were ordered out. The sign at the station said Flossenburg. It took a while for our numbed limbs to return to life. The flow of blood returning to our legs caused piercing pain while the sharp mountain air hurt our lungs. We were made to march in the direction of the new camp in columns of five.

Prisoners in striped camp uniforms were working along the sides of the road. We cautiously tried to find out about the conditions of the place that we were being marched to.

"It's not to bad, you will be all right," was the standard answer. We were encouraged. The prisoners we saw looked well fed, their uniforms looked clean, and we saw no beatings and heard no yelling. Some of the prisoners were landscaping the banks of the road leading to the Flossenburg camp with flowers and shrubs.

When we entered the camp, however, the picture changed. We were greeted by the camp authorities in stern and threatening tones, told the rules and herded into our barracks. There we were ordered to strip naked and turn in our clothing, keeping only our clogs and leather belts. We were issued a tin plate and a spoon. Frantically we tried to find hiding places for whatever we still owned that was worth hiding. We were assigned to our bunks, four or five to each bed. The only way we could manage that many was to lie crossways on the straw sack.

In the morning we were chased outside to find frost on the ground. We huddled together, leaning against the naked bodies of strangers just to keep warm. We stamped our feet and considered our new surroundings. The detail that brought in the black brew masquerading as coffee informed us that we were in the quarantine barracks, and that this was only a temporary phase until we were processed.

By the fourth day, our nakedness had reduced our senses to a cattle-like numbness. We had lost our self-esteem, always rushed in a group to seize our meager food ration—soup, a slice of bread and some hot liquid per day—and from having to run together like a herd of cattle from one spot in the yard to another.

We were lined up to have our hair, all of it, shorn or rather ripped out of our flesh with dull barber-clippers; the shearing of the pubic areas was especially painful. To make matters worst they slapped burning disinfectant on our bleeding skin. Then we were herded into a shower.

The hollow echoes of shouts and screams bouncing off the cement walls almost started a panic as it evoked the images and fears of what we already knew about the gassing facilities in other camps. After moments of terror the showerheads finally opened, and to our enormous relief it was hot water that rained down. The mood changed instantaneously. We were alive, and there was another day to be endured. "I told you they need us," said some of the optimists.

On our exit from the shower we were given freshly laundered shirts and for the first time the striped concentration camp uniform. That despised uniform was not the only radical departure from our existence in the camps in Poland. For the first time since our incarceration we were thrown in with other nationalities—people of other cultures, some of them historically hostile to the Jews. Until now, Jewish personnel internally administered the ghettos and the camps we knew. Even though we had suffered at their hands, and even though the pain was so much more difficult to accept because they were Jews, there were still avenues of appeal to their mercy; there was still hope for Jewish empathy and at least the opportunity to address them in Yiddish.

Now the in-camp leadership was in the hands of strangers, and most of them Germans, either red or green *Winkles*, so-called because of the red or green triangles worn over the breast of their K-Zet uniforms. Red stood for the political inmates, green for the criminal. Those grizzly veterans of life in concentration camps—some of the green *Winkles* were men with criminal records for murder; some were sex deviates, some just plain pathological killers—derived pleasure from inflicting pain and terror on others. They were now the extension of our German masters of life and death.

"We expect you to maintain order and cleanliness. If you fall out of line, we have ways to make you wish that you were dead." These were the words of the German Capos, and we knew that they meant every one of them.

And then came a startling statement: "Keep clean. If you should find a louse or another insect on your shirt, we will issue you a new one right away." Perplexed by this new emphasis on cleanliness, we picked up our clogs and our belts and marched to the barracks.

We were happy to finally have clothing on our backs, but in the process of gaining the striped suits, we had lost our identity. Numbers were issued to us and sewn on our chest, and underneath the number a red-and-yellow Star of David. We were no longer individual human beings with a name. *"Heftling Nummer so und so.""*"Prisoner number so and so." And each of us marked a Jew.

Other inmates were identified for their infractions; we were branded for who we were, Jews.

We settled into an aimless existence, milling around the quarantine area discussing our situation and digesting rumors. Occasionally we would be assigned some in-camp chores. Several men were picked for some maintenance work and came back to the barracks with information about the Flossenburg camp. It reportedly held twenty thousand prisoners, among them the Austrian government leaders from before the *Anschluss*. The barrack on the hill above us housed some women who were there to sexually serve the ranking prisoners, the camp elders, the block elders and the Capos when they distinguished themselves by acts of cruelty. And, for the first time, there were some crematoria on the premises.

The meager food ration and the occasional cruelty of the Capos in this camp caused some people to wish for transfer. Their wish was soon to be granted. One day, several weeks after we had arrived, our transport was assembled and the inmates were given a physical inspection.

This inspection consisted of a visual appraisal and an occasional squeeze of the top of the shoulder next to the collarbone—seemingly to determine the amount of flesh still attached to it. Then the prisoner was marked with a chemical pencil on the forehead, a combination of two numbers separated by a slash: 3/4, 2/3 and so on.

If by now we still were not sufficiently degraded, dehumanized and robbed of the last vestiges of individuality, this act of defacement reduced us still further, to the status of cattle in a herd. We had no idea what the figures meant, but we guessed that they had to do with how we would be separated.

The next day, after the roll call, the division according to the marks took place. A number of people were set aside to remain in Flossenburg, the rest was segregated into two groups. Uncle Henry, my father and I were in one group; Uncle Sol, my father's younger brother, was in the other. Uncle Sol desperately tried to get my father's attention, and his body language betrayed his anguish, begging for rescue.

Nearly three thousand of us inmates were assembled in columns on three sides of the Appel-Platz. In the center stood the dreaded SS colonel, the head of the camp, with his no less feared corps of adjutants overseeing the proceedings. Suddenly my father broke the ranks, shoving away my hand as I tried to stop him. He marched straight to the center of the square and, smartly clicking his wooden heels addressed the colonel.

The prisoners froze as we waited for the colonel to pull out his pistol and do what the SS usually did in such situation: shoot the Jew. Instead the colonel turned his back on my father, who in his best German was reporting; that he was an ex-noncommissioned officer in the Austrian army during World War I who had been working for the last two years in the defense plant in Mielec and who was now being separated from his brother. The colonel heard him out and then, amazingly, he barked to one of his aides: *"Las dem Juden sein Bruder haben!"* "Let the Jew have his brother!"

The hush became even quieter still. We all watched in amazement as Uncle Sol was added to our group. My father's five-foot-two figure grew larger before our very eyes.

Our group of about 900 was loaded into cattle cars and we traveled southwest toward Czechoslovakia. The other group, we later found out, went to the infamous camp Mathausen where less than five percent of them survived. The luckiest of the lot were those kept in Flossenburg. Most of them stayed there until the last days before liberation.

I do not remember how we arrived at the next destination. *Leitmeritz*, or *Litomerice* in Czech, was a cluster of barracks on a muddy plot of land. We were taken to our quarters, which must have been a barn or a warehouse before. As we were climbing to the second floor and preparing to find bunks on which to bed down, suddenly a mob of prisoners ascended with all kinds of implements in their hands, shouting and distributing blows on the unsuspecting new arrivals. We had no idea what was happening till we were able to distinguish the "battle cry" of the Polish rabble: *"Bij Zyda, bij Zyda,"* "Kill the Jew, Kill the Jew!" Blows from two-by-fours, ax handles and the wooden boards of bunk beds reigned upon the tired, hungry, bewildered group of prisoners.

Suddenly it dawned on us: We were experiencing a *Pogrom*, here in the common hell of a concentration camp. The Polish prisoners were venting their pathological anti-Semitism on the first Jews who dared to be brought into their camp. As if we had any choice in the matter! We were being bloodied before we were able to recover our senses and offer any resistance.

Someone ran out to get help. Finally the SS guards arrived with bayonets fixed on their carbines, ready to squelch the riot. "What happened here?" the officer in charge wanted to know. We told him what we knew. He shook his head in disbelief and shouted to the few Polish inmates still trapped on our floor: "We are the ones who do the killing here, and you do the work! Understand? And now get out and stay out, if one of the Jews gets hurt I will hang the lot of you!"

Again we tried to find bunks close to each other, this time as much for protection as for comfort. Some of my friends, who felt that it might be advantageous to stay close to the Friedmans, found beds close by.

Suddenly an animal-like cry rose over the din of the commotion. My father immediately recognized its source and ran in the direction that it came from. It was the mute, the *Styme*. He brought the mute with him and found a bed for him next to us. Then he went back to retrieve the blanket that someone wrestled from the *Styme*.

The *Styme* came to the camp in Mielec in 1942 with one of the transports from a small town. He was a young man in his early twenties, well built physically and neatly dressed. It was noted right away as he was being unloaded from the truck that he had difficulties communicating and that he did not hear the orders. My father realized that he was deaf, grabbed him away from the rest and put him to work in the kitchen.

Despite the fact that neither my father nor the mute knew conventional sign language, they were able to communicate. The *Styme* claimed that he was a very good tailor who had worked for elegant ladies and gentlemen in his town. So my father was able to place him in the little tailor shop on the camp premises. The mute was true to his word; he was a very good tailor.

Soon the Gestapo, the SS and the Werkschutz, who came to the camp tailor shop to have their uniforms made and fixed, insisted that the mute do the work. He acquired a sort of prominence and he basked in it like a peacock. The Germans showered food and favors on him and he felt content. Often my father had to be called in to be the interpreter between the mute and the Germans. They shared a unique ability to understand each other's mimicry, a particular trait amongst those less educated who had to find ways to complement the poverty of their language by descriptive hand gesturing.

Only once did the mute face danger in Mielec. Herring and Drozd invaded the camp on one of their drunken binges and Herring vented his anger at the tailors in the shop for not pressing his uniform properly. He shot two of them, one of whom was the father of my good friend Ignatz Brand. [But they spared the mute.] So now in these new surroundings of the Leitmeritz camp, my father continued to have the responsibility of taking care of the mute.

NORBERT FRIEDMAN

Fortunately for the *Stymer* there was a tailor shop in the camp and he found a refuge there.

Most of the prisoners in Leitmeritz worked digging tunnels. After the war, we heard rumors that it was uranium-rich ore used to produce heavy water in preparation for a nuclear device to be built by the Nazis. Only lately I had found out that we were building underground facilities for factories for the Auto Union AG Co. the Osram GmbH company and the Philips Company. The work conditions were hard and the walk to the tunnels a long slog. We had to march through parts of the Czech town in groups of two to three hundred, watched by the SS guards. Occasionally a Czech man or woman would surreptitiously sneak a small parcel with food or fruit to the passing inmates, risking their own safety. Sometimes they would place a brown bag containing a sandwich in the gutter by the road.

Those rare acts of caring and compassion were the talk of the camp long after they took place. Their nutritional value was dwarfed by their inspirational impact. The chances of anyone becoming a beneficiary of those acts of human kindness were minimal, but their uplifting effect for the entire group was enormous. We fed each other with the stories of those encounters so that they became part of the camp's myth and an almost spiritual source of comfort, courage and hope.

In Leitmeritz I was hit by a mysterious illness. I would get a high fever in the evening and shiver uncontrollably. By morning the fever would be gone, but I would feel weak and exhausted. A prisoner paramedic diagnosed it as malaria and put me in the sick bay for the night.

Next day a German non-commissioned officer inspected the dispensary and a deadly silence fell over the place. The orderlies were ashen with fear as he walked through the beds asking questions about the patients. When he left, a definite sigh of relief could be heard through the room.

"Who was it?" was my question.

"He is crazy," one orderly told me. "They say that he studied medicine and the war interrupted his studies. He now conducts medical experiments on patients. Sometimes he injects air or water into their veins to see how long they live after a certain dose. We were lucky today."

I told the story to my father, who came to visit me that evening, and said that I wanted to go to work next morning no matter what. In the morning, even though my friends had to support me during roll call, I reported to my work detail.

A few days later at work, a lorry ran over my friend Milek Salpeter's foot and crushed three of his toes. He was put in the dispensary and I worried myself sick over him. A week later our transport was told that we were being moved to another camp. We were issued a bowl of soup and a slice of bread. I grabbed my soup, ran to the dispensary and gave it to Milek. I was sure I would never see him again. I did not know that the next day the sick bay would be transferred back to Flossenburg where our mutual friend Ignatz Brand would take care of him.

It was also time to say good-by to the *Stymer*. It was best for him to stay in his newly found haven.

In 1980, at the funeral of my father, the eulogy delivered by his Rabbi revolved around the story of the deaf mute. The mute had come to the United States in 1978 to visit my father when he described his relationship with my father to the Rabbi. It seems that the mute was eventually transferred back to Flossenburg. He worked there until the camp was evacuated before the allied forces arrived. He was liberated in a different part of Germany than my father and I. Through the grapevine he found out where we were, and shortly after the war ended, he showed up to be with my father and to benefit from his protection.

In 1948, during the Israeli war of independence, my father volunteered to join the armed forces of the new country. He was then fifty years old, but declared his age to be ten years less than it was, and he got as far as Marseilles. There someone who knew him tipped off the Jewish authorities and they rejected my father as to old to fight. He went back to Paris where he eventually settled down and remarried. When the mute heard about it, he also went to Paris and my father got him a job there in a tailor shop. My father then found for him a suitable girl, also a mute, from a fine, well-to-do family. They were married, and the mute opened a large tailor shop and became prosperous in his own right. So he arranged for a visit to America to share his happiness with my father, who had come to the United States in 1956. He openly told everyone who would listen— or rather who would watch his gesturing, for he never mastered conventional sign language—that he owed his good fortune and his life to my father.

CHAPTER XXV

This time we were loaded onto open cattle cars, about 80 to 90 inmates per car, with two SS guards in every car. As usual we did not know our destination and neither did the SS guards at least they would not divulge it. Naturally the proximity we experienced allowed a certain intimacy to develop, even between such opposites as the SS and their imprisoned charges. The SS guard on our side of the car was a young man of about twenty. He would not engage in a conversation with us, but could not help but hear all the accounts of our misery that we tried to share with him. He must have become affected by our condition, for he seemed very uncomfortable whenever he was consuming his meager food rations in the midst of this starving and what must have seemed like a faceless and formless mass of striped shapes.

At night he laid down wearily in the center of our half of the car. By the second day he would eat only when the train stopped. He would get off, instructing the other guard to watch his prisoners. Once when he returned he brought back several heads of cabbage, which he had taken off a freight car on an another train. We all decided that he was a decent sort and profusely thanked him for his kindness. That night he again cleared some space around him and went to sleep.

In the morning when he got up and examined his backpack, he was startled to discover that the piece of bread he kept there was gone.

"Who is the *Schweinhund* that stole my bread?" he screamed, obviously shaken and disappointed by the lack of gratitude on the part of those whom he had tried to show kindliness.

We all silently examined each other; who could be the culprit? Who would dare to steal from the German? We were all desperate but we all still valued our lives, and we also appreciated merciful benevolence. I knew who the culprit was, but I said nothing. During the night I heard someone trying to muffle the sound of chewing, and I saw a residue of breadcrumbs next to Zoltan Rosner. I also knew the reckless nature of Zoltan's drive to survive at all cost.

Before we left Wieliczka, my father gave me for safekeeping the diamond stone from his engagement pinkie ring. It was concealed in a boiled potato with the skin intact. On our voyage from Wieliczka to Flossenburg the potato disappeared. I knew that it was Zoltan who took it. In Flossenburg he once approached me sheepishly and guiltily offered me half a ration of bread that he claimed to have gotten from somebody. Several times I saw him receiving portions of bread or an extra helping of soup from one of the Capos.

After the war I visited Zoltan in the Feldafing Displaced Persons camp. He had lost his wife of one year after childbirth. His sister was taking care of the infant and he was somewhat depressed.

On my visit he tried to impress me with his newly acquired wealth, obtained through dealings on the black market. We shared memories, drank schnapps and confided to each other our plans for the future. Before my departure Zoltan produced a beautiful one-carat diamond stone. Before putting the box with it into my hand, he asked me:

"Do you know what this is for?"

"Yes," I replied, "that is for the stone in the potato that you stole from me."

He looked shocked. "You knew all the time and you never said a word? Why?"

"You were my friend, and you were always so uncontrollably hungry," was my reply.

When in America, after my first son was born, Zoltan came to visit and brought a beautiful silver Kiddush cup for my son Gary. "This is for when you take him under the wedding canopy. You were always my most trustworthy friend," he conceded. "And here is something else."

Zoltan then produced a photograph of me, taken in Zawichost in the company of my four Polish friends who were involved with Michal Kraviec. On the back it was dedicated to his sister. I had sent this photograph to his sister when she was hiding out on Aryan papers through Mr. Jankowski while still in Mielec. The note read: "To my unknown yet so dear a friend." It is now the only photograph of myself taken during the war.

I used the Kiddush cup at my oldest son Gary's wedding, bringing many sad and curious memories to that happy occasion.

"ARBEIT MACHT FREI." "Work makes you free" The large sign on the gate to Dachau welcomed our group. It was the end of October 1944. We had walked all the way from the Allach rail station where we had been unloaded. We were cold and had not eaten for three days, except for the few leaves of

NORBERT FRIEDMAN

cabbage that the inmates in our car were fortunate to get through the mercy of our SS guard.

We were led to the tremendous *Appel Platz* and lined up. In the center stood several closed kettles of food; our starved senses could smell the boiled cabbage and the steam from boiled potatoes. Just as the Capos, most of them red *Winkles,* started to dish out the food—a few leaves of boiled cabbage and few boiled potatoes in jackets per starved inmate—the sirens started to wail.

"Air raid . . . air raid . . . quick into the trenches!" The lids were put back on the kettles, and the whole transport was chased into air-raid bunkers on the perimeter of the square. We were prodded by the truncheons of the camp Capos as we ran, longingly glancing back at the undistributed food. We sat in the ditches dug for just such occasions as this: to protect the prisoners from the never falling bombs. And now it was we who waited and prayed for the aircraft to come and bomb us: "Please take this place out, take us if you need to, but somebody please punish our tormentors."

Suddenly some inmates, who could not control their hunger in the presence of the food intended for them, broke from the trenches and ran toward the kettles. They never reached them, of course; the SS guards opened fire from the watchtowers, dotting the camp yard with the limp figures of the dead and wounded.

The aircraft arrived shortly, and as they were passing over us we threw our arms in the air and shouted: "Bomb, please bomb us! Us and this whole hellish incinerator of a senseless world!" The planes dropped their bombs about two miles from us, on a nearby industrial complex. It only increased our sense of having been totally abandoned by the world outside. "No one cares, no one gives a damn what is happening to us; we are forgotten and forsaken; woe is us!"

After the all-clear sound we were returned to the square. The dead were removed and we again lined up to receive what now was cold and bitter-tasting food. The irony of the incident was not lost on us; they chase us to the trenches to save our hide, so that they can be the ones to dispense death.

We were again quartered in quarantine barracks without any specific tasks. In the aimless days ahead we wandered about and discussed what the Germans might have in store for us. "Why are they moving us around so much? What are we doing here?" The camp was run mostly by political prisoners who had been here for years. They were uncommunicative and self-absorbed, paying little attention to us. We didn't realize that through the years the old prisoners had seen scores of transports like ours come and go, and that for them it would cause only pain to become friendly with any of us.

It was the beginning of November when we were notified to get ready for *Entlausung*, de-lousing, and a change of uniforms. At that time I had been an inmate of various camps for almost two and a half years. In the five years since the start of the war I had turned from an upright, innocent youngster into a cynical, rather hardened camp-wise veteran. I had been able to insulate my psyche with a protective shell from the things that I witnessed or had to participate in. I developed the prerequisites for survival: ignoring my physical condition, mastering pain and hunger. For self-protection I would escape into my world of yesterday by daydreaming of my home, its warmth and shelter.

Ever since arriving in Germany we had been searched and stripped of all private belongings. Our possessions consisted of the pajama-striped uniforms on our backs, a shirt underneath, wooden sandals with rubber uppers (that cut mercilessly into our insteps), and a ridiculous striped hat. On our rumps dangled a metal dish and in our pocket a metal spoon with one side of its handle thinned out by the inmates to serve as a cutting instrument. Everything else had to be turned in, or concealed; upon discovery it would be subject to confiscation.

The only treasures I had managed to save and conceal were wrapped in a piece of a rag: two items that served as my cherished link to civilized life, to normalcy and love. They were the picture of my mother and a tooth brush.

The one brought me visions of my home life, sweet memories of holidays and Shabbat evenings, the gentle embraces and the enveloping warmth of my mother's arms. And at times when it was difficult to remember her lovely face, it brought back her likeness to me.

The other item, my toothbrush; was the last vestige, the last tangible symbol of civilized life, of the normalcy of mundane rituals. In strictly practical terms, it served a limited purpose. But the act of brushing one's teeth daily, even with cold water, without any toothpaste or powder, against painfully bleeding and ulcerated gums and caverns of teeth that had been knocked out by the butts of German guns . . . even that simple ritual of brushing gave me the illusion of being a whole person, a human being.

For the *Entlausung*, and to receive new serial numbers, we were instructed to line up. The old-timers in the camp suggested entrusting them with any valuables that we might have on us, warning us about the severity of the searches. Those who trusted them never saw their possessions again. I went behind one of the barracks of the sick bay, and pretending to be performing some cleaning function; I hid my package under the barrack, making very carefully sure that no one saw me. After the showers and registration for new numbers (mine was 118250), I went to the place were I hid my treasured possessions to retrieve them. I put my hand under the barrack looking for the package; to my horror and dismay, it was gone. Feverishly I dug my fingers into the ground like a mad animal, scraping the hard earth, to no avail. Someone must have seen me putting the small parcel there and, expecting valuables removed it. I pounded my fists helplessly against the ground in fury, sobbing silently over my loss.

Afterwards I went into a severe depression. I had lost the means of contact and connection to my past and to being human. And there seemed no point in going on. I lost the will to live and to struggle; I wanted to end my life on the electrified barbed wire that surrounded Dachau. Only my father's efforts kept me from ending my misery.

Shortly after that we were assembled and put on a transport. Much of what would take place after my experience in Dachau would be lost to memory. The subsequent journeys to other camps are vaguely remembered and difficult to distinguish one from another: another train, another cattle car, more shouting, pushing, blows, blood and corpses. Still, there are some incidents that stand out clearly as signature memories of those camps.

I remember the next camp, Augsburg. The frequent air raids, just as we were about to eat our noon meal; The frantic efforts to hide our plate of soup somewhere before we had to run to the air shelters. Maybe I remember that because the soup in Augsburg was thick with noodles, and because most of the time when we rushed to retrieve it, it was gone, seized and devoured by someone else. We even suspected that the thievish inmates were in conspiracy with the SS who operated the air sirens.

I remember Augsburg for the many black-triangle Gypsies who dominated the camp's vital positions. I remember them going out to defuse the unexploded bombs, and the trucks coming back empty, without the defusing detail; their bodies would have been blown to pieces by some allied missile too tricky to defuse.

I remember Augsburg for the transport of Hungarian Jews that arrived there, the first Hungarian Jews we encountered. How we tried to educate them in the ways of camp survival. "Do not try to get into the food line a second time," we pleaded. "The beating that you will get will speed up your demise faster than hunger!" "Do not trade your bread rations for cigarettes, you need your strength; the German domination has lasted five years for us now and it is not going to end soon." We begged them to exercise self-restraint, to little avail. We were losing the Hungarian inmates at an alarming rate, alarming even by concentration camp standards.

I remember Augsburg for the first time that we were bombed directly, while I was working in a Messerschmitt plant. We were trying to get the machinery into a working order the plant had been bombed before.

The most distinct memory from Augsburg is of the attempted escape and the consequent hanging of three Russian POWs. It seems that these three Russians were captured shortly after their attempt. They were put between two rows of electrified barbered wire, and big red-and-white circular targets were sewn onto their uniforms. They were made to stand between the wires for a couple of days, while their case was reportedly being referred to some authorities.

Finally on the third day the whole camp was assembled. Three gallows were erected in the center of the camp's square. The three Russians were made to stand on stools while nooses were wrapped around their necks. An SS officer read the verdict from a document. We could not understand the procedure; either there were new laws concerning the prisoners or they had to die in this official fashion because they were military men.

The officer was about to finish reading when one of the prisoners spoke and the two others shouted: "*Kak zyvie Batushko Stalin, Kak zyvie Matushka Rosyia.*" "Long live Father Stalin, long live Mother Russia. For every one of us, thousands of you German dogs will perish." All together, they kicked the stools from under their feet, denying the Germans the satisfaction of executing them.

A hush fell over the assembled throng and then came a low murmur. Whether we were Russian or not, we were moved and inspired. This was a rare act of defiance, almost a signal for rebellion. The mass of Russians prisoners standing in one column started to sway like a field of wheat in the wind. But the SS reacted quickly. They fired some shots into the air, surrounded the Russian contingent and herded it back to the barracks.

The next camp was Horgau; it had to be near Augsburg for I do not remember having been transported from one to the other. I remember that in Horgau we had to commute to work by train. We had to wait at the station, where it was always wet and cold. The work required some technical knowledge, and an incident that etched itself deeply in my memory was the result of my father's unfamiliarity with some technical terminology. He later told me that while sorting some screws he had put the wrong parts in the wrong bin. As punishment, my father and another prisoner, he for a different infraction, were hung by their wrists lashed behind their backs, their feet dangling just above the ground. As we waited for the train to come and take us back to the camp, we all had to stand and watch their agony together, except that my agony and my helplessness were impossible to bear.

I was tempted to run out from the ranks and lie down under my father's feet to relieve his suffering, but he looked at me and with his eyes begged me not to do anything. He kept moving his head from side to side: No, no, be still. I suffered immensely as I stood there thinking of all the instances that he risked his life for others and me. My frustration and guilt were driving me insane. When the train finally arrived, after what seemed like an eternity of waiting, we were allowed to lower the two men from the poles from which they dangled. My father's shoulders were out of their sockets and he was in intense pain. I was able to place him in a sick bay for a couple days to recover. The head of the sick bay was a young erudite Polish man, Wlacek, very kind and very understanding.

After the war we read that Wlacek became an official in the ministry of education in Poland. In 1956 it was discovered that he was Jewish and we heard that he fled Poland and went to Israel.

CHAPTER XXVI

The vapors shrouding my memory, perhaps caused by my state of depression after the experience in Dachau, must have cleared after a while. My memories of the next camp, Leonberg, stand out rather clearly.

Leonberg was situated near the town of Stuttgart east of the Rhine River. I can see the layout of the camp. The barracks situated in the depression of the camp grounds, the trek uphill to the plant where fighter planes were built. The two tunnels that once were part of an *Autobahn,* a super highway, were closed and now housed the plant where the wings and fuselage of the new Messerschmidt 262 were being assembled. This revolutionary aircraft, we were told, was the first jet-propelled fighting machine of World War II.

We were assigned work details in the plant. I worked in one of the tunnels in the tooling department, while my father worked as a riveter's helper on the tail section of the aircraft in the other tunnel. There were passages from one tunnel to the other, and the tunnels were at least a couple of hundred of yards long.

In the morning when we assembled for the count we could hear the sound of heavy guns when the wind blew from the west. It gave us hope that the war's end and the allies were not far away.

My German *Meister*, my supervisor, appeared to be a decent man. He was proud of his skills, which probably kept him out of the army, and pleased by the fact that I understood the work and was able to be of use to him. The fact that he could delegate some assignments to me and trust that they would be carried out properly was changing his opinion of the Jews. *"Da gibts doch fahige Juden,"* he would say. "After all, there are some capable Jews."

I started a little business with him. Whenever possible I would make small cigarette and jewelry boxes and rings out of aluminum scrap and he would tell me what kind of engraving he wanted on them. A friend of mine, a talented artist would engrave them to order. My Meister probably sold them to the SS, for often he wanted the skull and bones engraved on them. The next most popular design that he asked for was the *Edelweiss*. For our efforts he would bring us some food, which my friend and I shared. Occasionally I would make for my own trade some boxes that the German did not know about. So now I became the breadwinner for my father and, if there was something left over, for my uncles, Henry and Sol.

All this ended one day when my supervisor's family was killed in an air bombing. He directed his anger for the loss against me, cursing the Jews who were the warmongers again and the cause of his misfortune. He chased me around our workstation, hurling tools and scrap metal at me. When he finally caught up with me, he laid me out with one blow of a wooden mallet. The next day he did not talk to me, maybe out of a sense of shame for his outburst or maybe because he was mourning his losses. From that day we never discussed making another cigarette box.

One day a transport from another camp arrived. As the prisoners were being counted we were all herded into one area, standing at attention, hats off. Some people from the transport seemed to be missing, and the checking and counting continued forever. Some distance away amongst the newcomers stood a person resembling someone from my past. Haggard, emaciated, his head shaven, he was unlike anyone I had ever known, yet he still evoked some vague memory. He also kept looking in my direction, a questioning look on his face.

Finally came the order *"Mitzen an!"* "Hats on!" and we ran into each other's arms. With our hats on, we had recognized each other immediately. It was my dearest childhood friend, Oskar Klausenstock, my schoolmate from the fourth grade on, my companion on the long walks to and from school, my comrade from the Zionist organization; my intellectual challenger, my alter ego. We had not seen each other since before the outbreak of war in 1939, back in Bielsko, and now the vagaries of the war had thrown us together again.

"Come on, let's find my dad!" I babbled like a little child that has found a long-lost toy.

"Who else is here with you?"

"Just my two uncles, you do not know them."

From then on we tried to stay together whenever possible, sharing our experiences since we had last seen each other. My father, who was so happy to see Oskar, now tried even harder to scrounge additional food for us. To accomplish this he volunteered to do chores after working hours around the camp's kitchen. Russian POWs ran the kitchen in Leonberg. It was hard to get anything out of them because they supported their own. To their Euro-Asian way of thinking there was little room for anyone else, especially the *Yevrey*, the Jew. Oskar worked in the same tunnel as my dad, and since he was mechanically inclined he would occasionally help my father when he found himself in technical difficulties.

It was a wet and cold winter; we were losing many prisoners to sickness and starvation. The *Musselmen*, the dregs of the camp universe, wandered around the camp looking for scraps of food and begging for drops of soup. People were dying on their feet, sitting in latrines, even standing in the food line. We had become expert at predicting how long one had to live: swollen ankles, three weeks, the swelling gone one more week. Living skeletons followed dying skeletons, who had a better pair of clogs, waiting for them to expire. Lice and other pests became our steady companions, keeping one from sleeping, transforming a person into a perpetual motion scratching machine.

We needed each other more then ever before. Talking to each other about our common past helped to maintain the last residue of a human behavior. Receiving material assistance from others, no matter how meager a spoonful of soup or crumb of bread, instilled hope and created precious bonds. In turn, the occasional ability to rise above one's own desperate needs to share a scrap of food with some other hopeless wretch ennobled the benefactor, made him seem more humane in his own eyes and therefore more worthy in the struggle to survive.

On the bunk across from mine slept a middle-aged Hungarian man, seemingly of a hassidic background. I would spot him praying whenever he could, a father of twin teen-aged sons who tried constantly to instill hope and trust in G-d in them. One night after the bread rations had been distributed, my dad noticed the twins grabbing their father's bread away from him. "You are old, you are not going to make it anyhow," they told him. Their father, as if paralyzed, did not resist; he could only shake his head in sadness, tears streaking down his cheeks. My father, sitting next to me, jumped off the bunk, grabbed the portion of bread from the two boys and returned it to the father. "Such children are no better than wild animals," he yelled at them. "They should be cursed."

I have not seen my father in such rage for a long time. Was it his fear of my ever abandoning him? Or did he feel that his sense of family loyalty—his credo—was under assault?

The Hungarian man gratefully took the bread portion from my father's hand. The tears still streaking down his face, he handed half of it back to his children.

NORBERT FRIEDMAN

The air strikes became more frequent and the sound of the big guns seemed to be getting louder. One day, after an air raid on the town of Stuttgart, a couple of slain horses were brought to the camp and their carcasses used in making the daily soup. The soup was dished out to eager and pushing inmates. In their desperation to survive, they hoped and believed that the nutrients, the faint blood and the scraps of horsemeat in that watery slop, would provide additional days of life.

As my portion of soup was being ladled I noticed a big jawbone in the kettle. I quickly made a deal with the Russian who was dispensing the soup, half a portion of bread for that bone. He agreed a little too eagerly. As I grabbed my soup and the bone, I spotted Oskar ahead of me and we found a secluded space behind the barracks. I had visions of heaps of marrow, life-giving marrow, enough for me, for Oskar, for my father and others. Enough to put on our bread rations to enjoy. As we turned the jawbone back and forth we found that there wasn't any meat left on it. We turned it from side to side; there was no orifice from which to suck the marrow. We decided we had to crack the damn bone to get to it.

A horse jawbone is a hard thing to crack. We started whacking it against a rock, then stopped. What if it cracks and all the marrow spills out? We looked for a rock to crack it with, found one in the stream that ran through the campsite and still could not crack it. Go find my dad, I said to Oskar, he will know how to break it. My Dad showed up shaking his head. "Throw that bone away. You should have known better, there is no marrow in this jaw bone."

Whenever an air alarm sounded while we were in the barracks, even if it was the middle of the night, we had to assemble quickly and march to the tunnels for the duration of the alarm. One nasty, cold and sleeting winter night the alarm sounded. I was not feeling well; I had a temperature and was shivering with fever. I decided to stay in the barrack, hide under the blanket on the upper tier of the bunk. I reasoned that no one would see me or miss me.

The alert lasted a long time. Lying securely under the blanket, I congratulated myself for my decision. When the all clear sounded and the light in the barrack came on, one of the barrack eldest showed up in the company of the most feared SS guard in the camp, known as the *Wurger*, the strangler. He pulled me down from the bunk. Someone had ratted on me.

The *Wurger* had come to the camp in Leonberg with a transport from Auschwitz, where he had established a reputation as a ruthless killer, one who really enjoyed murdering people. It was said that he derived sexual gratification from choking prisoners to death. He was not a big fellow, but how big did you have to be to choke a shrunken and helpless inmate? Around his neck he wore a bandage; some said he had boils on his neck, others that he suffered from some venereal disease. And now that the Wurger had me in his clutches, he did not even bother to use his hands. He pulled a board from under a straw mattress and started to whack me with it. When that board broke into splinters he pulled out another one. I do not know how many he used for I lost track of time and the sense of pain. I was prepared for my life to come to an end. Blood ran from my nose, mouth and ears; my elbows were numb from warding off blows. The beating must have lasted all the time that it took for the men to come back to the barracks, for it stopped when they arrived.

My father found me lying next to the bunk, listless and crying. He pulled me up and laid my head in his lap.

"Let me be," I pleaded. "I have no strength to go on, it is no use."

"Do not say it!" he admonished me. "You must not lose hope, redemption is near." He implored me: "Do you know what it is today? It's the last day of Hanukkah. It's your birthday, look," and he produced from his pocket a little folded paper envelope with fever-reducing medication. "That is for you my son."

And we hugged in a helpless, tearful embrace; silently understanding that we would never ever, abandon each other, till death parted us.

Years later I asked my father how he had known that it was Hanukkah and where he had found that medication. He told me that in the camp even under the worst conditions the faithful tried to keep track of the Jewish calendar, marking its passage and its holidays by whatever means they could. Some kept track by scratching the dates on the bottoms of their tin plates, some on scraps of paper. The Hungarian inmates who had arrived relatively late had been able to keep the dates in their heads. The source of the medication my father would not talk about. But I knew that it must have had cost him at least one portion of his bread ration. It was the most precious and meaningful birthday gift I have ever received.

Some time later came the order to evacuate the camp. It was nighttime, and we were roused from our bunks and told to line up in the dark for food distribution. We could smell the cabbage. We slurped the half-boiled, tepid soup and, following the counsel of my father, I saved my bread ration for later.

NORBERT FRIEDMAN

"You never know how long we will be underway," was his advice. We were led to the main highway and began to march in rows of five. With their usual viciousness the guards made us keep pace and alignment, sicked the dogs on us and banged us with the rifle butts.

We had been marching for about two hours when I felt a familiar pain in my gut. I knew instantly what it meant—cramps that were the forerunners of an attack of dysentery. Panic seized my throat. I knew that if I got permission to step out and relieve myself and the convoy passed me by, I would be shot. No guard would wait for a straggler. I began inching myself forward through the marching rows, and I noticed that there were others in a similar predicament, trying to run outside the column, falling under the blows of truncheons and gun butts. I used whatever language I was being cursed in to apologize as I moved forward, breaking the rows of the marchers.

When I neared the front of the column I tried to get permission of the guard in his area, asking to be allowed to step out and relieve myself. I exaggerated the rank of the SS man; that and the fact that I spoke fluent German were probably in my favor, and I was allowed to step out. I squatted quickly as the excrement gushed out of my body. I groped for some grass in the dark to clean myself, pulled up my pants and joined the column. Soon the pains came again, as I expected they would, and I tried to repeat the routine of making my way forwards. This time the pains reached their climax before I had passed even the middle of the column. In a cold sweat I joined the frantic efforts of others to get permission to step out. It seemed that the same culprit struck most of the marchers: the under-cooked cabbage soup.

The guards were becoming increasingly annoyed with the situation, as they wanted no delay in transporting the convoy. You could hear frequent shouting and rifle fire indicating executions of those who could not keep up with the pace of the marchers. As I squatted down this time, I pushed what was now only liquid from my intestine and immediately ran forward. When the next attack hit me, I decided to control it rather than risk another departure from the column. The pains were excruciating. My testicles felt like they were being drawn into my bowels. I could feel my face flushing hot. My fists clenched spasmodically as I fought the desire of my body. The shouting of the guards, the barking of the dogs, the flashlights' beams dancing from the stragglers on the roadside to the rows of the marchers, the sudden rifle shots—all framed my agony in a hellish and macabre nightmare. I finally released my body from its struggle. The discharge ran down my ulcerated legs, the acid liquid burning my wounds. Tears of shame and degradation streaked down my cheeks. I tried to find some familiar silhouette amongst the marchers; I felt so alone and so afraid to die.

Gray dawn was breaking; one could distinguish details of the road and see the houses of a hamlet. The convoy slowed. My limbs ached and my knees quivered; I felt weak and feverish. I was dehydrated, my mouth was dry and the hunger pain in my stomach, no stranger to me in the last six years, seemed this time to pull the skin of my back towards the flesh of my hollow belly. There seemed to be no room for anything except for the pain of emptiness.

I considered consuming the bread ration I had saved, repeatedly touching my pocket where the treasure rested. Although I was toughened and disciplined by my experiences, I was tempted to give in. I only resisted because I knew that if I ate it, it would pass quickly through my body, replaying the agony of the past hours, leaving no benefit behind. Instead I tried to get into a rhythm, void of thinking, an almost mechanical stride, eyes downcast, taking one step at a time.

In front of me one of the marchers collapsed. The SS-man who was guarding that section appointed another prisoner and me to carry the fallen fellow. Apparently the guards had orders not to shoot while we were marching through the village.

I took the blanket which I carried rolled up on my neck, laid it out on the ground, and took hold of the body's legs while the other prisoner grabbed the arms. We put the ailing man on the blanket to carry him, struggling with the weight. The man was ashen, his features collapsed around his facial bone structure, a sure sign that his end was near. After a while my arms began to feel wooden from carrying the load. I found myself hoping that the man would expire soon.

Unexpectedly the living corpse opened his eyes, looked at me pointedly, and as soon as we passed near an SS guard, let out a faint scream: *"Herr officier, Herr officier, er hat mein Broat gestholen"* "Officer, Officer, he stole my bread, he has it in his pocket." With a feeble hand motion he indicated the bulge in the pocket of my striped camp jacket.

The German's hand shot out in one violent motion, striking me across the face and bloodying my nose. *"Du Schwein . . . du Sauschwein"* "You pig . . . you sow pig . . . You steal bread from your sick comrade?" the SS man cried in earnest indignation. "Give it back to him!"

I put my end of the blanket on the ground and handed the dying man the ration of bread which I was saving to feed my empty stomach. I continued to carry the skeleton-like apparition with increased contempt and ill feelings toward it.

As we trekked on, the man carrying the front of the blanket initiated a conversation in German. We both felt a need to communicate. We were coupled by an accident of fate, the dying man a hyphen between us. The man carrying the blanket with me appeared older. He said he was from Luxembourg, a teacher who was thrown into the concentration camp for anti-Nazi sentiments. His name was Ernest and he seemed like a decent sort.

We were apparently heading toward a railroad station, marching beside twisted tracks and wreckage of bombed-out railroad cars, some still burning. The fatigued prisoners and guards stepped over strewn debris. The convoy, in disarray now, appeared much shorter than when we started out. An order was given to halt. It looked as though the officers in front were asking whether they would be able to put the transport on some kind of train to get us to our destination.

As we stopped to rest, the man we carried closed his eyes, twitched and gave up the ghost, his hands still convulsively clutching my portion of bread. We summoned the guard, who told us to lay the corpse near the tracks. We slowly laid the man down and straightened his limbs. I bent over him and forcibly opened the fingers that held what was rightfully mine—the life-prolonging portion of bread, now defiled by contact with death.

"If there were two loaves, the one unclean and the other clean, and a man ate one of them," Rabbi Jose asks, in either case both are declared unclean."

Oh G-d, dear G-d, why now . . . . Why do you bewilder me with your teachings now? I know how low I have fallen . . .

And you do not lift me up, but make me look into the depth of the pit of my despair.

Ernest looked at the piece of bread in my hand and asked when I was going to eat it. So I told him about my disorder and of my fear of what would happen if I consumed it. "Come with me," Ernest said, and led me to one of the burning freight cars. He told me to put my slice of bread into the smoldering coal. "Burn it to charcoal, then eat it! It will stabilize your stomach."

Ernest did not say so, but the begging longing look in his eyes betrayed his deep hunger. I broke off a portion of the ration, handed it to my newly found friend and put the rest of it into the glowing coal of the burning wreck. Before the order came to assemble and fall in again, I was able to consume the charred bread. I almost choked on the dry burnt crust. I wiped the black smudges of my face with the sleeves of my jacket. My mouth was dryer now then before and my tongue cleaved to my palate.

We lined up, again in rows of five, and walked to the main highway. The tracks were all bombed out and there was no chance for us to move by rail. We marched for the rest of the day on our empty stomachs. We had some much-needed water at one of the infrequent stops.

CHAPTER XXVII

I do not remember how or from where we arrived in the next camp, called Kaufering. I do remember Kaufering for three things.

One was that we spent the first night in a meadow in a torrential rain. Water reached almost the tops of our supine bodies, and rifle shots rang out whenever a prisoner tried to raise his head. Oskar and I tried to keep each other awake so as not to drown in the deluge.

The second was the panic and chaos as they squeezed us into a hutch so small we could hardly breathe. The evaporation from the soaked clothing robbed us of our body heat and the Russian horde robbed us of whatever else there was to be taken.

The last memory from Kaufering is a faint recollection of seeing some female prisoners from a distance and not being able to get close enough to find out whether they were the women of our lives, or had some information about our mothers, sisters and sweethearts.

The next camp in my memory, a satellite of camp Natzweiler, was a place where sometimes on weekends they rewarded us with a container of jellied snails, which we traded, my father and I, to the French or Luxembourg prisoners for a bit of soup or bread. I also think that it was the place where my father collapsed unloading sacks of cement, and where I on shaky legs tried to carry his load along with mine so as not to endanger him. When a merciful SS guard found out what I was doing, he sat my father down and had him count the sacks as they were being unloaded, in order to make him appear useful.

In March they moved us again, this time to Ganacker camp in Bavaria, which had the worst accommodations we had encountered. The camp was attached to an airfield to which we marched daily over a distance of several kilometers. The war was winding down, and the conditions for concentration camp inmates deteriorated beyond description. We were placed in underground hovels, sleeping on bunks carved out of the earth and sprinkled with a bit of straw. Cold and dampness never left us; the meager rations never stilled our hunger. Nights were only nightmarish intervals between hellish days of hard labor.

The SS guards in this camp were especially vicious and cruel. They were also feeling the pinch caused by the lack of food supplies. Then, on the morning of the 13th of April 1945, their behavior seemed to change. Instead of shouting and beating us, they only prodded us with their gun butts; the bark of their voices became less abrasive. On the way to the airstrip they even joked among themselves. All this created a chilling premonition among the prisoners; something was up, we thought, that did not bode well for us.

We found out what was going on when we got to the airstrip. *"Los, los,"* The guards were shouting gleefully, your end is at hand. *"Eure Juden Freund is vereckt, Roosevelt is tot."* "Roosevelt, the friend of the Jews is dead." Ironically we had no evidence of Roosevelt's friendship, but if they rejoiced so much, it had to be bad for us.

That morning's labor seemed heavier than usual, for the hopelessness of our situation had grown even bleaker. Then, around noon, the sirens at the airport sounded an air alert. The guards hit the bunkers on the perimeters of the airfield. The *Luftwaffen* women, whose job was to operate the anti-aircraft guns, ran to their positions. Feverishly the pilots and their crews ran to their planes and pushed them against buildings to shield them from diving aircraft.

It was ironic that the air squadron at this airfield flew the fearsome Messerschmidt 262s, the first jet fighter planes, but there was no fuel to get them up into air. We lay down on the ground, vulnerable, unprotected, and expecting as usual an over-flight of bombers on their way to more important targets. We had long ago resigned ourselves to the fact that neither the R.A.F., which flew at night, nor the American Air Force, which flew by day, cared about our prayers that we be bombed and our camps be destroyed. The fighter planes (I think that they were the American P-51 Mustangs) came in low this time, making one sortie, and then took off. We thought we had been ignored once again. The women soldiers shot their allocated meager ration of flack ammo and ran to their bunkers.

Moments later, however, the planes came back in a steep descent. With incendiary bombs they picked out the parked Messerschmidt aircraft, one at a time. Their tracer bullets accurately strafed the bunkers where the guards were cowering. They flew over the prone prisoners, and we could have sworn that they tipped their wings.

NORBERT FRIEDMAN

The planes on the ground were burning and our guards stayed in their bunkers. We arose, and in the bedlam and confusion of the situation we ran not to freedom but to the mounds of earth were the turnips, potatoes and sugar beets were stored for the winter. We lay on our bellies and dug with our fingers. Then we carried the life-promising booty to the burning planes and baked them among the exploding ammunition. We danced around the wreckage of the planes, mindless of the danger. A dance macabre performed by wretched, emaciated living corpses, celebrating the death and destruction being visited on their tormentors.

Ten days later, on the night of April 23rd, we went to sleep as usual, hoping to surrender our worn, starved bodies to the escape of slumber, huddling our gaunt forms close to each other for warmth. The sparse layer of straw covering the earth bunks in the underground dwellings offered little protection from the dampness of the ground, and the thin blankets offered no comfort from the penetrating cold. The bleakness of the night was not much better then the harshness of the day's travail.

Only the occasional humming of aircraft overhead and the heaving of the ground as the planes delivered their deadly load onto the soil of Germany offered any faint hope or consolation. The camp's lights were out and only the sound of the steps of a passing guard interrupted the stillness.

Suddenly shrill whistles and shouts shattered the quiet night. *"Auf . . . Auf . . . Aufstehen!"* "Up . . . up . . . Get up!" *"Antreten,"* "fall in!" The prisoners automatically jumped up from their resting-places and with robot-like movements tried to push their swollen feet into wooden sandals. They fastened the metal dishes to their rumps and ran quickly outside so as not to be found in the bunkers by the Capos or the SS and be beaten or shot.

I had trouble following the others. My lacerated legs were hurting me tonight, and I was looking for something with which to wipe the oozing puss. I briefly entertained the notion of not going out, of hiding some place. Maybe this was the final hour, I told myself; maybe they were calling out the prisoners to liquidate us before the allied forces could arrive. Rumors to that effect were circulating in the camp: certainly the Germans wanted no witnesses to their atrocities. But in the confusion I could not find my father or Oskar to share my plan with.

My musing was interrupted by the shouts of a Capo who bent down to look and stuck his head into my bunker. *"Raus . . . raus . . . antreten!"* "Out . . . out . . . fall in, or I will fix your ass."

I climbed out of the bunker and lined up with the others, again in rows of five abreast. After we were counted, the Capos went into the bunkers to check for stragglers and came out carrying the prisoners' blankets.

We found ourselves on a long march, very much like the one from Leonberg, except that this time my stomach, although empty, did not suffer from a disorder. After two days of marching we were losing inmates at a staggering rate. In the evening of the second day we were placed in a school building in a small town. As we were pushed into the large assembly hall, we could see by our shrunken numbers how many of the original convoy were gone. Sure we had noticed the people falling and collapsing, we had heard the shots, but we had no idea that two-thirds of the transport had been lost.

In the middle of the night we were awakened and given a watery gruel of boiled farina. Our numbed bodies lifted themselves from the floor of the auditorium, and with awkward strides we tried to get our balance. We received the hot liquid and proceeded to slurp it, and then we sank back into a stupefied slumber. We were awakened at the crack of dawn after what seemed like a wretchedly short rest. We marched out into the cold of the morning and proceeded on the highway toward our still unknown destination. Oskar was running high fever and could hardly drag his feet. My father was concerned about his ability to go on. At one of our stops, he suggested that Oskar should lie down in the roadside ditch where we would cover him with branches and leaves as if he had died—just as we had been doing for others who succumbed on this march of the dead. Oskar agreed and we left him in the roadside trench, doubting we would ever see him again. I was terribly burdened by the uncertainty of the fate of my best friend.

The sound of the big guns seemed to come from much closer now, and the guards appeared much more nervous. My father alerted his two brothers and me, telling us to remain wary and watch for an opportune moment to make a dash for freedom. The SS Commandant, who had passed us several times in the boat of a motorcycle driven by a soldier, again drove by the column of marchers. This time he was accompanied by the *Lager Elterster,* the elder of the prisoners, who was known to the inmates as a tough, mean German. He was wearing a green triangle, which indicated that he was a criminal offender who had probably been incarcerated for a long time.

The motorcycle drove on ahead, and when it returned more than an hour later, the transport was led to a clearing in the woods. The SS Commandant explained that we were surrounded by enemy forces and that every SS guard was to take 5 or 6 prisoners and hide with them in some farmhouse. When the glorious, victorious German army had vanquished the foe, we would reassemble.

It was a ruse, as we were to learn later, arranged by the SS Commandant and the *Lager Elterst,* the camp elder. They had struck a deal between them: The lives of the prisoners, in exchange for a promise of an appeal for clemency from the allied forces for the German officer.

As the SS officer spoke, some of the guards started to sneak away and disappear in the woods. Uncle Sol, of all the people, wanted to run after the *Wurger* to take revenge and to give vent to all his pent-up emotions. My father stopped him, saying: "Don't look for trouble now." Instead, my father turned to a tall, middle-aged SS guard and asked him if he would go with us. Having been with some of the guards for a long time, we had learned much about them by observing them in different situations. This particular man must have been a Hungarian, for he spoke German poorly with a marked Hungarian syntax and accent. We never saw him harming or even yelling at anybody. My father promised the Hungarian SS man that we would protect him when necessary if he would protect us now.

The man was happy to oblige. He was indeed from Hungary; in 1944 he had declared himself an ethnic German to obtain the advantages that the *Volksdeutsche* were entitled to. But he was drafted into the "home army," according to him, which later became incorporated into the *Wermacht* and then the *Waffen* SS. And so he became a concentration camp guard. My father, Uncle Henry, Uncle Sol, five others and I formed a group, and under the protection of the Hungarian we marched in search of a save haven.

In the evening we reached a village and sneaked quietly into a barn. We bedded down in the hay, hoping the Hungarian would watch over us, and fell asleep in total exhaustion.

Next morning, Szalos, which was the guard's first name, went out to scrounge for some food. He was gone for a long time and when he came back he was very unsettled. He had met some other SS guards in the village, and they had told him that an order was supposedly issued from the SS headquarters in Berlin: Guards were not to leave any trace of the concentration camps or their inmates. The SS were now looking for any prisoners from the convoy, intending to slaughter them.

He had brought some bread and eggs, which we devoured. We could see the farmhouse from the barn and the women who worked around it. Once one of them came into the barn to fetch something, and we held our breath till she left, hoping to stay undetected.

Next day we observed a frightening incident. About a hundred yards from the farmhouse, two very young boys in German home army uniforms were guarding an insignificant bridge over a stream, which powered the mill next to the farmhouse. The *Wurger*, who could be clearly identified by the white rag around his neck, seemed, in the company of another SS man, to be ordering the boys to do something. When they refused he shot them both. A few minutes later an explosion rocked the air as the two SS men blew up the small bridge, which the two local boys had refused to do.

We spent the next day in fear that the SS would find our hide-away; that would have meant our end. The conclusion of our suffering was so close; it was both more precious and more difficult to imagine than ever. The fear of doing something now that might jeopardize that freedom was overwhelming and paralyzing.

On the morning of May first we were awakened as usual by the crowing of the roosters. This day, however, the sound of the heavy guns was coming closer and closer. Suddenly the guns fell silent and an ominous quiet fell over the area. We sat up, shook the straw out of our crumbled rags and crawled toward the wall of the barn to look through the cracks. During the night snow had fallen and the ground was covered by a white blanket of flakes. The rising sun's rays brilliantly bounced off this virgin garment as if heralding a new day and a new era. The innocent snow, by covering the blood-soaked raiment of Cain, seemed able to proclaim a new beginning.

Some time later we heard a strange rumbling. The barn actually shook, and we ran to the other side of it to peek through the boards. We saw an amazing sight: three large tanks slowly rolling toward the village. On the side of the tanks were five-pointed stars and soldiers marched behind them.

"Russians, Russians," we cried at first, misled by the five-pointed stars.

"No, no, *Americaner*," Szalos corrected us. We embraced, and, knee deep in hay, danced crazily. And then suddenly we stopped and looked at each other.

Who were we?

We were free! Free!

Free? Free at last?

Free of that ever-present fear that we would not make it, that we would not know the end to this nightmare and would never live to tell others about it.

NORBERT FRIEDMAN

There we stood motionless, haggard and dirty human scarecrows, draped with rags loosely hanging down from our shapeless, bony frames.

Each of us had been transformed by our experiences. All of us had been violated, befouled. Only a handful of us were saved from among the martyred multitude, and so very few of us were fit to be beatified. And yes, all of us were morally soiled. We just stood there in cliques of two or three, contemplating our first wobbly, infant-like steps into freedom.

In our numbness we were unable to totally comprehend the enormity of the moment. The gates of the Gehenna had finally opened and the caged beings were unable to leave.

And I stood alone, knowing that I would need to separate myself from this group and all the experiences that I had shared with them. At the time, I didn't understand why, or how, but the feeling was certain.

After a couple of hours we could not wait any longer. We were free, and we wanted to know what it meant. After a huddle, I was chosen to go into the village to find out what the situation was. After all, I was the only one who knew the sound of English from watching all those American movies that I always bragged about. I don't know why my group expected that the few words I knew ("I love you," "Good-bye darling") would help me talk to American soldiers.

I started out slowly, unaccustomed to walking without an SS guard. I kept glancing back over my shoulder in fearful disbelief that I was free, dragging my swollen lacerated legs. The wooden soles of my clogs drummed out the cantata of the long-awaited and now wearily received promise of freedom, here on the cobblestones of a Bavarian hamlet.

The Village Square was crowded with American soldiers and their vehicles. Some soldiers leaned against the trees, some against the buildings in the square; others sat on their helmets, most of them chewing on some kind of food.

My appearance did not go unnoticed. The reaction of the GIs at the sight of this emaciated, 80-pound apparition, garbed in a tattered, striped K-Zet uniform, was one of embarrassed surprise. At once they would stop eating and watch the silent, confused, severely pained image slowly traveling in circles, perplexed and dazed, trying to assess the setting around it.

The silence in the square was broken when one of the soldiers called out to me in broken German from the GI manual: "Commen sie her!" I approached him and told him in German that I was Polish. I was not yet sure that it was safe to admit being Jewish, although the badge under my serial number, the little red and yellow Star of David, would have given me away.

A Polish-speaking sergeant approached and questioned me: Who was I? Where was I coming from? Upon hearing my story and relating it to others, he proceeded to comfort me, and heap upon me, in merciful compassion all kinds of food. He and other soldiers loaded the C- and K-rations into my skinny arms, which tried but could not hold them.

In terror, tears streaking down my face, I watched their precious expression of life-giving generosity fall to the ground, the cans clanking onto the cobblestones and rolling away. The soldiers got down on their knees, picked up the food, put it in a packsack and handed it to me.

It was that act of kindness, of gentle caring compassion from a military authority, so far the opposite from the behavior from those warriors I had lived under, those brutal products of a hateful totalitarian tyranny. That pure gesture of a helping hand and an instinctive goodness made a powerful impact on my battered, worn-out, cynical shell. That warming sense of a man's comforting pity gave birth at that moment to a new expectation. I was flooded by a hope born of all the dreams I had dreamed during the nightmarish midnight of our Golgotha, a confluence of all my yearnings for a better, cleaner, undefiled world—a world free of the downtrodden and the victimized, of the brutal and the arrogant.

For me the sight of those imposing, stalwart and yet benevolent liberators embodied the promise of justice forthcoming, justice for all the wrongs for which we had been the targets. In their gentle generosity they represented a promise of a humane, healing providence—a promise they nobly fulfilled.

Sun Rays at dawn of a new day.

NORBERT FRIEDMAN

Of all of the experiences I tried to record in the last few pages, the moment I realized that I was free was the most difficult to reconstruct. No matter how hard I tried I could not describe the feeling of freedom to my satisfaction. Anything I wrote sounded incomplete and somehow unfaithful to what I "should" have felt. After speaking with others who experienced similar moments, and were also unable to describe them satisfactorily, the reason dawned on me. I could not recall what should have been the expected emotions simply because they were not there. At that very moment of liberation, the others and I were simply incapable of experiencing the feeling of liberation that we had yearned and hungered for during all those months and years of captivity.

CHAPTER XXVIII

May 1, 1945 was a beautiful and sunny spring day in southern Bavaria, the earth slowly warming under the rays of the rising sun. And yet I, the newly liberated, was facing a future whose course I was unable to map. For years I had been denied the challenge of planning for myself, and now I seemed to have lost the ability to do so, or to imagine what my goals might be. A vacant chaos and an almost primeval social landscape seemed to face me.

I should have felt something extraordinary to mark this moment, this culmination of all my strivings, the realization of six years of dreaming and hoping. There should have been a rush of emotions, of overwhelming joy, of exhilaration, of trembling sensations; I was alive, finally I was free!

I do not remember any such ebullience.

The worn shell of a body housed a numbed, spiritless wretch who was unable to comprehend the significance of the moment. As I went through the hazily remembered activities of the following days, I acted more by instinctive reflexes than by rational reasoning.

For three days my father was able to keep from our group the supplies I had brought from the merciful GI's. He was trying to bring us back to normal gastronomical functions slowly by feeding us first some bread dunked in warm, diluted milk and later some broth and boiled chicken. And by doing so, he might have saved our lives, for we learned later that many survivors died *after* the liberation. Some died because their process of decline was already irreversible, but others died because they could not handle the richness of normal food or because they overate.

Finally he could not keep them from the food any longer. The members of our little group dragged it out of the barn and spread it on the ground, falling upon the strangely packaged supplies like a herd of wild animals. My father finally shoved everyone away. He told them not to open anything and not to eat it. "The food may be too rich for us," he said. "Wait a few more days till we normalize our stomachs. I remember what happened after we came out of the trenches in World War I. People died from overeating."

"But it belongs to all of us!" cried Michael G., citing the unwritten code of the camps. "Give us our share and we will split it. We want to find our own place to stay anyhow."

"Me too," piped up Chaim D.

"You can have your share and you can leave whenever you want," replied my father, "but remember what I told you. Be careful of what and how much you eat. Lack of hunger control will kill you quicker than hunger."

They divided the supplies, more according to volume than food value; after all, we did not know what the labels "C rations" or "K rations" meant, or what these packages contained. Spam, ham and limas, processed cheese—to us it was all just American food and all equally precious.

Michael G. took with him his brother Buziu and his brother-in-law Dolek Z. and went in one direction, eventually-finding shelter in a farmhouse a half kilometer away. Chaim D. and his brother wondered off in the other direction, eventually winding up in the town of Egenfelden a few kilometers away.

While all this was happening I stood to the side, detached and bewildered, my comrades apparently having turned into hyenas. I had brought the provisions, and now they in their hunger and greed could not wait to divvy it up and run. Three years of common suffering and struggle for survival and all the loyalties forged in the perilous climate of camp existence were tested and forgotten at the first sign of safety and security. Those few cans of food represented to them a fleeting promise toward independent living, the first grubstake for their future. I saw in their actions all the negative kinds of behavior so prevalent in the camps. I saw the things that I abhorred both in them and in myself, and I knew that if I wanted to "repossess" my old self I would have to leave them and their old camp ways. I did not know how or when, but I knew I would have to do it as soon as I regained my physical strength.

A week after the liberation we all walked to the town of Egenfelden. The ex-inmates passing our farm told us that everyone congregated there to hear all the latest news.

It was May eighth; the walls of the town were plastered with official announcements in both English and German: Germany had surrendered, and the war was indisputably over. The bilingual proclamations were signed by the Commander of the Allied Forces, General Eisenhower.

As we stood there someone yelled that they had found a warehouse of the German army and that the American soldiers had broken down the door and were distributing clothing to the former inmates. We ran as fast as we could, some of us ex-camp prisoners feverishly shed their hated striped uniforms

SUN RAYS AT MIDNIGHT

even as they ran. At the warehouse they exchanged them for civilian clothing and shoes, many of them walking away with extra pairs hanging over their shoulders.

The American soldiers were trying as best they could to keep order among the pushing throng. Our group—my father, my two uncles and myself— outfitted ourselves in new underwear, socks and shoes, but we did not shed our KZ uniforms. After all, they were our only proof of identification. They proclaimed to the outside world our victimization and legitimized our claim to what we felt entitled to, preferential treatment from either the Americans or the Germans.

We gathered news about who had survived the march and where some of our comrades had settled down. Inmates talked about going back to their homes and searched lists of names on the bulletin boards for members of their families.

We went back to the farm in which we had made our temporary home. The old farmer, his wife and two of the women who lived on the farm had moved to the farmhand's quarters. The farmer's flourmill was inactive; the paddle wheels used to power the mill stood motionless, water slowly trickling down from the dam.

One afternoon, a couple days after our trip to Egenfelden, two Army trucks pulled off the road, which was frequently traveled by American personnel. They parked near the dam, and we saw four soldiers who got out and threw hand grenades into the millpond. As we heard the explosions we understood the reason for their action. We watched as they picked stunned fish out of the pond, started a bonfire, and sat around it in a circle as they opened provisions and fried the fish.

The soldiers were about a hundred yards from where we could observe them. My father turned to me and instructed me to go and invite them into the farmhouse. "They should not have to eat outside like gypsies," he said.

My father's idea that I had learned English from my prewar attendance of American movies again prompted him to choose me as the messenger. As I was nearing the circle of seated soldiers I realized that they were black. I had never seen a black person except in a Shirley Temple movie and on a prewar *"Suchard"* chocolate advertisement. I felt uneasy without knowing why.

They saw me coming, and must have noticed my striped KZ uniform, for they greeted me with a friendly Hi! And with hand gestures invited me to sit down.

"Hello!" I said, barely able to get the words out. But following my father's instructions I tried to invite them to join us by a combination of gesticulation, trying to make German sound like English and body language. They refused, insisting instead that I join them. I shook my head, confused, and ran back to my father.

"*Nu,* What happened?" he asked.

"Pa, you do not want them, they are a strange people," I blurted out. *"Wilde Menschen,"* wild men. "They eat fish with marmalade." (I did not know about cranberry sauce). I continued describing what I thought I had seen. "And they are black!"

"So what?" My father responded impatiently "they are American soldiers, they fought to liberate us." Then he continued: "Come on with me we will bring them into the house. They should not be eating in the fields."

We walked back to where the soldiers were sitting. My father's familiarity with the sign language of the deaf and his obvious seniority of age, coupled with his determination not to take no for an answer, finally swayed the GIs and they returned with us to the farmhouse. My father served chicken soup, boiled chicken and potatoes, while the soldiers brought in various canned foods and opened a bottle of "Four Roses" whiskey.

We could not speak English and they did not know any other language, so we ate, drank and laughed at each other's attempts to communicate. They were part of a transportation company and said they had seen combat. One of the soldiers finally got up from the bench and told a story. He happened to be a fabulous mime; his facial expressions spoke volumes, his arms and body seemed to be rubber bands. He told us—or at least we thought he told us— about a young black man who took his girl on a date at a restaurant. The boy tried to impress the girl by catering to her every whim, ordering the best food and drink. When it came time to pay, he pretended to have forgotten his wallet, and had to wash dishes in the restaurant as his date left him behind in a fit of pique. We rolled with laughter in response to that story, amused by its simple innocence. It gave us our first demonstration of levity since we had been liberated. We were buoyed by our ability to communicate with the Americans despite the language barrier.

It was getting late and my father invited the soldiers to spend the night in the house. I was to share my room with the storyteller; he produced a business card that read Norman C. Norman, Attorney at Law. We went upstairs to my room. As Norman stripped to wash up in the small water basin, the moonlight that came through the window shone on his black athletic body, clad only in army shorts. The bulging muscles on his perfectly formed torso made him look like a black Apollo.

We went to sleep, and when I awoke in the morning, he was gone, along with his companions. I went over to his bed and I checked the sheets; there had to be some trace of the black shining texture I believed I had seen on his body. He must have had applied something (shoe polish, maybe?) to make it so strikingly black and shining. But there was no trace of any such thing on the sheets, and I could not ask him about it.

A couple of days later a truck arrived, driven by two of the soldiers, but Norman C. Norman was not one of them. The soldiers instructed us to open the double gate to the barn. They drove the truck in and proceeded to unload provisions: sacks of sugar, salt, and flour; boxes with large cans of lard; canned fruit, coffee, powdered milk and eggs; cartons with boxes of K and C rations, containing small packages of a few cigarettes each. They seemed to have everything the American army was issuing as rations. "It's for you!" they said, pointing at us. They did not stay this time, but the memory of their genuine concern and kindness, which came from the core of their hearts, would stay with me forever and create a lifelong empathy for their race.

We secured the barn by putting a chain and a padlock on the gate—probably the first time that the barn had been so protected. My father was in charge of its treasure, except for one item that I had secretly removed and hidden, a chunk of chocolate. I had not seen or eaten chocolate during the six years of the war, and now I had such a craving for it that I concealed it even from my father. I did not realize that stuffing myself with what turned out to be cooking chocolate would cause such a severe case of constipation that eventually I had to seek a doctor's assistance. My greed cured my craving for chocolate, and to this day I stay away from it.

We settled down to a facsimile of normal life. Slowly we began to regain physical strength; the skeletons began to take on the semblance of normal human beings. The numbness of spirit was still there, but we were beginning to think of things other than food and sleep. In particular, we began to wonder what had happened to our families and how we could learn about their fate. There was also much talk of repatriation, of going back home, but not so much among the Jews from Poland. We heard disturbing snippets of news about Jews not being welcome when they returned, about finding that their homes and possessions had been appropriated by their former neighbors. Instead of friendly expressions of welcome from their neighbors, they found death threats. Instead of settling back into a peaceful life they found themselves sneaking back out of the places of their birth under cover of darkness; the places where they had spent their childhood and youthful years and where they thought they belonged.

Meanwhile, in the days immediately following liberation, in some areas of Germany where the American army had liberated prisoners from the concentration camps, the Army commanders were so shocked and revolted by the atrocities of the SS that some of them gave the survivors *Cart Blanche* to take revenge. The Jewish survivors, freed on the soil of the tormentors who had brought about the destruction of their lives and their world, had the opportunity to take vengeance with their own hands. But strangely enough, they did not. They spilled no blood, sought no revenge. They did seek justice for those who were personally responsible for their affliction. But they themselves inflicted no punishment.

The infrastructure for handling the hundreds of thousands of liberated persons was still not in place. The American authorities did the best they could—although not always judiciously at first. In some cases they gave the German authorities jurisdiction over the survivors, creating consternation and resentment; in some cases they even created Displaced Persons camps on the premises of what had been concentration camps, causing pain and dismay. In hindsight, it is hard to believe that they could have displayed such a lack of sensitivity and psychological expertise.

For my own needs, I bought a bicycle from a German farmer, who had hidden it in a barn. I learned about the bicycle from one of the women in the farmhouse we were living in. She was a neighbor of the farmer who carried a grudge against him, and she betrayed his secret to me. In return for the bicycle I gave him a can of coffee and some cigarettes. It might have been worth a lot more, but he was not going to argue with an ex-concentration camp inmate, fearful that I might take it from him with no compensation at all. I rode into town almost every day to look at the bulletin board where people were putting up their names and the names of people they were looking for. I also bartered some of the victuals the soldiers had left us for items of everyday use. On one such trip, a former fellow inmate stopped me to say that he thought he had seen my friend Oskar Klausenstock in an American uniform. An American company was stationed in one of the school buildings in town, and I hurried there immediately. I stopped the first GI I saw and, pointing to my striped uniform tried to find out if he knew of anyone by the name of Oskar.

"Yes, Yes!" he said, gesturing. "Come with me." And soon I was standing with Oskar, looking fit in his American Army uniform—my friend whom we had last seen buried in a ditch on the death march.

He told me the story: During the evening, after the convoy of prisoners from the death march had passed, Oskar got up from his concealment and wandered about. Good fortune brought him to a camp of American prisoners of war. The German guards, who sensed the imminent end of the war and were trying to ingratiate themselves with the Americans, let him into the camp, where the medic diagnosed pneumonia and treated Oskar until the camp was liberated by American troops a few days later. When the American POWs went home to the States, Oskar went to work for the company that liberated him.

He was still working for that outfit, and after a lengthy discussion I decided to join him. It was my first step in taking a direction—an almost forgotten ability. It also gave me an opportunity to separate myself from those who traveled the road of pain with me. I felt it would help me to shed what I considered a taint of slavery, of worthlessness, which had been so effectively drummed into my consciousness by my oppressors. I began to peel off the stigma of being an *Untermensch,* a sub-human that the German propaganda machine had tried to pin on me. By wearing an American uniform I might even be able to exercise authority over the conquered Hun.

I was introduced to a Captain Nieland, who hailed from Chicago and whose mother was of Polish extraction. He spoke a halting Polish, yet good enough to make me feel comfortable. I was given the coveted American uniform, without any insignia, the same as Oskar wore. I joined him in working as an interpreter; the Captain spoke English and Polish, we spoke Polish and German, and Oskar had learned some English before the war. I also helped out in the kitchen. My father made no comment when I told him about my decision to work for the Americans. I knew he would rather see me do that than join those who were wandering around aimlessly.

When the captain asked for my name, I told him it was Norbert Volny—to Oskar's shock and surprise. Volny means free in Polish—it was an idea that came to me instinctively as a way of emphasizing a new beginning. I also wanted to divorce myself from all that was associated with my family name, which I felt had been soiled by my Uncle Henry's conduct in the Mielec camp.

I had been visiting the farmhouse almost every day and had started a friendly relationship with a Hungarian refugee girl. She was pretty and lively, such a contrast to the drabness we saw around us. Her looks reminded me of my friend Hanka from Tarnow, the girl I was still in love with but had not seen or heard from for three years.

Tina, as I nicknamed her (her full name was Christina), had wandered into Germany as part of a Hungarian caravan that followed the German Army in an attempt to escape the advancing Russians. Her group must have been German sympathizers or maybe even members of the defunct Hungarian Army, but I asked her no questions. I was looking for my first post-war love experience.

One morning, after a couple of weeks of working for Captain Nieland's company, he informed us that we were pulling out that afternoon for a little town some 30 kilometers away. I asked permission to say good-bye to my father. "Go, but you have to be back by two o'clock sharp. That's when we're shoving off." I jumped on my bike and peddled to my father's house. I said good-bye, promising to visit him as often as I could. "You can do whatever you want with my share of the provisions the black soldiers gave us," I added. I waived to my uncles and went looking for Tina.

I found her in the village square, trading some of the goodies I had given her, the chocolate bars and cigarettes, for a colorful blouse. I told her that I was leaving with the army, but that I hoped to be able to visit soon.

"Oh, nein mein Schatz!" "Oh, no my darling!" she exclaimed in German, the language that we spoke in (I found Hungarian an impossible language to learn). "Come, we must say good-bye properly to each other," and she led me to the very same barn where we were hidden before liberation. There, where I had experienced the first sensation of freedom, I was now being promised carnal love again for the first time since before incarceration. We undressed each other slowly, intending to savor the moment. We explored our bodies with tenderness and anticipation, but there was no physical response on my part. Tina was reassuring at first, covering my body with kisses, but then, having aroused herself with the foreplay, fiercely tried to get me to satisfy her. She dug her nails into my shoulders and raked them down my backside. I felt blood trickling down my body as my cheeks burned in the shame of failure. Crushed, I disengaged myself from Tina's embrace to put my clothes on. "I'm sorry," I whimpered. "I like you; maybe the next time when I come to see you," was all I could say.

"Don't bother," was her short reply. "I'm going back to Hungary. It was nice knowing you; some day you will be a man again."

I mounted the bicycle to get back to Oskar and the company. I knew I was late, but I still hoped to catch them. I peddled furiously, the shame of my experience burning a hole in my self-esteem. Not only had the Germans robbed me of all that I was, of my innocence, my freedom, my home and my family. They had also robbed me of my pride and my manhood.

The company was ready to leave and the captain was furious, angrily instructing me to throw my bicycle on a truck and join Oskar and the rest of the company. "Were the hell have you been? We almost left without you." My hand wandered to my back under my shirt, gently touching my bloody scars.

I sat next to Oskar in the truck as the convoy moved along. "Why were you late?" he asked. "You know the Cap does not like tardiness. What happened?"

"Oh, I had to say good-bye to my father and Tina," I said lamely. The next day, when we were taking a shower at our new location, Oskar saw the marks on my back and nodded knowingly. "That's why you were late yesterday, you s.o.b." he said jokingly. "At least you could have taken me along." I did not volunteer the details of the encounter, preferring to let him think what he wanted to.

We settled into our new location, a small village. As best we could figure out our outfit, which was part of the First Army, had moved there to look for members of SS units that had dispersed in the area. Oskar spent most of his time traveling with the captain, interrogating the villagers in the vicinity. I helped out by supervising the German personnel who were assigned to perform kitchen duties for the company.

Slowly I began to learn to communicate with the GI's, picking up American idiomatic expressions and trying to use them at the appropriate times. The guys, as I learned to call them, encouraged me, sometimes bursting out in good-natured laughter at my mistakes. I thought I was making progress in learning the English language, but of course what I was learning was GI slang: Ain'tcha, can'tcha, don'tcha, won'tcha; I get, I got, ain't got. The all-encompassing phrases did help in making myself understood to the gang, but the captain turned up his nose when I tried to speak to him in this kind of English. "Here is a book," he would suggest, "try to read it. It will help you to speak properly." Oskar, who remembered some grammatical basics from before the war, would encourage me to speak English and correct me.

The interaction with the GI's had a healing effect on both of us. Their natural informality, regardless of their rank; their healthy, happy demeanor, even when performing the most mundane tasks; their banter when tossing the football around and repetitive baseball chatter during a pick-up game or playing catch—all of this had a therapeutic effect on us. I took it is as a symptom of a simpler, more honest, benign world, a world where one could expect fair rewards and equal treatment for one's effort.

We stayed in that location for a few weeks. Oskar's ingenuity in tracking people down (the GI's were helpless at this) helped to capture eight SS men. Then we moved again, this time to the city of Regensburg. Untouched by the ravages of the war, Regensburg excited Oskar's intellectual curiosity, with its ancient churches and Gothic cathedrals. We must have been regaining some interest in the life around us, for we spent some of our free time visiting points of interest. Sometimes we would take a GI or two with us. Most of them, however, preferred to spend their free time looking for *Freuleins,* despite the fact that fraternization with German girls was off limits.

We were stationed in a large school building, not far from where the Danube and Regen rivers converged. The meals were served in the schoolyard in full view of the Germans, who would gather at chow time, hungrily watching through the iron grates in hopes that someone would throw some leftovers their way. Their luck depended on who was the head cook on the given shift. Some of them, who bore deep animosity toward the Germans, would taunt them by throwing the leftovers into the garbage, scornfully watching as the disappointed, humiliated, and hungry crowd turned and left.

Usually those were the same guys who would gleefully grind their discarded cigarettes into the ground just to watch the dismay on the faces of those who followed them in the hope of gleaning a final puff or two. Occasionally a compassionate cook in charge of the meal distribution would scrape the leftovers into a can and hand it to a hopeful German through the opening in the gate. The most coveted item was the coffee grinds. Throughout the war years, real coffee had been unavailable to the Germans, who now would brew them over again and again, or trade them on the black market.

Those begging for the handouts were mostly women and a few children. The men, even the elderly, who had not been in the POW camps, would not come to plead for food, although would pick up discarded cigarette butts. One young girl in her twenties, who always stood to the side with a metal can, wordlessly stretching it out when the scraps were handed out, caught my eye. She was always dressed neatly and somehow retained a dignified posture even when appealing for compassion. When the GI's called out suggestive propositions she would gracefully turn on her heels and turn away.

One evening I approached the gate and asked her name. She was startled to have been addressed in fluent German and instinctively replied, Trudy. She had ash blond hair that fell in waves around her pretty face. Her figure was concealed by the loosely hanging clothing, but I could see her shapely, though muscular, bare legs and nice feet in leather sandals.

"Tell you what Trudy," I continued in German, "come tonight at seven and I will bring you some food and coffee." She looked at me quizzically, but promised to show up. It was already well after six. I went into the kitchen, threw into a bag some cans of Spam and sardines, a few little plastic bags of Nescafe, half a loaf of white bread and a couple of packs of cigarettes. I watched through the kitchen window and saw her arrive at exactly seven. She casually walked past the gate, discretely glancing in the direction of the schoolyard. I walked out and coolly left the yard. "Follow me around the fence," I suggested, and there I handed her the package.

"*Danke,*" "thanks," was her simple response. Then she said "Would you like to take a walk with me?"

"Sure, why not?" was my reply.

"Let me drop off the bag with my mother," she continued. "I live right across the street. I'll be right back, I promise," she smiled shyly.

"O.K.," I said. "Go." I believed that she would return, why wouldn't she? She came running back a few moments later. I thought that I noticed that her hair had been combed and a trace of lipstick applied.

"You put make-up on, didn't you?" I asked.

"You noticed, how nice." She continued, "Who are you? You are not an American, your German is too good for you to be an 'Ami' (the Germans' nickname for Americans) and you are not a German, who are you?"

"You don't want to know," was my reply. "No, really, who are you, why won't you tell me?"

Void of words to reply, I rolled up my sleeve and showed her the tattoo on my right wrist: the large letters KL. Startled, Trudy turned her head and started running back toward her house. I caught her just before she reached the door. I grabbed her by her shoulders and turned her toward me. Tears stained her face and she was trying to control her weeping. "Please forgive me, forgive me, I'm sorry," was all that she could utter.

"Stop it, stop it, I am not angry with you," I pleaded. She put her head on my shoulder and sobbed. "Please do not cry, I'm all right, you had nothing to do with it," I said, hoping to comfort her, even though I knew nothing of her role during the war. She calmed down, and we stood there not knowing what to say next.

NORBERT FRIEDMAN

"I must go now," she declared, "my mother will worry."

"Listen, meet me here tomorrow night at seven, I'll try to bring you some stuff. What would you like?"

"Sugar, if you have some," and with that she planted a kiss on my mouth and ran up the stairs.

The next day I prepared a much larger package, including the sugar and some other hard-to-get items, such as soap, toothpaste and spices. I met Trudy in front of her house, and again she took the parcel up to her apartment before she came down to walk with me. We walked a long way this time. She told me about her family. Her father had been killed on the Russian front, and her younger brother was a prisoner of war held by the Americans. She swore that they were not Nazis, although she did belong to the *"Bundes Madchen,"* the girls' counterpart of the *"Hitler-Jugend,"* the boys' Nazi youth movement. "Everyone had to," she insisted. She said that her parents were very religious, and that her mother went every day to church to pray for her son's safe return. During the war she had heard something about the Jewish problem, and her family wondered about the gradual disappearance of their Jewish neighbors, but she had had no inkling of the situation that was now being described by the Americans and some of the survivors who settled in Regensburg.

Was it really that bad? Could I tell her something about it?

Except for sharing some of my experiences with those GIs who were willing to listen, or an occasional brief reference in my conversations with Oskar (we did not need to elaborate to each other; a few words, a name, a locality would instantly recreate a specific incident or the whole specter of our experience) I had had no occasion up to now to recount the details of my odyssey. And I was not willing to reopen all the wounds just to satisfy a German girl's curiosity. Trudy accepted in silence some of the facts that I was able or willing to share with her.

When I asked her whether she would want to meet me the next day, she shook her head in the affirmative and squeezed my hand firmly. "You don't have to bring anything, please," she murmured. Next day I took several packs of cigarettes and went to where the black marketers congregated to barter the cigarettes for a pair of nylon stockings. I kept the package of stockings separate from the parcel of food, planning to give the stockings to Trudy at the end of the evening.

That evening, however, Trudy asked me to come up and meet her mother. I really did not want to; I had no interest in meeting her old lady, as the GIs would say. But Trudy insisted. Her mother looked much older then I expected, her gray hair hanging in straight strands down her head. She must have been

SUN RAYS AT MIDNIGHT

good-looking at one time, however; her *Deutsche Haus Frau,* German housewife, features betrayed a once-handsome face. As I entered the neatly furnished apartment, I noted pictures of men in German Army uniforms lined up on the dresser. I was glad not to see any in an SS or SA uniform. Her mother served us some tea and fresh biscuits. She graciously thanked me for my generosity, displaying the same trait of dignity that I noticed in Trudy. To my relief she asked no questions about my past. All she wanted to know was where I came from and where I had learned to speak German. She left the room shortly after we had tea.

Trudy pointed out her father's and her brother's pictures to me, all ordinary looking Germans, I thought. Then she insisted on showing me their apartment and led me to her bedroom. We sat on the bed, where she obviously expected my advances. Weary of my miserable experience with Tina the Hungarian, I led the obviously disappointed girl back to the living room. I cast about for some way to break the sense of rejection that she obviously was feeling and remembered the pair of nylon stocking. The shriek of delight was so loud that her alarmed mother came running from her bedroom to see what happened.

"Mutti, Mutti shau dier ein," "Momy, Momy look! Nylon stockings!" And in front of her mother, Trudy planted a passionate kiss on my mouth. Her mother showed no trace of embarrassment; the only person who was uncomfortable was I. From that time on, however, our relationship made quick strides.

Next day was Sunday, and we went for a stroll along the Regen River. It was a lovely summer day, with other couples strolling along with us, mostly GIs with their German *Freuleins,* wearily looking out for MPs who might check their passes. Trudy and I found a secluded spot and after some conversation wound up necking (again, a term I learned from the Gis). Trudy noted my guarded attitude, went silent for a spell and then very frankly asked: "Is there something wrong with you sexually, or you just do not like me?"

"Oh, no," I protested vigorously. And lacking any further excuse, I told her about my disappointment with Tina, at the same time assuring her that I really did not like Tina as much as I liked her.

Again she went silent for a moment, and then started to reassure me. "You should not worry; you were undernourished for so long. You told me that you were only 40 kilos when you were liberated, and besides, they put saltpeter in your food so that you should loose your sex drive. You will be all right, you'll see." (How did she know about that? I wondered later.)

NORBERT FRIEDMAN

She started to give me passionate caresses and kisses that were meant to communicate tenderness and affection. I began to yield to her, feeling a peaceful sensation and a growing sense of fondness for her.

"Come," Trudy urged me; "we will go home. Mother went to see her friend, and then they are going to church together. They will have a coffee klatch. She took some Nescafe with her. Come on, we will be alone."

Holding her hand, I followed Trudy to her place. She led me straight to her bedroom and partially undressed me. We lay next to each other in a soft, gentle embrace. The inner peace I felt at the banks of the river had enveloped me and gradually liberated me from my fears, my insecurity, and my hidden pain. We made love in an almost motionless manner. As I kissed Trudy's face I tasted the salty flavor of her tears. After a while we made love again, and then again, each time in a more joyous and reckless mood. We heard her mother come home, but Trudy did not care and apparently neither did her mother, for she was surely able to hear us and yet never reacted.

I went back to the barracks early in the morning. The guard on duty, who knew me well, teased me and said, "Take a pro soldier, take a pro," referring to the prophylactics the army distributed to the GIs. I tried not to disturb Oskar, but he was awake and wanted to hear all about my night out. I was in a buoyant mood and I did not mind the ribbing of the guard or the funny comments that Oskar made in response to my story.

I felt as though a tremendous burden had fallen from my shoulders. I had been liberated from the nameless concerns and fears about myself. This unsophisticated, caring German girl had given me back my manhood, my identity, my confidence and in some way even my freedom.

We made love now whenever and wherever we could. She was free and natural in giving herself, making no demands and asking no questions. She had no illusions about the future or permanence of this relationship, and neither did I. But there was a radical change in my demeanor. I whistled I laughed, I had a good word for everyone; my feet were lighter, I was happy. For the first time in ages I expected the sun to shine every day.

One afternoon Oskar and I went swimming where the rivers Danube and Regen merged. The flow was very strong. Oskar, daring and brave as he was, ventured into the current, while I stayed closer to shore. It might have saved my life. Suddenly I felt a paralyzing pain in my right side. I yelled for help, and

238

some soldiers swimming nearby dragged me to shore and covered me to keep me warm while someone ran to fetch help.

The company medic was a young, not very experienced practitioner. He examined me and diagnosed my ailment as appendicitis. He insisted that I could not be admitted to an Army hospital, and had me taken in a Jeep to nearest German hospital instead. Oskar told me later that the captain was furious when he found out. "How could you take this man to a German hospital," he yelled at the young medic. "They killed his people!"

The hospital was run by a religious order and the nursing personel were nuns in their habits. It was overcrowded with ailing soldiers. It made no difference to them that I was a Jewish concentration camp survivor. I was put in a large hall with all the rank-less German soldiers and with some old patients with no families to look after them. The hall looked to me like a church sanctuary, with all the crosses and a small altar at one end.

The doctor who came to see me was an elderly man who examined me very deliberately and had me taken into the Roentgen room for x-rays. "You do not have appendicitis," was his verdict, "you have gallstones. We will have to operate."

"Oh, no!" I yelled. "YOU are not going to operate on me! I do not trust you, I do not believe that you will put me together again!" The visions of all the sick bays in the camps, and the evil that was done there, flashed before my eyes. The doctor looked at me thoughtfully, picked up my right wrist, looked at my tattoo and concluded: "I understand, I will come to see you later and we will talk, meanwhile take this for the pain."

He did come back, and he sat at my bedside. He asked me about what I was doing in Regensburg, how long I had been interned in concentration camps and which ones. He explained to me that the stones he had seen had most likely formed recently—probably the result of the rich American food that my constitution was unable to process. He felt that with some medication and a strict diet I could be released in a few weeks. Before he left he quietly revealed, "My teacher and mentor in the medical school was Jewish. They killed him in Buchenwald, *Die Schweinhunde,* the bastards."

In the evening they brought me some boiled vegetable leaves and kohlrabi.

"Is this my diet?" I asked the stern-looking nun.

"No," she snapped back, "that is what everyone eats. The Americans took everything from us."

Oskar came to see me the next day and brought me some bad news: the company was moving out to another location. He promised that he would try to come to see me when possible.

NORBERT FRIEDMAN

"I brought you some cigarettes and chocolate, you should be able to use them to buy whatever you might need. By the way, your girlfriend Trudy came by this morning asking for you. Should I tell her where you are?"

"Yes, by all means! And leave my bike with her when you push on." Was my buddy trying to use my situation to help me end this relationship? Is that why he had not told Trudy where I was? When Oskar left I felt uneasy and abandoned, I hated the men around me; they were all *Krauts* and I didn't want to be under German authority again.

The next morning Trudy came to see me. Oskar had told her about my condition and she brought me some boiled porridge sweetened with condensed milk. I was not sure whether it was all right for me to eat it, but I was hungry; I had not touched my food the night before. I took from under my bed the things that Oskar had brought me and gave them to Trudy.

"You must not do that," she protested, "you might need them yourself."

After a couple of hours the nun passed by and told her she had to leave. Trudy released my hand, gently kissed me and promised to come the next day. She did come then, and every day after that, managing to bring me the food that I was allowed to eat. She must have been using all the provisions I had given her to trade for chicken, meat and vegetables.

My stay in the hospital, and the long hours of just lying in bed, gave me plenty of time for thinking. For the first time I was able to reflect on the enormity of my losses. I knew that I would never see my mother or my brother again. Most likely there were no other relatives on either side of my families who had survived the catastrophe.

In addition to that, it seemed that we had little to look forward to in our homelands. I based this conclusion on the experience of Uncle Sol, who had tried to return home. He had gone back to Poland, planning to go to the village of Wielopole where we had left our families in 1942. Ten miles before he got there, he was told to turn back or face the threat of being killed by the peasants, who did not want anyone to come back to claim their possessions. He was also told that all the Jews from that area had been taken away to the Belzec extermination camp and that there were no survivors there. I suspected that most of my youthful friends had not survived the cataclysm either. In other words, the world as I once knew it did not exist. During the sleepless hours of the night I could see only a vacuum, a dark void of uncharted future, stretching before me.

On the tenth day of my stay in the hospital Oskar drove up with a sergeant from a different outfit. His insignia indicated that he was from the 4th Armored

Division. Oskar told me that he was now stationed on a baronial estate and the old company had left for the Czech border. Captain Nieland had left some German *Reichsmarks* for Oskar to give me in case I had to pay for my hospital stay. Our new employer was Company "B" of the 35th Tank Battalion, 4th Armored, part of the Third Army. Oskar had told the company commander about me, and it was he who gave him the jeep and the driver to come and see me. Oskar introduced the soldier to me. "This is Little Red, the captain's driver," he said. "Wait till you meet Big Red."

The estate was about 60 kilometers away. Oskar left me an address where I could notify him when I was ready to leave the hospital. Again he left me cigarettes, chocolate and a can of coffee, and said good-bye in his best GI lingo. "It ought to last you till they let you go. Get well soon for Christ's sake, I miss you. You're gonna love the new guys."

When Trudy came the next day I gave her the stuff Oskar had brought me, all except two packs of cigarettes and two bars of chocolate. I saved those for the doctor, who was coming to see me quite frequently.

A week later he finally announced that I would be ready to leave in a couple of days. I told him I had to stay until I could reach Oskar and he could come for me. I wrote a note to Oskar under the address he gave me and asked Trudy to mail it. She looked at it and shook her head. "Do you have any idea how long the mail takes nowadays? I will take the bike and tell Oskar myself."

"Are you crazy?" I protested. "It is one hundred twenty kilometers [75 miles] round trip. You will kill yourself, or if not, someone else will kill you. The roads are not safe yet."

"Don't worry, I'll go, sleep over and come back the next day." There was no changing her mind. She was determined to do it for me, even though she certainly knew that my departure meant the end of our relationship.

She left the next morning and returned a day later with Oskar. Fortunately he was able to give her and the bike a lift in the jeep on the way back. We said a passionate good-bye to each other, promising to keep in touch. Of course we had little opportunity to do so.

It was eighteen months before I had a chance to see Trudy again. She introduced me then to her fiancee, who had been a school friend of hers and whom she started to date when he came back from the POW camp shortly after I left. He knew about Trudy and me, but he shyly shook my hand and invited me to their wedding.

That was the last I saw of Trudy. I remained forever beholden to her for our affair and the tender way in which she brought about my healing.

NORBERT FRIEDMAN

CHAPTER XXIX

Oskar helped me get out of the Jeep and led me to our "pad"—an apartment off the estate, across from a church which stood on the other side of the square. It was a large room, with a bathroom and shower in the hall. The furniture consisted of two Army cots, a table and some chairs covered by pillows and Army blankets. I saw boxes of cigarettes, canned food and Coca-Cola bottles, a shelf with some books and a sewing machine. "That's it, that's all we own," Oskar said.

"Where are our KZ uniforms?" I asked.

"They are gone," announced Oskar. "I got rid of them. It's time to start a new life. Can you walk?"

"Sure, I'm all right," I bragged. "OK, then let's go to the mansion, it's only a five-minute walk."

On the way Oskar briefed me about the company commander, Captain Kingsley, and about Lieutenant Sakowski, who was Jewish. The master sergeant's name was Cox, and he was a Canadian and a professional soldier.

We reached the estate and the main building where we found the captain in the music room. He was having a cup of coffee and a piece of cake. Oskar smartly saluted: "Captain, this is Norbert, I told you about him."

"Sit down, sit down, how do you feel?" were his first words. "You want a cup of coffee?"

"No I cannot have coffee," I said, "I have to watch my diet."

"How about you, Oskar?" he said. When Oskar agreed, he told him, "Well, go into the kitchen and tell Wesley or whoever is there to give you a cup and bring another one for me, and also another piece of cake."

When Oskar left the room he continued, "They bake a lousy cake, but what the hell, they were not drafted as bakers."

I liked the man immediately. His blue eyes had a friendly twinkle and he had an air of informality. He smoked continuously. He was from Buffalo, he told me, a high-school teacher in civilian life. I did not know where Buffalo was or the significance of his being a high-school teacher, but I nodded knowingly, impressed by his friendliness.

Oskar brought in the coffee and the captain again inquired how I was feeling and when would I like to start working. "Take your time, there is no rush, Oskar can work for two," he joked. "Seriously, take a day or two, get acquainted. You will be taking care of the officer's mess. Go get some rest, I'll see you around." That sounded like a dismissal so we got up and saluted as we left. "Don't salute me, you're not soldiers for Christ's sake!"

Outside, Oskar asked me what I thought about our new boss. I said that Captain Kingsley seemed like a remarkable man, something I found to be true on more than one occasion.

"Come along, I'll introduce you now to Anne-Marie, my girl-friend. She is from Vienna and lives nearby. She also has a very nice friend. Her name is Magie; she is also from Austria. They are very elegant, educated women. Their husbands are missing or something."

The women lived up a flight of stairs in a very small and crowded apartment, their sleeping accommodations separated from each other by a curtain. The one bed in the first room also served as a couch, for there was room for only two more chairs and a small table. Anne-Marie was slim and tall, her aristocratic face framed by dark hair. She moved easily with fluid gestures, projecting a sense of self-confidence. Magie was much shorter and on the plump side. She did not say much, but would smile approvingly at whatever anyone else said.

"Ah, so you are Norbert. Oskar has told us so much about you. We like you already, even before we met you." I did not realize it at first, but Anne-Marie was speaking English to me—not perfect English, but better than mine. Oskar was right she was an educated lady, a producer of educational films in Vienna, she said. (Later we found out that they were German propaganda films.) Magie's English was very poor and she did not volunteer any information about herself. The women smoked a lot of American cigarettes. They told us that they had wound up in Germany after fleeing the advancing Russian Army. They were terrified of the "Ruskies," as they called them, who were rumored to treat the conquered Germans very roughly, especially the women.

I was very tired, and Oskar and I promised to see the women the next day. I fell asleep while Oskar was describing in detail his relationship with Anne-Marie and what a wonderful lover she was.

We got up early to join the GIs in the chow line. It was a beautiful summer morning and the line extended through half the yard. Except for the toast there was nothing for me to eat there. Bacon and eggs, butter and coffee were all off limits.

This is Big Red; Oskar told when we reached the end of the line. Big Red was not large, as I had expected, but he was given this name to distinguish him from Little Red. Both were recognized members of the outfit, one the captain's driver, the other the boss in the kitchen. Big Red, Joe Collangelo was the only redheaded Italian I ever met, and he was the first and dearest American friend I was to have. He held the rank of sergeant and was second in charge of the kitchen after the mess sergeant, who was known as Wesley the Weasel.

"What's the matter, you don't like our chow?" Red remarked good-naturedly, looking at my plate, which held only the two pieces of toast. "I'm just kidding. Oskar told me about your problems. Go into the kitchen, and when I'm finished here I'll fix you up something."

I went into the kitchen and found a chair next to a small desk in a corner. Oskar went out to find out about his schedule for the day and I was waiting there alone when a sergeant walked over and yelled at me, "Who the hell are you? Get up! You're sitting in my chair!"

This was my introduction to Wesley the Weasel. At that moment Big Red walked into the kitchen and took control. "Simmer down Wesley," he said. "This is Norbert and he's going to work with me. You got a beef, go see the Cap." Wesley must have been afraid of Red for he turned on his heel and left the kitchen mumbling.

So I started two different relationships, one of rancor and animosity with Mess Sergeant Wesley the Weasel, the other of a deep friendship with Red that has continued till his passing.

"Come on what can I make you, what can you eat?" Red asked me. I recited to him the list of all the forbidden items the German doctor had given me: no fried foods, no raw vegetables or fruits, no caffeine and no alcohol, at least for a while.

"Holy shit! Didn't he know you're with the army? Don't worry, I'll take care of you." He brought out some marmalade, opened a large container of canned fruit (just to dish out a few spoonfuls) and brought me some milk. "Here, eat slowly, we'll find plenty that you can eat."

There was caring and concern in the tone of his voice and a shielding demeanor toward Oskar and myself that spread through the whole company. He was perhaps more protective of me because of my perceived infirmity. This bunch of war-hardened veterans, survivors of many momentous tank battles, heroes of the Bastogne campaign, elite troops of General Patton's Third

Army—they exhibited such genuine interest and touching concern for our welfare that I renamed them "The Gentle Giants."

Coupled with their comradeship, they accepted us as equals and tolerated the quirks in our behavior, oddities which were the result both of our pre-war culture and of our nightmarish experiences. They slowly restored in us a confidence in ourselves and in our values. The GIs did not pry, but gently led us to share our past with them, drawing us out by telling us about their own homes, their families and about America the Beautiful. Theirs was a tale of love, of admiration and of longing to get back, to what was to them the best place in the world. They differed in the parts of the country they came from, but not in the values they professed and exhibited: their love of athletic competition, especially baseball; their dedication to the concept of fair play in sports and in everyday conduct; their deference to what was right and what was wrong; their tendency to root for the underdog. All of these impressed me as the basic components of democracy—maybe not the theory that is taught in political science courses, but the one I have learned from the hearts of the American people.

The healing effect on both my physical condition and my battered psyche of these wonderful young warriors, fresh from fighting to free the world of evil, is a debt that I and my children will forever be repaying to the American society.

The baronial estate on which we were stationed was the property of the *"Graf Arco Von Valley,"* the Earl Arco Von Valley. It lay somewhere in the vicinity of the town of Landau. A brook ran through the large property, which was adorned with classical statues and beautiful shrubbery; the many gazebos offered the opportunity for privacy and rest. The round, main building housed many rooms; the former ballroom now served as the officers' mess. Magnificent works of art graced that wing as well as the music room and other rooms of the estate.

Oskar and I had permission to use the gardens and stroll through the property in the company of our female friends, Anne-Marie and Magie. The GIs were housed in several other adjacent buildings and the grounds were off limits to them. The two young original inhabitants, heirs to the estate, lived in what once were the servants quarters.

Our friendships with Anne-Marie and Magie contributed in a large measure to the development of our cultural growth. Both women were civilized and educated in the classics, as well as in art and music. They re-educated us in the social graces we had forgotten, the little things that distinguish a boor from a civilized creature: the way you handle a fork and a knife, how you conduct yourself in public. I learned something from them about classical composers and writers and about culture in general. But I could not get an answer to one important question: How could such a cultured and civilized people as the German nation, commit such barbaric crimes?

Our relationship with the two women came to an abrupt end when Anne-Marie's husband showed up suddenly. He had been released from an American POW camp and he immediately moved in with the women. We did not see them for a couple of weeks, and then Magie showed up and asked us if we would come up for coffee. She did not answer my question why was I being ignored just because Anne-Marie's husband had returned. According to Magie, he knew about Oskar's relationship with Anne-Marie, but had not quite accepted it yet. Oskar would not hear of going up to visit them. He said to me, "The bastard eats my food, smokes my cigarettes and sleeps with MY woman, and has the gall to bitch. Doesn't he know that he lost this war?"

A while later Company B left the estate and moved to the town of Simbach/Inn. The town was situated on the German side of the Inn River; on the other side was Austria. We could see the town on the Austrian banks—Braunau, the birthplace of Hitler. Our company patrolled the border and manned an outpost bridge a few miles from the town.

Captain Kingsley began to press Oskar and myself about our plans for the future. When we told him that we would like to emigrate to the United States he was delighted. But Oskar and I, despite declaring our intention and filling out our immigration applications for the American Consul, were not completely sure about our intentions. More and more survivors were opting to go to Palestine. The underground organization *Bricha* was smuggling people in from Poland and other countries in Eastern Europe to transit camps in Germany; from there they were moved, albeit illegally, to Palestine. On occasion they asked Oskar and myself to help them cross the border from Austria to Germany.

The American occupation of West Germany had by now become a routine, orderly bureaucratic operation. Displaced Person camps were set up for the survivors. They were run by the UNRRA, the United Nations Relief and Rehabilitation Agency, and staffed by volunteers from the United States, Great Britain, Canada and France. People in the DP camps were offered opportunities to attend religious schools, prepare for life in Palestine with the help of Zionist organizations, study at trade training centers run by the ORT, watch artistic presentations, or take part in social dances and soccer competitions.

Those who were not fortunate enough to find their pre-war spouses or sweethearts sooner or later engaged in courtship. Boys and girls whose youth was interrupted in violent ways, who never had the chance to experience the dreams and the romance of adolescence, were drawn to each other in search of warmth, love and companionship. With awkward tenderness they sought each other out to silently share the scars of their individual tragedies. In their quest to build families they would join in matrimony in anticipation of new lives either in Israel, the United States, Canada or Australia.

For Oskar and myself the decision of where to go was difficult for several reasons. We had grown up in Poland dreaming of one day finding ourselves in Palestine. The dream was nurtured by the history of our people and the liturgy of our prayers, and crystallized in the anti-Semitic incidents of pre-war Poland. The dream did not die with our liberation, even though the dreamers had been transformed by their abuse. Many of us were numbed, tired, listless, callous and disinterested. We considered ourselves poor assets for the new and needy land of Palestine, so we finally opted instead for the promise and comfort of America.

The captain was delighted, and then gave us a piece of advice. If you go to America he insisted, you should get an education. Knowledge is capital that no one can take away from you. We confessed that our formal education had been interrupted at an early stage, but he said he would get us a tutor who would be able to get us ready for college.

And so it happened that the captain engaged Professor Stachowsky to tutor Oskar and myself for college entrance exams. Professor Stachowsky (we called him professor, though we did not know if he really was one) was either a Russian or Ukrainian refugee. He spoke several languages fluently, including Latin, English and German. He claimed to have a medical degree and to specialize in ENT, the ear, nose and throat discipline (he later became director of the UNRRA hospital in Regensburg) and had a very good knowledge of the subjects we believed were necessary to get into a German university. He was also married to a beautiful woman, Tatyana. Their four-year-old daughter already spoke four languages. Every evening he would spend time with Oskar and me, cramming into us history, literature, algebra, science and Latin. We swallowed six years of Latin in six months! The captain paid him for his services with items from the PX and food rations from the kitchen.

The day soon came when we were told that the company would have to turn in its tanks at a gathering point in Landshut, Bavaria. Although Oskar and I meanwhile gained admission to Johan Wolfgang Geothe University in Frankfurt/M, we were sad to see them go. The veteran soldiers started going back to the States, with the order determined by points of seniority or other assets. Big Red and a few others were due to leave soon. The time had come for us to say good-bye to what we often referred to later as our convalescence. We were parting with that element of America we had come to love so much and hoped someday to become part of. The healing process was over. There was a world out there to face and a life to rebuild.

CHAPTER XXX

Once we had left the protective shelter of the US Army we had to find ways to fend for ourselves. We needed lodgings, food and clothing. Those of the survivors who opted for living in the displaced persons camps were provided for by the UNRRA; those who chose to settle in towns also registered with the relief organization and drew rations through its offices. My father, who had settled in the area where we were liberated, was helpful in supporting Oskar and me with packages of food from the countryside.

Many of us supplemented our earnings by way of the black market. No one honored the German legal restrictions; we had nothing but disdain for the authorities. Bypassing their laws was simply to us an exercise in cleverness and gamesmanship. It was common practice to lie or misrepresent the facts to gain preferential treatment or access to certain resources.

When I was asked for proof of having completed high school in order to enter the university, I produced an affidavit stating that I had attended the gymnasium in Krakow (only partly true: I had attended the vocational school, an annex to the gymnasium) and a secret high school in Warsaw. I had no qualms about my deceit. These same authorities had taken my youth, my early life, and my opportunity for education. They had violated all the laws governing civilized conduct, leaving me with no home and no country to protect my rights. I had become a stateless orphan in a state where no one cared about my fate.

Once again, I had to survive in a German world. It was a new environment, with new circumstances, but it was still run by the Germans. And this time I was going to get the better of them.

Oskar and I, we were admitted to the International Student Hostel on the Zeppelin Allee, not far from the Johan Wolfgang Geothe University. The hostel housed students from different countries that had fallen victims to the Nazi onslaught. Students from Poland, Lithuania, Latvia, the Balkans and other countries lived and studied side by side, not always harmoniously. Oskar and I, we drew food rations at the nearby displaced person camp of Zeilzheim and once a day, at noon, we would go to the Jewish Community Center kitchen for a hot meal. At the university itself, about 90 Jewish students had enrolled during the previous semester and lived either in the DP camp in Zeilzheim or had found accommodation in private German homes.

Those Jewish university students were part of a remarkable post-war phenomenon. About one thousand of them had decided to resume their academic studies after the war. All of the students—victims of the Holocaust, orphaned by the savagery of the persecution, subjected to the most horrific atrocities—they still thirsted for knowledge and entered German universities at Munich, Marburg, Heidelberg, Frankfurt and Goettingen. Most of them opted for medicine and eventually became physicians.

I met some of them at a reunion in the Catskill Mountains in New York State in the late 1990s. Most had achieved distinction in their respective communities, serving in various prominent capacities. These altruistic healers, born of man's evil disregard for other human beings, were a testimony to the indestructible nobility of the human spirit.

I had decided to enroll in the philosophy department, specifically the philology subdivision, with an eye toward journalism. Oskar wanted to go into medicine, but since those courses were oversubscribed, he was advised to enroll in some other discipline and transfer to medicine after one semester. So he joined me in the philology courses.

At the induction ceremony, the president of the university addressed the new student body, speaking of the dawn of a new era; of the responsibility of the new generation to build a new and more just world, free of bias and prejudice; of the need to forgive and forget. At the end of his address, however, his true sense of Germanic superiority emerged as he issued instructions to the assembly: The German students were to remain in the main auditorium, while the foreign students would go to Auditorium "B" to receive their *Studien-Buch,* the record of enrollment and attendance. So much for the new era and the new German sense of equality.

The bulk of the German student body consisted not of recent high school graduates but of war-veterans—ex-Wermacht, Luftwaffe, Marine and sometimes SS Waffen; mostly officers, whose education had been interrupted by orders to fight for the Fatherland. The lives of foreign students at German universities were not made easy by the chauvinism of their native colleagues. This became clear from my first day in the classroom, I had no idea what subjects to choose from the great variety that were offered, I followed Oskar's suggestions to enroll in a course on Thackeray's essays. I think he got this idea because he had once read Thackeray's *Vanity Fair*. We did not know that this particular seminar was designed for juniors and seniors who were well advanced in the study of English literature. When we entered the classroom, about twenty students already sat around a large table, with Professor Sanders, our teacher, in the middle. As we took two chairs and found a place for ourselves, the students eyed us with cool curiosity. Obviously this was a close-knit group, and the two newcomers did not fit their mold.

They were studying a thin book of Thackeray's essays. Each student was asked to read a sentence, and a short discussion followed. When my turn came, the professor pushed his book toward me and asked me to read.

I felt very uncomfortable from the first moment we sat down. The 19th-century English sounded unfamiliar to my ear. I was accustomed to the sound of American GI slang and to the written style of the Stars and Stripes newspaper. I tried to read the assigned sentence, but toward the end my voice drifted and the last few words were hardly audible. An embarrassed silence fell over the room.

Professor Sanders, a German, was an acknowledged authority on languages in the European academic community. We were later told that he had taught at Oxford University before the war. He had written many works, some of which became textbooks on philology. He was an expert on Beowulf, spoke nine languages and knew six alphabets. He had a slightly hunched back and was known for his cryptic sarcasm.

He looked at me quizzically and asked, "*Mein Herr,* Sir, where have you learned your English?" I must have turned crimson, but I was not about to confess that the source of my expertise was my friends on "kitchen patrol" in the U.S. Army.

"In Poland," I replied bluntly.

"There is room for improvement," was his curt response. I was not going to let this German mentor (I was then totally unaware of his prominence) have the last word, so I replied, "That is, what I came here for, improvement."

Needless to say, we dropped the course, but that was not the end of my relationship with Professor Sanders. I went on to chose a course of his in Elizabethan literature intended for freshmen. Assignments had to be turned in for grading, and mine were all coming back un-graded, each with a simple note from him: "Illegible." Unless my work was graded, he would not sign my *Studien-Buch* and I would not get credit for the course. As the end of the semester approached, I knew I had to do something.

NORBERT FRIEDMAN

The protocol at German universities at that time was to stand three feet in front of a professor and ask for permission to speak. I, however, brazenly walked up to Professor Sanders' desk and, holding all my rejected papers in my hand, unceremoniously addressed him.

"*Herr Professor,* I understand that you speak nine languages."

"*Ja,*" was his laconic reply.

"I understand that you know six alphabets."

Again, a brief "*Ja.*"

"Then it should be easier for you to learn a new alphabet than for me to change my handwriting."

A long, tense silence followed. I frankly expected him to tell me to leave the classroom and perhaps the university. At last he took a scrap of paper, wrote an address on it, and handed it to me. "Come to see me at such and such a time."

I went to find him at the appointed time. The building with the address he gave was bombed out, as were most of the houses on that street. I carefully ascended three flights of stairs, rubble still hanging over the staircase. The entrance to Professor Sanders' apartment was by way of a balcony; the door hung partly off its hinges, leaning against the entrance. I knocked on the door and was asked to come in. I had to lift the door a little before I could swing it aside.

It was a cold December afternoon, and the temperature inside the room was only slightly warmer than the outside. The professor sat on a couch, wrapped in a German army blanket and eating from a jar of boiled nettle, correcting papers. I was momentarily taken aback: this world-renowned authority on languages, this giant in the world of academia, living in such poor conditions. I was humbled by his resolve to continue working in his profession as if everything were perfectly normal.

He invited me to sit down and without glancing at the papers I had brought with me, he asked me about my background and what had prompted me to enter a German university. We talked for a long time as the smell from his terrible pipe tobacco filled the cold air. Then he looked at my papers and had me read some lines in order to familiarize himself with my handwriting. Then he asked me to come back next week. I left, immensely impressed by his determination to go on despite very meager compensation. He had told me that his salary was enough to buy what was available through his ration cards, not enough for anything on the black market.

As I thought about him, I felt that although his country had lost the war, his people had not been defeated. A people who were determined to rebuild from this rubble and who still had pride in their work would re-emerge to claim their prominence.

Next week, when I went to Zeilzheim to claim my rations, I also bought additional items to take to professor Sanders, making sure that I had a couple of packs of decent American pipe tobacco. I took the carton of provisions when I went to see him. He was visibly moved by my thoughtfulness, but that in no way affected his grading of my work. He brewed some tea and pointed out the many errors in my work.

We developed a more than cordial relationship. He was very helpful in the coming years advising me on the choice of subjects. He suggested that since I intended to go to America and pursue a career in journalism, I should concentrate on American literature and the American political system. He pointed out the professors who taught those subjects best. I had the sense that he was a German patriot longing for the years of pre-Nazi era and the German academic prominence of those days.

In 1948 I accepted the position of the president of the Jewish Students Union in Frankfurt/M, a job that involved assuring financial aid for the Jewish students from the German authorities. For the sake of finishing my studies, with an eye toward a Ph.D. in philology, I had twice extended my visa to the United States, each time for the maximum time of six months. In January of 1950 I was called to the American consulate and told that this was my last chance to take advantage of the opportunity to go to America. The consul convinced me that I would be able to finish my studies in the USA if I so desired, and that if I should miss this opportunity, I would have to re-apply and wait for another three years.

So in May of 1950, I and 2,000 other DPs (we preferred to call ourselves Delayed Pilgrims rather than Displaced Persons) boarded the liberty ship *General W. G. Hahn,* originally designed to carry 500 army personnel, and left for New Orleans.

On Monday June 6th, 1950, St. Norbert's day on the Christian calendar, I stepped on the soil of my Promised Land, the United States of America.

EPILOGUE

The large school auditorium was quiet and empty. It was set up for about 150 students, and I still had about 20 minutes before they would arrive. It was my practice to use the time to leaf through index cards containing questions that the students had been asked to submit in advance of the day's assembly.

Over the years I had spoken to so many assemblies, small and large, from 5th graders through university graduates. I had spoken with countless groups in my capacity as a gallery educator at Manhattan's *Museum of Jewish Heritage, A Living Memorial to the Holocaust.* I had found that the subject of my presentation and the presence of a survivor would sometimes intimidate the students and thwart a productive question-and answer-period.

As I looked at the questions, most of them similar or identical to the thousands of others that I had been asked to address through the years, thoughts and memories raced through my mind. How had I made this journey from suffering prisoner to gallery educator? How had I survived at all?

I understand that an individual who suffers the loss of a dear one undergoes certain stages of emotion: Anger, depression, denial, hopefully acceptance. But, what about a person, who has lost almost all of his dear ones in his life? What about someone who will never again know the world that was torn from him and destroyed by the twisted cruelty of deranged mind?

I have thought about the stages of my own bereavement. First I remember bewilderment, a never-before-known sense of shock and numbness. I remember sadness, an all-encompassing, sky-darkening cloud of sorrow. I vividly recall the overwhelming feeling of bitterness toward the whole world for its abandonment and silence. And I remember my own silence, a self-imposed reticence, for me the most difficult of all burdens to bear. And I'm painfully aware of the always-present sense of guilt for having survived at all, when so many others perished.

I remember the first time I dared to speak publicly about my experience. In 1969, my spiritual leader, Rabbi Abraham M. Moseson of blessed memory, insisted that I give testimony and share my experiences with my congregation on Long Island. In his wisdom, he knew the therapeutic value of confession. He knew that the heart whose bitter poison had to be drained of its venom in order to keep beating normally. (To quote a survivor interviewed in the *Shoa* documentary by Claude Lanzmann: "If you licked it [the heart], the poison would kill you.")

Now I sat in the auditorium wondering when I had lost my self-pity, that urgent need for empathy that had characterized my earlier presentations. Had the process been gradual, or had I had a sudden revelation? I know that to some extent my audiences had helped, because it became obvious to me that although I can never totally leave the prison of my nightmares, I can—and must—join the children and young people in trying to build a better world for them. And I know that the process of writing these memoirs helped as well.

I began to write them when my children were able to understand that a part of my life had differed significantly from the lives of most other people. I had decided to leave my children and grandchildren some record of my life, even though the attempt was by its very nature doomed from the start. It was doomed not only because I did not have the good fortune to be trained as a writer in the English language, or because it was not easy to find time and energy to write. More important, I knew it was fated to be at best an incomplete, inadequate, impaired and sometimes even romanticized recording of events. I realized that I might be able to relate the factual outlines of things as they happened, but that I could never recreate the sense of fear, apprehension and confusion that filled those years. I could never express the pain of despair and hopelessness; the degradation and dehumanization; the terror and the withdrawal from pathological sadism and bestiality. I could not even depict the eventual numbness, the self-doubt, unworthiness, cynicism and resignation, the not-always-successful attempt to crawl into a protective shell of indifference.

My first words on paper were memories of childhood, which I intended as a kind of family tree about the ancestors my children would never know. I realized that without telling the story of my childhood and European relatives my narrative would be incomplete. For I firmly believe that we are who we are because of what we have been. That early part of the story served my children, I hope, and it served me as well in organizing and motivating the longer narrative you have before you.

The liberty ship *General W. G. Hahn* delivered me and hundreds of other immigrants to the port of New Orleans in June of 1950. I made my way by train to Atlanta, where the HIAS, the Jewish agency which helped to bring survivors to the American shores, purported to have employment secured for me. Pursuing my dream of becoming a journalist, I applied for a job on the *Atlanta Journal*. The personnel manager, however, took me out for a cup of coffee and pointed out the absurdity of my trying to get a position on a major newspaper. In a few words he exposed my self-deception for what it was. "You are not an American, you are not a Southerner, and you are Jewish. If I give you a job, you will be stuck in the copy room forever, making forty dollars a week. If you have skills in other fields, try to get a job there."

So I faced reality and went to work in a machine shop, where I did know my way around. I was able to utilize the skills acquired in the Jewish Vocational School in Krakow and honed while working in machine shops before and during the war. I also attended night courses at Georgia Tech to learn American technical terminology. I was in love with America and I wanted to be more American that anyone born here. I inhaled and devoured everything about the country: the style of clothing, the songs, the mode of talking, the infatuation with sports, the pursuit of success.

In 1951, I left Atlanta and found employment in New Jersey. At that time the Korean War was on and jobs were not easy to find. So I was fortunate to find this position through a friend.

But the job was only part of my good fortune in moving to New Jersey. A relative of mine introduced me to her best friend, whose name was Marilyn, and I fell in love immediately.

During all my years in Germany I had never dated a Jewish girl, though I had many female Jewish friends. I had made a conscious decision that the mother of my children would be an American and not a survivor. I believed that it would be bad enough for one parent to suffer from morbid moods and other results of a tragic past.

We were married on January 16, 1955. When my wife became pregnant, I made her leave her job and started thinking about running my own business. I started a small machine shop of my own and kept my regular job at the same time. I would work for thirty-six hours in a row, sleep for eight or ten hours, and then repeat the process again. I followed that schedule for over a year. Then, from the money I had saved and a loan from my friends, I bought some more equipment and opened my own business, the Automatic Screw Machine shop, in Jamaica, Queens. This was America as it had been promised to me by those GIs in Germany: If you worked hard enough and did a slightly better job than the other guy, there was no limit to your rewards.

My oldest son was born in 1958, my second son in 1963 and my youngest in 1965. Unfortunately, my middle child, Stuart Lawrence, suffered brain injury at birth. For four years until his death, my wife Marilyn, my oldest son Gary, and I suffered all the agony that a retarded child can bring to a family. Dear God, I thought; is there never going to be an end to being tested by You? I compared myself to Job, pondering my tribulations.

I brought my father, his new wife and her daughter from France in 1956. My wonderful stepmother created a warm grand-parental home for my children and my stepsister Irene an extended family to love again. Meanwhile, my friends in the survivor community were rebuilding their own lives. My social life, however, revolved around my family and my wife's family, with little social interaction with my fellow survivors.

In 1968 I moved my family to Long Island to be closer to my machine shop in Queens. By then my sons knew of my past. They had already asked, "Dad what is this KL on your and grandpa's wrist?" And I had told them: KL for *Konzentration-Lager,* Concentration Camp.

In 1969 I gave my first public testimony, a traumatic and cathartic encounter. I chose to speak about the heroism of Hamek Schildkraut. The experience of barring my soul in public about events suppressed for so long, unsettled me deeply. After that, young students from my congregation would often ask me to speak to classes in their schools.

My children were growing up aware of both my past and my sense of indebtedness to America. From adolescence on, they felt a sense of gratitude and social obligation, which they have carried on into their professional lives. In their parents' and grandparents' homes they have witnessed a life of traditional religious observance, something I expect them to continue.

In 1951, two ex-inmates, who had come to the camp in Mielec from the camp in Budzyn with the group of Jewish POWs, reported Uncle Henry to the INS, the Immigration and Naturalization Services, accusing him of collaboration with the Nazis while acting as the Commandant of the Ordnungsdienst in Mielec.

This was not the first post-war confrontation Uncle Henry had had with ex-inmates. The pain, ire and resentment of concentration camp survivors towards Jews who were in authority in the camps was a natural and expected reaction. The leaders were the focus and targets of all the anger and resentment the survivors felt toward all authority, whether German or Jewish; authority that was associated with the inhuman injustice they were forced to endure. In the years immediately after the war, many ex-Capos had been hunted down, assaulted and even executed by embittered survivors.

As a result, Uncle Henry was arrested and placed in Ellis Island, subject to deportation proceedings. I was then working the night shift at the Edison Storage Battery Co. in N.J., and I went to Ellis Island to find out about Uncle Henry's predicament.

At the office of the Immigration legal department, the person in charge of Uncle Henry's case was Inspector Shaughnessey, a handsome, middle aged, self-assured bureaucrat. When I inquired about the indictment he told me that it was basically an open-and-shut case. Uncle Henry wore a uniform issued by the Germans and he executed their orders; he was therefore a collaborator and consequently subject to deportation. There would be hearings, he said, but that was only routine; there was no question about his guilt. Uncle Henry had basically admitted that he was the commandant of the camp in Mielec. Could I get an attorney? I asked. Of course, but I would have to let him know in seven days.

I went to the luncheonette on the premises to have a bite. I picked up a tray and sat at an empty table. A woman with her own tray came to my table and asked if she could sit "Of course," I answered.

"I saw you talking to Shaughnessey," she said, "and I heard you speaking about your uncle. You had better get a lawyer."

"Who are you, if I may ask?"

"I'm the court stenographer," she replied. I told her that I did not have the money to pay for a lawyer, and besides, I did not know of any attorney who would be familiar first-hand with the conditions in the concentration camps, especially the one in Mielec.

"Why don't you act as his attorney?" was her surprising suggestion. "You have a right to ask to serve as a Friend of the Court, which gives you basically all the rights of an attorney." I was startled to hear this and I was also suspicious about her motives. After all, she was an employee of the immigration authorities. "Why are you telling me this?" I finally asked.

"I don't like that self-righteous SOB," she said, meaning Shaughnessey. "Go to a library and familiarize yourself with the immigration and naturalization laws. They are the opposite of our civil and criminal laws; you are guilty until proven innocent. And try to learn how to conduct yourself in the proceedings." As I was leaving she grabbed my hand. "Please, don't tell him that you spoke to me."

I went right back to Shaughnessey's office and I asked for a postponement.

"Do you have a lawyer?" was his question.

"No, but I would like to serve as a Friend of the Court."

He looked at me with suspicion. "OK, you got two weeks. What do you know about defending someone in court?"

"Nothing except the truth," was my reply.

"OK, I'll see you in two weeks."

That was not much time for me to prepare for a trial. I went to the public library in Newark, told the librarian of my predicament and took home a load of books that she recommended. I absorbed only some of the basic information I thought I needed and decided to rely mostly on my common sense and intimate knowledge of the Mielec situation.

At the first hearing, the charges were read and I requested the right to submit witnesses for Uncle Henry and to cross-examine the two accusers. During the several hearings that followed I brought friends from the camp who now lived in New York or New Jersey. They all responded to my questioning, testifying that Uncle Henry was never guilty of causing anyone's death; to the contrary, they stated that in several instances he had saved people's lives by risking his own. True, they said, he used to yell, and was not smart in using the right language. He sometimes even hit people, but someone had to keep order. Their key statement was that, unlike what had often happened in other camps, this Capo had no one's blood on his hands.

The interrogation of the two accusers was a little more complex, requiring more prodding and skillful questioning. Finally, I got both of them to admit that they would have turned other people over to the Germans if doing so would had save their own lives.

I felt that I had vindicated Uncle Henry of the charges against him and I was sure that Shaughnessey would rule in his favor. Some time later I got a frantic call from Uncle Henry, saying that he had been found guilty and was waiting to be scheduled for deportation. I went out to Ellis Island in a foul mood, sorely disappointed with the American system.

Inspector Shaughnessey was the sole judge and jury in this case, and I thought that he did not have the mental or professional capacity to understand it. I was sure that I had proven Uncle Henry innocent of the charges, yet he was still to be deported.

Before seeing Shaughnessey I sought the counsel of the court stenographer. Her advice was, "Get a lawyer to issue a writ of *Habeas Corpus* so he can go home. Once he's home it can take months before they are able to deport him;

right now they don't know what country they can send him to. And get the lawyer to write an appeal, or better yet write one yourself. You did a hell of a job at the hearings."

I found an attorney in the Bronx who issued a writ of *Habeas Corpus*. Uncle Henry was allowed to go home after a couple of weeks, and I started to write the appeal.

It was the fist time that I had really tried to describe the rights and wrongs of that fateful period to those who had not been there. Six years into my freedom, all the events I had witnessed were still very fresh in my mind. I had witnessed human nature under the most trying conditions, watching people make the most difficult choices. I had learned that in most instances the drive to survive overcame moral and ethical imperatives.

I found myself wondering, what would have been my response had Herring lived and had to face a postwar tribunal? How would I have handled the moral complexity of that situation? Would I have testified on his behalf in gratitude for saving my father's life?

I felt again that brief, powerful link between us when he talked about his lost father and poured drinks for both of us: Would that unique spark have been rekindled? If he were facing a trial, would I have turned my face away, pointed a finger at him, and gained retribution for all my murdered comrades?

When seeking justice, can the wanton taking of innocent human lives be forgiven—or the penalty lessened—because of one instant of merciful compassion?

Are humans capable of rendering just judgment for deeds that outrage and astound us? Do crimes committed under barbarous and uncivil circumstances require uncommon canons of justice?

Is anyone innocent enough to pass judgment? Does the potential for evil in every one of us disqualify us from passing judgment?

I tried to face those questions, but found that the only answers to them were additional questions that were just as difficult. At least I bore them in mind as I wrote my appeal, and maybe they were helpful. I had the attorney's secretary correct my orthographic errors and sent it to Washington.

In May of 1952, Uncle Henry received a short, official document marked A-7-405 009 (t) from the United States Department of Justice, Immigration and Naturalization Service. It read:

Dear Sir: Please be advised that under date of April 18, 1952 the Commissioner of Immigration and Naturalization ordered that the deportation proceedings against you be terminated. Signed P.A. Esperdy, Acting District Director, New York District.

I went to Ellis Island to pick up some things that Uncle Henry had left there. They were not really important, but I wanted the satisfaction of facing Inspector Shaughnessey one last time. I saw the court stenographer first and she told me how rare it was for a decision of an Immigration Inspector to be reversed and how pleased she was that Shaughnessey was beaten.

I saw Shaughnessey in his office and could not hide my glee. "I told you," I said, "that you really did not have a case." But he gave me little satisfaction. He simply said, "I wouldn't mind loosing to another professional, but loosing to a layman irks me no end."

Uncle Henry, however, was never really free. He lived out his life in obscurity, hiding from the public eye in a small community on the Jersey shore, always fearful that someone may hunt him down for his sin of having served as a lackey of the Germans.

I turned to the first index card and the often-asked question "How did you survive?" stared me in the face. I always found that question difficult to answer. As I have said in the introduction: I knew that it was not my youth or my physical condition that was the reason for my survival, hundreds of thousands of others as young and as healthy as I was perished. Besides, in the course of events my youth vanished and my good health faded. I knew that it was not my guile or street smarts that kept me alive, for thousands of others more cunning that I, with more life experience, did not live to see the day of liberation. And I knew that it was not my vocational skills that saved me. Some people who had inferior professional qualifications lived, many others with skills immeasurably greater than mine did not.

If I dismissed divine providence or random luck, I would have to point to another reason that was at least partly responsible for my survival. That was the ability to seek out and to cleave to those rare people who showed genuine integrity and human compassion when all around them were only human suffering and evil deeds.

When I summon my courage, face and exorcise the demons of my childhood, when I cast out the ghosts that had once plagued my relationship with my father. I'm compelled to give the credit for my survival to him, his efforts and his amazing metamorphosis from a young, not always dependable parent and husband, to a reliable protector and provider, not only for myself, but also for others. In retrospect, I must also consider the fact, that his will and courage during the years in the camps was a result of his dedication to ensuring my welfare and survival.

At my father's funeral in March of 1980, the many friends of mine, co-travelers through the journey of pain who attended the interment had one common consolation in the form of the following observation. Not, "Sorry that you had lost your father," but; "You do not know how fortunate you were, to have had a father with you!"

I kept leafing through the index cards, disregarding the questions that would be answered in the course of my presentation. The next one that caught my eye asked another common question: "Did you ever see Hitler?" Early in my career as a public speaker I would ignore that question, or answer it with a curt, No! It was not until later, when I was asked to assist at an Anne Frank exhibit, that its importance became clear to me.

I was going through an orientation session with volunteers who were to become guides for that exhibit, which was being shown at a community college on Long Island. Some twenty students, mostly women, were in the group of prospective docents. It intrigued me that none of them was Jewish. I decided to interview them and ask why they had volunteered. What I heard, although not so explicitly expressed, was that they were attracted to Ann Frank as an icon of humane goodness. Perhaps they were responding to the words in the diary: "In spite of everything I still believe that people are really good at heart."

It struck me that their motives were exactly opposite of what motivated the children to ask about Adolf Hitler. Anne Frank and Adolf Hitler were both icons, one of evil and the other of goodness. The fascination with evil was as much a characteristic of human nature as the attraction to decency was. The whole struggle, the entire conflict that humans had to deal with during the Holocaust, was the titanic wrestling match between those forces. In the case of evil, the objective was not to banish it, but at least temporarily to get the upper hand.

I checked my watch. There were still 10 minutes before the students would start coming in. I kept going through the questions on the cards. I was amazed at the insight and sensitivity of some and the banality of others.

"Do you still believe in God?" was the most frequent query. Or, "Did you believe that there was a God while in the Holocaust?"

The question after all did not differ much from the question of a young friend of mine, Dr. Aaron Haas, who was a child of survivors and a lecturer, scholar and writer, mostly on the subject of the post-Holocaust second generation. He once asked me how it was that despite my experiences, I had retained my faith in Man and God—unlike the majority of survivors after the war. How could I keep my faith despite witnessing the apparent negation of everything that others and I were taught and practiced in our daily liturgy? Despite the fact that everything we had been taught ("God the Savior, the Redeemer, the Merciful, the Just and Compassionate, God the Omnipotent") had collapsed into a heap of confused and scrambled aphorisms.

I told him and the children that I had kept my faith because of those rare instances when man's spirit rose like a hope-inspiring vision; when I had seen the magnificence of man's soul rise from the swamp and muck of ordinary existence. I told him and the children about Rabbi Schenken's courage and Reb Mayer's altruistic act and my friend Michal Krawiec's courage and the many other small and large acts of heroism that sustained my strength during the terrors of the Holocaust.

But I could not tell the children about my deeper burden, about my struggle with the complexities of the experience. Sometimes the whole infernal memory of the Shoa becomes obscured in a mystical shroud where one gropes in futility for answers to the enigma of creation; its purpose, its mysteries, the unavoidable question of its termination. I could not expect the children to wrestle with mysteries so deep, subjects that tradition did not allow my friends and myself to contemplate until we were at least 40 years of age and married.

Tradition, to which we so often turn for answers, describes the condition of the Jews under the Roman occupation of Israel in the second century C.E. In the tractate HAGIGAH 14b it states: Four men entered the Garden, or *PARDES*, Ben Azzai, Ben Zoma, Elisha Ben Abouya, and Rabbi Akiva. Sages consider the *PARDES* a figurative expression for the mystical realm of theosophy.

Eli Wiesel in his book *Sages and Dreamers* writes in wonderful detail about this story:

"These four men under the leadership of Rabbi Akiba. These four, amongst the most learned in the annals of Jewish thought, had started out on a mystical adventure to seek and find mystery of G'd and his universe through study."

Tradition tells us that Rabbi Akiva issued a warning: "Do not speak falsehood when you confront the transparent whiteness of the marble" (in my reading:

NORBERT FRIEDMAN

" . . . of your epiphany"). The men entered the garden, discovered the mystery of creation, and did not heed this warning:

Ben Azzai looked and died.

Ben Zoma looked and lost his mind.

Elisha Ben Abouya lost his faith and became an informer against his own people.

Only Rabbi Akiva emerged unscathed.

Does the experience of the Holocaust offer a parallel to this story? Does finding the mystery of G'd have a dark side? Is the discovery of truth too much for us to bear? After all, every coin has two sides; a mirror cannot reflect without its dark side.

During the Holocaust, almost two thousand years after the original story, a whole people encountered the PARDES.

And what they found was Darkness, miasma and inferno.

Most of the people lost their lives.

Some lost their sanity.

Many lost their faith.

Were any of those who survived able to emerge as they had entered?

Are there any Rabbi Akivas left?

Would Reb Mayer Katz have been such a man, had he survived?

Soon the students would enter; once again I would be facing the future while recounting the past. How many would be receptive to the message I always tried to convey? I remembered an incident that shines among my recollections of encounters with young people.

One afternoon I was leading a group of high school seniors through the exhibits at the museum. The group was a part of an organization called "Bridges to Humanity," and included students from different ethnic backgrounds in New York City. The students in my group came from two ethnic groups, Jewish and Afro-American. Our tour was called "From Hate to Humanity." In the hour and half allocated for the tour, I tried my best to demonstrate to the students the tragic effects of bias, discrimination and prejudice on a society and, in the case of the Holocaust, on much of the world.

I wove my personal experiences into the events of the Shoa, stressing the personal courage by the righteous rescuers and those who practiced spiritual resistance when physical action was impossible. I tried to impress on them the danger created for a society when one segment for reasons of difference, be it race, color, religion, nationality or sexual orientation, is categorized as *Untermenschen*, sub-humans. How such labeling permits that segment of society to be mistreated, disenfranchised, and stripped of its rights; how it opens opportunities for intellectual and physical harm and eventually leads to genocide.

When we reached the end of the tour, I invited the youngsters to pose questions. One young man, a student from a Jewish religious school, asked me why I was engaged in this task when it obviously resulted in an emotional drain on my physical resources. I paraphrased the Talmudic dictum that "If you save one human life, it is as if you had saved the whole world."

I told him that if one young person should leave the museum a better human being, than they were when they entered, my task would have been worth the effort.

Then a beautiful young Afro-American student, who had seemed to be detached and uninterested during the whole tour, came forward and pointed to her chest. She burst out in a teary voice "I'm that person."

The school bell rang, rousing me from my reverie. The students guided by their teachers, most of whom were familiar to me from previous visits to this school, started to settle into their respective seats. I saw the usual faces that one encounters in white suburbia.

On this lovely spring day it would be difficult at first to create a point of reference to that dark era that I was to speak about. But I trusted in my tested ability; I would attempt to draw positive lessons from a most tragic epoch in man's history. I would take them along on my journey through the bottom-most trough of man's behavior. And a few days later, when I would receive the usual batch of letters from this audience, I would be looking for the one letter that would reward all my efforts. The one that would say: "Mr. Friedman, I'll never hate again."

NORBERT FRIEDMAN

Norbert Friedman's maternal grandparents, Esther Bochner/Mandelbaum and
Hersh Mandelbaum, Krakow, Poland circa 1926

Norbert's parents, Gusta and Josef Friedman, Krakow circa 1919

NORBERT FRIEDMAN

Post-war picture of the house on Josefa 16, Krakow, Poland.

SUN RAYS AT MIDNIGHT

Aunt Pepka and Uncle Srulek Szwetzreich, circa 1912

NORBERT FRIEDMAN

Aunt Pepka, Uncle David and Aunt Rozia, circa 1914

From left to right, standing, Uncle Michal Erlich, Aunt Hela Bochner, Gerd's mother, Gerd's grandmother, his aunt, his grandfather, Uncle Jacob, his wife Lola and Gerd's father, David. Sitting, Cousin Gerd and Aunt Selma. Teplitz Schoenau, Czechoslovakia circa 1930

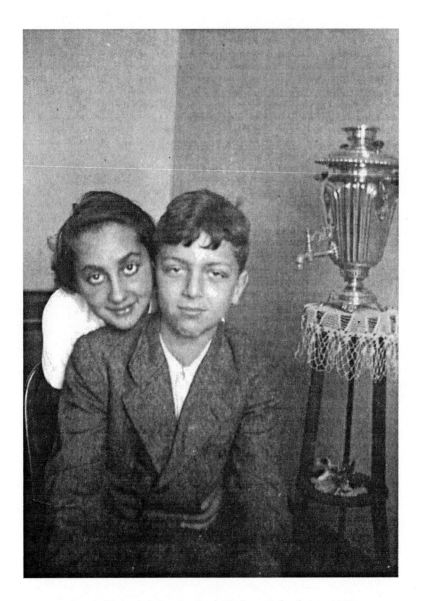

Cousin Tosia and Cousin Gerd, Krakow, Poland circa 1937

Norbert's fourth grade class, Norbert is #16 center of picture—of the forty-two youngsters in the picture, less than ten survived the Shoah-Bielsko, Poland, 1931

Outing of the Szomer Hatzair group of Bielsko-Biala, circa 1935

Norbert, center, with his Polish friends in Zawichost, Poland, circa 1941

NORBERT FRIEDMAN

Cousin Lusia, Uncle Henry's daughter, Lwow, Poland, circa 1941

Norbert in American Army uniform while working for Company "B", 35th Tank Battalion, 4th Armored, 3rd Army. Adldorf, Germany, spring 1946.

NORBERT FRIEDMAN

BESCHEINIGUNG

Es wird hiermit bescheinigt, daß

Herr
~~Frau~~
~~Fr.~~
~~xx~~ Norbert Friedman

in Frankfurt/~~M~~-ain

geb. am 20.12.22 zu Krakau

i. d. Zeit vom: 1940 bis: 1945

in dem ~~KZ-Lager, Zuchthaus, Gefängnis, Gestapogefängnis~~ *)
Ghetto: Krakau und Tarnow und
KZ: Pustkow, Mielce, Flossenburg und Dachau

inhaftiert gewesen ist.

Er (Sie) gilt somit als ~~politisch~~, rassisch ~~und religiös~~ Verfolgte(r).

~~Diese Bescheinigung verleiht nicht gleiche Rechte wie solche den verschleppten Personen der Vereinten Nationen zustehen, noch gewährt sie Sonder- oder Vorzugsrechte gemäß den Vorschriften der amerikanischen Militärregierung.~~

Ministerium für pol. Befreiung
für das Land Hessen
In Auftrag

Wiesbaden, den 2.12.48 (Siegel)

*) Nichtzutreffendes streichen.

Norbert's ID issued to Ex-inmates of concentration camps.

Norbert and his friend Oskar Klausenstock, now Dr. Oskar Klausenstock,
on an outing on Lake Chiemsee, Bavaria, Germany, circa 1948.

Norbert and Marilyn, Wedding Picture. Newark, NJ, Jan. 16, 1955

50th Wedding Anniversary of Marilyn and Norbert, Boca Raton, Fl. Jan. 2005. Standing from left, Dr. Julie Zweig, David's wife and their son Gavin. Sons, David and Gary, Grandson Colin and Noelle, Gary's wife. Sitting from leftt, Marilyn and Norbert with Julie's and David's daughters Joelle and Carolyn.

NORBERT FRIEDMAN